Cyberscience 2.0

T0136806

Interaktiva

Series of the Center for Media and Interactivity (ZMI),
Gießen, Volume 11

Edited by Christoph Bieber, Claus Leggewie and Henning Lobin

Michael Nentwich is the director of the Institute of Technology Assessment
(ITA) of the Austrian Academy of Sciences and the author of *Cyberscience. Research in the Age of the Internet.*

René König is a sociologist at the Institute of Technology Assessment and System
Analysis (ITAS) of the Karlsruhe Institue of Technology (KIT).

Michael Nentwich, René König

Cyberscience 2.0

Research in the Age of Digital Social Networks

Campus Verlag
Frankfurt/New York

Bibliographic Information published by the Deutsche Nationalbibliothek.
The Deutsche Nationalbibliothek lists this publication in the Deutsche Nationalbibliografie; detailed bibliographic data are available in the Internet at http://dnb.d-nb.de
ISBN 978-3-593-39518-0

All rights reserved. No part of this book may be reproduced or transmitted in any form or by any means, electronic or mechanical, including photocopying, recording, or by any information storage and retrieval system, without permission in writing from the publishers.
Copyright © 2012 Campus Verlag GmbH, Frankfurt-on-Main
Cover design: Campus Verlag, Frankfurt-on-Main
Printing office and bookbinder: CPI buchbuecher.de, Birkach
Printed on acid free paper.
Printed in Germany

This book is also available as an E-Book.
For further information:
www.campus.de
www.press.uchicago.edu

Contents

Preface

This book is the result of the research carried out by the two authors between 2008 and 2011 in the framework of the project "Interactive Science. Internal Science Communication via Digital Media", funded by the German Volkswagen Foundation under its program "Key Issues in the Humanities" (project number II/83099). In this joint project, led by the Center for Interactive Media (ZMI) of the University of Gießen, four subprojects explored the theme from various angles. The authors formed the Vienna-based team at the Institute of Technology Assessment (ITA) of the Austrian Academy of Sciences within the sub-project "Collaborative Knowledge Management and Democratization of Science". We focused on several emerging promising Internet platforms that potentially have an impact on science and research. Our initial plan to write a series of short portraits of many of these tools quickly evolved into a much more challenging task. We felt the need to deliver more in-depth presentations and preliminary analyses of our case studies: social network sites, microblogging, collaborative knowledge production platforms, virtual worlds, and search engines. For the present book, we have built on these five reports (in German) and extended the analysis by comparing these tools and drawing meta-level conclusions.

Very special thanks go to *Ernest Braun*, the first technology assessor in Austria and founder of ITA in 1988, emeritus professor of physics and technology policy at the University of Aston in Birmingham. He accompanied the genesis of this book over the last months and invested a great deal of effort into this manuscript, both on the level of language and by raising critical questions to us. It was challenging and fruitful to have Ernest on board who cannot be accused of being a computer addict and Web 2.0 aficionado.

Furthermore, we are very grateful to our colleagues in the overall project for their feedback and input over time, in particular to *Christoph Bieber,*

Gerd Fritz, Thomas Gloning, Claus Leggewie, Henning Lobin, Sibylle Peters, and *Jan Schmirmund.* We also gladly acknowledge the major input by *Jana Herwig* and *Axel Kittenberger* to our interim report on microblogging, which was the basis for section 2.2. In addition, special thanks go to *Walter Peissl, Stefan Strauß, Georg Aichholzer, Cornelius Puschmann, Peter Haber, Ulrich Riehm, Astrid Mager, Ellen Fischer,* and *Karen Kastenhofer* for commenting on some parts of the manuscript, but we certainly take the responsibility for the final text and its remaining shortcomings. Many thanks also go out to our interview partners and all the others who took their time to answer our questions, in particular *Payal Arora* who helped us with many details. We are indebted to the Institute of Technology Assessment and Systems Analysis (ITAS) in Karlsruhe for making it possible for one of us to concentrate fully on this text for several months, while the other had to split his attention between this book and his managerial tasks related to ITA, which has undergone an important external evaluation and was affected by a major institutional crisis of its mother institution, right during the hot phase of finalizing this text. Michael sends his thanks also to the students of his recent seminars on cyberscience at the University of Vienna who inspired him with challenging questions. René would like to express special thanks to his colleagues at ITAS, in particular the "421 bike crew", for their warm and helpful welcome and working environment. Last, but not least, we gratefully acknowledge the support of the Campus team, which handled the production process in a very professional and amiable manner.

Michael Nentwich
René König
Vienna/Karlsruhe, December 2011

1 Introduction

In the early part of the 21st century one of us coined the term "cyberscience" (Nentwich 2003) to describe the trend of applying information and communication technologies (ICT) to scientific research. Scholars tended increasingly to use the Internet not only to exchange e-mails, but also to participate in online debates, cooperate at distance, use remote databases, simulate and model reality on their computers, and teaching their students with the web. These developments have not come to a halt since the early days but have accelerated and diversified ever since. As will be discussed in section 1.1, the Internet has today become an essential tool for everyday scholarly communication; academic work without the use of the Internet is now as unthinkable as writing an academic paper on a typewriter, especially for young researchers. The emergence of Web 2.0 opened up new opportunities, seized not only by the general Internet community worldwide, but increasingly also by researchers and academic teachers. During the same period powerful commercial actors continued the development of the Internet and made it a different place compared to its early days.

This book focuses on these latest trends and addresses two interrelated research questions: *What role does the digital social culture triggered by Web 2.0 play in the academic world at present and what are the potentials of platforms such as Twitter, Facebook, and Wikipedia? What impact will the emerging socio-technical practices have?*

We approach an answer to these questions in three steps. First, we will review the status quo of how cyberscience developed (1.1) and which new tools and platforms evolved over the last decade with the potential to serve the academic communities (1.2); as a basis for our empirical research and subsequent analysis, we will present our conceptual framework (1.3). Second, we will present five empirical case studies, discussing promising fields of the developments in recent years when it comes to analyze the potential impact on academia: social network sites such as Facebook and similar sites specifically dedicated to research communities (2.1); microblogging with a focus on Twitter (2.2); collaborative knowledge resources, exemplified by various projects of the Wikimedia foundation, namely Wikipedia, Wikibooks, and Wikiversity (2.3); virtual worlds, in particular the rise and fall of Second Life (2.4); finally the most prominent and ubiquitously used universal search engine Google Web Search as well as Google Scholar and Google Books, which are of special interest for academia (2.5). In a third step, we will analyze the empirical material of chapter 2 in the light of our conceptual framework identifying the following key issues: the crucial role of interactivity (3.1); the blurring boundary between academia and the public (3.2); academic quality in the age of Web 2.0 (3.3); the problem of multiple channels and information overload (3.4); transparency and privacy (3.5); and finally potentially democratizing effects emerging from the participatory possibilities of the new platforms (3.6). The book closes with an outlook and overall conclusions, in which we put the analyzed developments into perspective (4.)

1.1 Cyberscience 1.0 Revisited

The notion of cyberscience first appeared in the literature fifteen years ago (Wouters 1996; Thagard 1997); it was later conceptualized and defined "as scientific activities taking place in the information and communication space that is coming into existence with the help of information and communication technologies, a space in which scientists increasingly circulate while remaining at their desks" (Nentwich 1999, transl.). The study *Cyberscience: Research in the Age of the Internet* (Nentwich 2003) demonstrated empirically and analytically, in detail way, that (1) the transition from traditional science to cyberscience has the potential to bring about changes in all dimensions of scientific activity, including organizational space, and that (2) the changes in science that are occurring in this way are qualitative in nature. At that time, the main focus of the analysis was still on the transition to an electronic publication system (e-journals, multimedia, hypertext, quality control, and digital libraries) and on Internet-based forms of communication and cooperation (e-mail, electronic conferences, groupware, virtual institutes, collaboratories). Even by then, though, it was clear that this object of research was a moving target; today, hardly a day goes by without the appearance of new e-journals, innovative forms of cyber-cooperation, and novel Internet tools and services, all of which at least have the potential to change the way in which scientists work—this dynamic character of the field is one of the main reasons for writing this book. Before looking in more detail at the latest Web 2.0 related developments (below 1.2), we give a brief overview of the status quo of the maturing cyberscience.

One of the most visible impacts of the evolution of cyberscience relates to the *scholarly publication* system. Academic publishing is not what it used to be before the advent of the Internet: In most fields, electronic journals emerged, the publishing houses offer their paper journals also online, huge digital working paper archives give access to the research literature at an early stage, and research libraries slowly turn into "cybraries" (Okerson 1997) providing access to digital repositories of all sorts. Furthermore, we can observe new forms of scholarly publications that would not have been possible in the traditional paper environment, but can only be realized in digital formats. While genuine (strong) hypertexts, which would present knowledge differently, are not frequent, the weak form of electronic texts with multiple links becomes the norm. In enhanced versions of journal articles, multimedia elements like small video clips enhance the ways to convey messages to the reader; and communicating research results via (annotated) databases becomes ever more common (Hey and Trefethen 2008, 16). Since 2003, the open access movement has gained in strength and challenges the commercial scholarly publishing system. Today, an estimated 20 to 25 percent (Björk et al. 2009; Björk et al. 2010; Gargouri et al. 2010) of all research literature in journals is available online *and* open access.

Nowadays by far the most usual form of *direct communication* between researchers is via e-mail, almost universally replacing traditional mail. Voice-over-IP services, such as Skype, have taken over traditional phone calls in some fields. By contrast, video conferencing in academia is still in its infancy, only a few research communities such as high-energy physicists use them more frequently. One of the reasons is that the technical equipment and bandwidth necessary to achieve good quality is generally not available or very expensive, which is a problem in most fields of research. Chatting seems to be a communication channel used by the younger generation of researchers and often as a side-channel to the audio-video conferencing software Skype or within a social network site (see below).

Software supporting *collaboration of groups at a distance*, often subsumed under the umbrella term "groupware", have not yet "taken off", so-called "collaboratories" (Olson et al. 2008) or virtual institutes are not the norm. Most project groups or co-authors still use e-mail as their main tool for exchanging files, only few started to use wikis or other platforms—despite their abundant availability.

The *methods of research* are increasingly influenced by the use of ICT. In some fields, such as astronomy, climate and pharmaceutical research, distributed computing, i.e. the organized use of a large number of computers distributed worldwide to perform computational tasks too expensive or even too large for supercomputers, is widespread. In the social sciences Internet surveys have become an important tool for empirical research and increasingly so even for topics that are not directly connected to the Internet use per se. Research databases, stored not locally, but on the web, are a popular tool. In general, novel methods relying on ICT are developed and often referred to as "digital humanities" or "digital methods".

When it comes to *teaching*, many universities nowadays provide e-learning platforms to administer classes, communicate with the students and exchange files and other resources. Many also broadcast their lectures online, making them available at any time to a larger audience. However, distant learning is far from replacing traditional face-to-face methods on a macro level.

To sum up, since the turn of the millennium, cyberscience matured and is now ubiquitous. Practically all researchers of most fields are cyberscientists as they spend a considerable and increasing amount of time not only in front of a computer screen, but also communicating with their objects of research, their peers, and the extra-academic world (Gibbons et al. 1994, 36ff.). In contrast to this, "traditional science" persists only in small niches. There is no doubt we live in the age of cyberscience. But what is next?

1.2 Web 2.0 and Cyberscience

1.2.1 The Internet is becoming a social space

The term Web 2.0 seems to have been used for the first time in a magazine for IT managers at the end of 2003 (Knorr 2003). It originally referred to a new software model (web services and outsourcing), and by extension to an economic model in which the software is no longer tested at considerable expense in closed user groups before being commercially released, but remains in a kind of permanent "beta status" and is constantly being improved by active users and on the basis of the feedback they provide. As this happens, it is quite possible for new versions of a software to appear on a daily basis (see for example O'Reilly 2005). These innovations and groupings of services have been hyped as a new phase of the Internet; the decimal term 2.0 is taken from software jargon, where it is used to refer to a new, significantly revised version. One of the most important technical characteristics of these innovations is that the web is now seen as a "platform" rather than just as a way of storing data on a large scale. From the point of view of the users, it is no longer just the content but in part the software itself that is no longer to be found on the local computer. This means that the goal of interactive access from any location is on the way to being attained. The new software architecture makes it possible, to an unprecedented degree, not only to combine content from different points in the network, but also software modules. They are fused and recombined to become what are known as "mash-ups", i.e. Internet pages where the different parts (graphics, text, the contents of databanks, software, interactive elements, etc.) come from different sources.

The most important characteristic of Web 2.0[1] in the present context relates to the "*architecture of participation*" (O'Reilly 2005). This means that contributions are made in a decentralized way, both by the programmers and by the users. In this context, Bruns (2008) speaks of "produsage", observing that today the traditional distinction between production, distribution and reception would no longer be adequate (in section 3.2 we will come back to this thesis in the light of our empirical findings of chapter 2).

---

1 This is not the place to present the ongoing conceptual debate around the term "Web 2.0": see e.g. Berners-Lee (2006) and his critique of the term referring to the original concept of Web 1.0, and e.g. Wu Song (2010) for a deeper theoretical and critical perspective on the concept. Despite its historical and theoretical weaknesses, we decided to use it for pragmatic reasons, simply because it is widely used.

The term "crowdsourcing" originally described outsourcing the development of software modules to programmers working online, without pay-
ment, in their spare time. It has become a popular term and principle
which is now used in a number of different settings.[2] Today various kinds
of content such as texts, videos and pictures are increasingly developed by
the users themselves with the help of Web 2.0 technology. The term commonly applied in this context is "user-generated content". Instead of aiming at a mere passive consumption of content, Web 2.0 developers try to
take advantage of the interactive functions of their tools, also for shaping
the technology itself. It is very difficult to use the conventional language of
copyright to capture the result of this process. Consequently, this development is associated with the "open content" movement, which supports
the reuse of software in different settings without restrictions. Scientists,
too, now speak of "science commons" as part of the "creative commons"
(Wilbanks 2005).

Here are some examples of typical Web 2.0 applications. Recently especially social network sites such as Facebook gained a lot of attention. They
are mainly used for identity management, self-marketing and networking,
i.e. getting in touch with others with shared interests (see 2.1). There are
also Web 2.0 applications which make it possible for users to become authors themselves in an uncomplicated way, in particular web diaries or
"weblogs" ("blogs" for short). Microblogging services enable users to send
short messages that resemble diary entries (see 2.2.), and there are various
kinds of wikis, which are collaborative and, unlike earlier groupware applications, public forums where written contributions can be posted. The
best-known example is Wikipedia, a global, free encyclopedia compiled,
potentially, by all its users (see 2.3). Another group of typical Web 2.0
applications which also serves as a way of sharing knowledge without creating primary content is "social bookmarking", which is the collection of
links to websites and online publications on related themes. This results in
so-called "folksonomies", which in the new web are replacing and complementing the traditional taxonomies centrally controlled and updated by
specialists: By means of "collaborative tagging" or "social tagging", users
allocate web content descriptors without reference to any rules and so
make it accessible to others; this means that the tagged elements (e.g. web-

---

2 For example, Bry and Herwig (2009, 31) also use "crowdsourcing" with regard to the
concept of "open innovation" to refer to the outsourcing of "research work to a large,
barely defined crowd of people".

sites or publications) are collated in a comprehensive, albeit "unprofessional" way via the volume and weighting generated by the frequency with which the tags are allocated (see Bruns 2008). Podcasts, series of audio or video data made available online, are also counted as part of Web 2.0 to the extent that they are often not produced by professional mass media (however such professional radio content is also increasingly becoming available as "podcasts"). Virtual worlds are another area of Web 2.0, and are also shaped and characterized by their users and their behavior (see 2.4).

We can sum up by saying that what has become known as Web 2.0 largely builds on the elements that were part of the early Internet phase and which foster interactivity and the joint production of content. The early Internet was to a great extent a top-down medium—with some exceptions such as chatting services or discussion lists—in which established providers or those in the course of establishing themselves, but at any rate relatively few providers, made content available (classic "one-to-many" communication). The main focus of what is now emerging is that in addition to the traditional forms of communication, which continue to exist, practically every user can become a provider ("many-to-many" communication). Although this was already possible in the early time of the web, the new applications make this process much easier. Moreover, the much greater bandwidth of most Internet connections has now made many of the new services widely usable for the first time and so made them relevant to society as a whole (at least in developed countries). Together with the emergence of new social networks and online communities, this phenomenon is evidence of the Internet's development towards a social space. However, it remains to be seen if the expectations caused by this development are fulfilled.

1.2.2 Social media, digital social networks and digital social culture

Many connect this development with terms such as *social media* (Kaplan and Haenlein 2010), *digitally enabled social networks* or *digital social networks* (DSN) (e.g. Grange and Benbasat 2009; Nordan et al. 2009; Bampo et al. 2008). According to Kaplan and Haenlein (2010) the concept of social media refers to "a group of Internet-based applications that build on the ideological and technological foundations of Web 2.0, and that allow the creation and exchange of user-generated content". This also supports novel forms of social interaction. Social interactions are the building blocks of social networks, which are more or less stable social structures made up of network entities or nodes (individuals and/or organizations). These nodes are connected by one or more specific types of interdependency, such as friendship, kinship, common interest, financial exchange, dislike, sexual relationships, or relationships of beliefs, knowledge or prestige. Expanding to the digital world, we understand by DSN with Grange and Benbasat (2009) "web applications that enable people to create social networks, i.e., when users—or their representation in virtual environments—are network entities connected to each other by links of various nature, such as awareness, friendship, proximity, mutual interest, etc.". These networks may either relate to existing non-digital or offline networks, or expand on them, or be fully independent from any pre-existing network outside the digital space. The term DSN contains three important elements: *digital* describes the specific technical shape which determines the communicative possibilities; *social* refers to the interactive practices between the users; and *networks* points to the significance of interlinked web-like structures. On the one hand, these can be the outcome of such practices; on the other hand, existing offline networks pre-structure these digitally-mediated networks.

DSN are on the rise and have become important factors in many fields of modern societies, from journalism to business—not least in academia—challenging established structures. Due to their digital nature, ICT play a significant role in intermediating between the involved actors. While DSN could already be established with tools available in the early Internet, in particular by means of e-mail listserv or web-based forums, the interactive and participatory nature of Web 2.0 technologies is particularly suited to support building them. Note, however, that further technologies also profoundly shape these networks, e.g. search engines like Google—that is why we included them in our case studies alongside typical Web 2.0 platforms.

DSN contribute to an emerging *digital social culture*. By this we mean the specific networking and communicative activity and behavior of humans online and intertwined with the offline world. We observe new patterns of written communication in a blended synchronous-asynchronous mode, with even new terminologies, new social norms with regard to responsiveness and timeliness, novel kinds of assessing the usefulness and quality of resources, ad-hoc forms of collaboration with a high degree of work-sharing, etc. All this contributes to the slow evolution of a new kind of culture in the sense of customs, "how-tos", and standard practices.

1.2.3 On the path to cyberscience 2.0?

When we first studied the phenomenon of cyberscience in 2003, Web 2.0 was still in its infancy. Today, it is everywhere: millions of people all over the world, including many scientists, have become part of the rapidly growing digital social networks that are fostering the development of the new services. Elements of some of the phenomena, that we would today subsume under the blanket term Web 2.0, were already visible in 2003: some academic journals were experimenting with open review procedures, known as "open peer commentary" or "open peer review" (Pöschl 2004, 2007; Nentwich 2003, 371ff.; 2005b). There was also discussion of the possibility that the knowledge accumulated by the sciences could be stored in new kinds of hyper-databanks which would be collectively maintained and updated (Nentwich 2003, 270ff.). Even at that time, there was extensive discussion of the way in which readers could also become, to a certain extent, authors, or "wreaders", which meant that there would be an increase in multiple authorship and, thus, a situation in which texts could no longer be attributed to particular authors. By then it was possible to discern that the new media had the potential to, as it were, open new windows in the ivory tower of science and to contribute to the removal of the traditional, strict distinction between communication within science and communication between science and the outside world.

In 2003, these considerations were still largely speculative. Now that Web 2.0 services have arrived, they have become of much more immediate concern. If one looks at the new phenomena, described briefly above, it rapidly becomes clear that the changes set in motion by e-mail, e-mail discussion lists, video conferences, groupware etc., which led us to speak of cyberscience—the digital communicative space of researchers—are now being strengthened or are providing, for the first time, the means by which this new form of science can establish itself.

It is quite clear that the setting up of collaborative knowledge resources (or net-based collaborative writing) is a development with great potential for use in science, and this is emphasized by the fact that scientists are already showing great interest in it. Virtual worlds could enrich distance communication in science, which has up until now largely been based on written texts, and it could even be the breakthrough that will make it possible to organize electronic conferences. Simultaneously, completely new forms of micro-publication are coming into existence, and so far there has been very little investigation of the effects these might have on formal and informal communication between scientists. Finally, the tools that make it easier to share information are also of interest for the scientific enterprise, which relies on cooperation and the availability of information and the building blocks of knowledge, both in its overall constitution and within smaller working groups.

These observations—shared by a few other scholars (e.g. Hey and Trefethen 2008, 28; Bry and Herwig 2009; Waldrop 2008)—present us with a good opportunity to ask what new potential and what specific influence the new Web 2.0 services will have on science. We propose to use *"cyberscience 2.0"* to refer to forms of science influenced by Web 2.0 and to employ "Peer Review 2.0" in an analogous way in relation to potential changes in the academic quality control system (Nentwich and König 2010). Similarly, the term "Scholarship 2.0" has been coined to refer to new forms of academic publication,[3] and so has "Science 2.0"—this latter concept, however, is in our view sometimes used merely to provide a contrast with "Science 1.0", i.e. traditional science before the advent of the Internet, and so corresponds more closely to cyberscience (1.0). It is true, though, that the expression "Science 2.0" also appears in connection with Web 2.0 sites such as ResearchGate, which explicitly applies the model of the new Web 2.0 social networks to the setting up of a scientific community (see below 2.5). Waldrop (2008), on the other hand, speaks of Science 2.0 explicitly in the context of Web 2.0, and defines it as follows: "Science 2.0 generally refers to new practices of scientists who post raw experimental results, nascent theories, claims of discovery and draft papers on the web for others to see and comment on." The parallel German concept "Wissenschaft 2.0" is used in a similar way (e.g. by Bry and Herwig 2009). The future of libraries is discussed by using the terms "Bibliothek 2.0" (see Danowski and Heller 2006) or "Library 2.0" (Casey and Savastinuk 2006) in relation to Web 2.0 applications. Finally, one also sometimes comes across the term Publication 2.0 (for example, in one of the ResearchGate groups), which is used to mean academic publication using either open peer review or open access.

In view of the considerations summarized above, which had already been put forward before the appearance of what is now known as Web 2.0, there is no particular reason to adhere to the concepts as these authors use them. Similarly, Tim Berners-Lee has criticized the concept of Web 2.0 on

---

3 scholarship20.blogspot.com. Note: All URLs given in footnotes have been retrieved on 30 November 2011, if not stated otherwise.

the grounds that the same conception of a network was the basis of the original web, that is "1.0" (Berners-Lee 2006). The question of whether or not the label cyberscience 2.0 is indeed appropriate, on the grounds that qualitatively new aspects have been added, and whether for this reason the conceptual demarcation (and fashionable creation of concepts derived from software development) is justified, will be examined in the course of this book (see in particular our conclusions in chapter 4).

1.3 Conceptual Framework and Methods

With a view to answering our main research questions—What role does the digital social culture, triggered by Web 2.0, play in the academic world at present and what are the potentials of platforms such as Twitter, Facebook, and Wikipedia? What impact will the emerging socio-technical practices have?—we apply and only marginally adapt the same exploratory approaches and the same conceptual framework that have been developed for and applied by the previous cyberscience study (Nentwich 2003, 1ff. and 21ff.; 2005a). In this section we briefly summarize this framework and our empirical instruments.

1.3.1 Modeling scholarly activities and ICT impact on academia

As in the previous study our main object of research, our dependent variable in a broad sense, is the scholarly communication system (1); the "independent", though dynamically changing, variable are the information and communication technologies, which are in this study mainly the emerging Web 2.0 platforms (2); furthermore, we will have to cope with a series of intervening variables that influences the changes under way (3).

(1) The scholarly communication system consists of a series of actors (all researchers worldwide) and their institutional, research and communication infrastructure. Our main focus is on the typical scholarly activities performed within this system. All of these activities are of a communicative nature and we may distinguish (with Gibbons et al. 1994, 36ff.) three layers of communication: with the object of research, with other researchers (and research-related) staff, and with the external world. From a proce-

dural point of view, we distinguish the following types of scholarly activities:

- *Knowledge production:* At the heart of all research activity lies the systematic and creative processes of producing new knowledge. These include information gathering, data production and processing, analysis, and data management.
- *Communication (knowledge processing):* The knowledge produced in the laboratories, in the field, and on the desks is constantly processed among the researchers: they exchange it and collaborate around it, they discuss and evaluate it in seminars, at conferences and in the framework of formal quality control procedures.
- *Distribution of knowledge:* Once produced and evaluated, the knowledge is published and informs further researchers, is used in teaching, and possibly implemented, for instance in a product or as policy advice.

To these scholarly activities, directly related to the research processes, we may add the *institutional settings* in which these activities take place. These relate to the organizational setup, such as the types of research institutions, the technical equipment, recruitment procedures, fund raising and project acquisition, etc.

In this model of scholarly activity the elements partly overlap. For instance, knowledge representation, i.e. the way research results are presented in written or other forms, is part both of producing and of processing knowledge; likewise publishing research results belongs both to knowledge processing and distribution. These activities are not linear "steps" to be performed in succession (production—communication—distribution), but are part of an iterative process. For instance, a preliminary result of the production phase is being discussed among colleagues; the discussion challenges the result and leads to further research. This is especially the case in the context of Web 2.0 as pointed out e.g. in the concept of "produsage" (Bruns 2008). We are not denying these instances of blurring, but we believe that a general separation of these typical activities is still appropriate for analytical purposes (we will come back to this issue in section 3.2). In Figure 1 the overall picture of scholarly activities and their framework conditions is visualized.

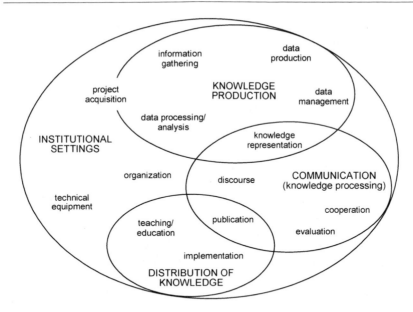

Figure 1: Types of scholarly activities and framework conditions

Source: Nentwich 2003, 24

As previously noted, one of the main results of the earlier cyberscience study (Nentwich 2003) is that, in principle, all of these types of scholarly activities and framework conditions are somehow affected by the widespread diffusion of ICT, in particular the Internet, in science and research. In this book, we assess whether this also holds true for the new Web 2.0 platforms and other maturing Internet services. Therefore, when we present our case studies in chapter 2, we will use the above model (and figure) in order to find out in which field of scholarly activity the respective platform or service may potentially influence the overall picture.

(2) The case studies will be devoted to describing and analyzing the development of the independent variables in this study, i.e. the various ICT applications, such as microblogging platforms or social network sites. Along the diffusion path, the technological tools become gradually adapted to the needs of academia. For instance, users' feedback will be acknowledged by the developers, which is particularly likely in a Web 2.0 environment (see above 1.2); or scholars and scientists "appropriate" the tools in a way not expected by the designers (we will present such examples in chapter 2). In other words, although set as the main independent variable in our

model (because what is available is mainly developed outside academia), technology can also be viewed as a dependent variable as it is further socially shaped inside academia (Nentwich 2005a, 545). Which technologies become further developed and get used not only depends on the characteristics of the technologies, but also on the nature and aim of the social groups that are using them (cf. MacKenzie and Wajcman 1988; Walsh and Bayma 1996, 361).

(3) In the second main part of this book (the third chapter), when we assess the potentials and possible impacts of these applications, we will deal with a number of intervening factors, which will influence the diffusion processes and the way technologies are shaped. We distinguish three types of intervening factors (Nentwich 2003, 38ff.):

–   *Institutional factors:* Diffusion research and science and technology studies have pointed out that institutions in a broad sense play an important role in explaining diffusion and shaping processes of technologies. Among these variables we may distinguish general co-ordinates (e.g. law and politics, the disciplinary environment), economic factors (such as research budgets, application orientation), and cultural parameters (e.g. the prestige of paper-bound publishing, professional cultures). These factors may play out differently for academia as a whole and at the disciplinary level.
–   *Technical and functional factors:* A major outcome of diffusion research (Rogers 1995, 16) is that some innovations will be adopted more rapidly than others if they offer a positive cost-benefit advantage over the earlier technology. We distinguish between the purely technical factors (such as the attractiveness of the innovative features, reliability, bandwidth, standards) and functional aspects (e.g. the pace of discovery in a field, time pressure, visual orientation, type of data generation, etc.).
–   *Actor-related factors:* Individual and, even more important, collective actors are the basic units adopting innovation; therefore factors such as reputation, experience, peripheral status (both on the individual and the organizational level), funding, institutional inertia, etc. play a decisive role. Furthermore, the history of innovation has highlighted the importance of agency, i.e. the existence of (cyber-)entrepreneurs.

As mentioned above, these intervening variables are important when it comes to understanding how and why certain technological innovations diffuse into the daily lives of cyberscientists and others do not and how they are shaped during the processes of appropriation by those who use them. These factors already played a role when we analyzed the development from the traditional (i.e. pre-Internet) scholarly communication system to the status quo at the beginning of the 21st century; they are also an essential part of the explanation of how and why cyberscience as we know it today (see above 1.1) came about; and they will be at the heart of our analysis about the possible future(s) of cyberscience 2.0. Figure 2 summarize this model of change.

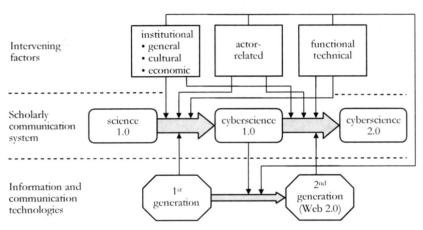

Figure 2: Modeling Web 2.0-induced changes of the scholarly communication system

Source: adapted from Nentwich 2003, 38

1.3.2 Methods applied

In this study, we applied the typical methods of empirical social research with a focus on the following four main approaches:

– *Review of the research literature:* There is a growing corpus of literature from different disciplines relevant to our research questions. We tried to consider and incorporate it in our case studies. Some fields are well-researched and could not be represented by us in detail. For other fields we had to draw on grey literature, in particular Internet publications such as blogs, because they were hardly researched so far.
– *Internet enquiry* Most of our empirical work was to explore the web and the platforms systematically (similar to Nentwich 2003, 12). We followed a large number of links with a view to exploring the mainstream

as well as the cutting-edge and already defunct new platforms and usage patterns. In addition we studied in-depth the operating modes, guidelines and terms of reference of these platforms. The results of this Internet research is recorded in the link collection "Cyberlinks".[4]

- *Participatory observation:* During the past three years the authors opened a number of accounts on those new Web 2.0 platforms—and used them actively—in order to be able to observe in close-up how they function, what activities the users (fellow researchers) perform, and what usage patterns emerge. In some cases, we staged small (social) experiments by intervening in the platforms, e.g. by creating a "group" in a social network site, inviting others to join, and then observing their behavior and activities.

- *Interviews:* Occasionally we conducted non-structured interviews with experts in the field or particularly active members of certain platforms, using the telephone, e-mail or web-based mailing tools within the platforms in question to communicate with the interviewees. In most instances, we asked a few very particular questions regarding usage practices in order to complement our observations of the platforms.

At this point the stage is set for the first main part of this study, the rich and analytical description of research-related Web 2.0 platforms and further important applications that have the potential to influence how present-day cyberscientists might work in the future.

---

4 www.oeaw.ac.at/ita/cyberlinks.htm.

2 Case Studies

Although the Web 2.0 is less than a decade old, it is nevertheless a rich and diversified environment. The academic profession can choose among an increasing number of dynamically evolving tools and platforms. The wealth of instruments that are potentially useful for academia include tools related to

- *knowledge production:* social bookmarking (e.g. Delicious), search engines (e.g. Google), wikis and collaborative writing (e.g. Etherpad, Google Docs), shared online libraries (e.g. Zotero, Mendeley, Cite-u-like), virtual labs (e.g. MyExperiment), automated translation services (e.g. Google Translator);
- *knowledge processing (direct communication and collaboration):* microblogging, video-conferencing (e.g. Skype), chatting, wikis, social network sites, shared workspaces, shared online libraries, crowdsourcing (e.g. Wikipedia, SETI);
- *knowledge distribution and publishing:* science blogging, microblogging (e.g. Twitter), open peer review, virtual worlds (e.g. Second Life), podcasts, video-blogs, information aggregators (e.g. Reddit, Digg, RSS), outreach portals (e.g. TED), recommender systems (e.g. Amazon), early publication systems (e.g. Nature precedings, Slideshare), open data sharing (e.g. BioTorrent), e-teaching (e.g. Sciencecourseware; Video-lectures);
- *institutional environment:* social network sites (e.g. Academia.edu, ResearchGate), virtual worlds, crowd-funding (e.g. Flattr).[5]

In the above list we included only a few examples. This study could not cover all of those instruments in-depth, but instead we focus on five empirical case studies of some central Internet platforms that have a consider-

---

5 For URLs of all examples given in this list see www.oeaw.ac.at/ita/cyberlinks.htm.

able potential to influence the way science and research will be done in the future. According to our interest in the latest Internet developments, we mainly look at typical Web 2.0 services of influential Internet actors and their platforms. We start with social network sites, including Facebook and a number of science-specific platforms (2.1), followed by an analysis of microblogging with special attention to Twitter (2.2) and Wikipedia and other platforms of the Wikimedia Foundation that may be of interest to researchers (2.3). The next subsection focuses on virtual worlds, in particular on Second Life, and on what activities researchers may develop in them (2.4). The last case study puts an additional influential Internet player center-stage, namely Google with its web search and the special services Google Scholar and Google Books (2.5).[6] Although, these Google services stem from the Web 1.0 era and cannot be categorized as Web 2.0, we add them because they shape Internet-mediated research not least by giving access to Web 2.0 content. Furthermore, the latest search engines include user-data to rank search results, thus including a typical element of the Web 2.0.

Our platform-oriented approach necessarily leaves out certain developments. For example, we could not analyze in a deep case study the countless science-related blogs, which certainly play an important role in cyberscience 2.0 (but see 3.2 for their role in blurring the boundaries between academia and the public sphere). However, we believe our case selection represents an adequate variety of the emerging trends and their impact on academia, which we shall discuss from a broader perspective in chapter 3. Moreover, they should shed light on influential platforms which are not part of institutionalized ICT infrastructure initiatives for academia (this has been studied in greater detail by Borgmann 2007; Dutton and Jeffreys 2010).

---

6 These case studies are based on five related research reports Herwig et al. (2009), König and Nentwich (2008, 2009, 2010), Nentwich and König (2011), and a working paper Nentwich (2009). For the purpose of this book, the empirical information has been carefully updated and partly expanded in the first half of 2011, the presentation structured in a new and mostly uniform way, and the analysis further developed.

2.1 Social Network Sites

During the first decade of the new Millennium, social network sites (SNS) have become a fundamental part of the web. At the time of writing, the most popular network Facebook has now more members than there are inhabitants of Europe[7] and it is one of the most frequented web sites in the world.[8] SNS offer novel communicative possibilities; above all they link-up its members and map their offline networks. This seems to offer an attractive potential for academic communication as well.

While it is undisputed that the well-known examples like Facebook, MySpace or the newcomer Google+ are SNS, the exact definition is less clear and unequivocal. Different authors use different versions of the term, from "social network services" or "sites" to "social network*ing*", "network-ing platforms", "social network communities" and many more (cf. e.g. Mack et al. 2007; similar in German: Richter and Koch 2007; Schmidt 2009, 23). In most cases these terms are used synonymously. However, some authors also discuss differences:

"We chose not to employ the term 'networking' for two reasons: emphasis and scope. 'Networking' emphasizes relationship initiation, often between strangers. While networking is possible on these sites, it is not the primary practice on many of them, nor is it what differentiates them from other forms of computer-mediated communication (CMC)." (Boyd and Ellison 2007)

We shall leave open at this point whether Body and Ellison are right in assuming that SNS would prefer not to initiate relationships (see also Beer 2008; Fuchs 2009, 4ff.) and will follow, for pragmatic reasons, the termi-nology of these authors, because the term "social network site(s)" seems to be most widely used. Note, though, that the terms are not used uniformly in the literature, probably resulting from the technical complexity of the various platforms. Accordingly the cited literature in this chapter some-times diverges from our understanding of the term. As SNS have multiple functions it is difficult to set a selective definition, hence it depends on the specific definition whether a platform will be counted as a SNS. For in-stance, Schmidt (2009, 23) focuses in his definition on the possibility to set up a personal "profile" with information about oneself, such as interests

---

7 www.socialmediaschweiz.ch/html/landerberichte.html.
8 In June 2011 Alexa has put Facebook on the second rank on its list of global top sites: alexa.com/topsites.

and activities, within a digital space that can usually only be reached after registration. Starting from this profile, users initiate and entertain social relationships to others, making them explicit through interlinking; the members interact and navigate on the platform, which is basically formed by these networks of "contacts" or "friends" (as they are called e.g. in Facebook). We find it necessary to focus on the central function of *profiles* in order to distinguish SNS from other services. Networking alone is also a characteristic of other platforms that are typically not seen as SNS, such as the voice-over-IP service Skype or the microblogging service Twitter. As for the latter, the profiles are minimalist and the timeline of messages, not the profile is at the center of the platform (cf. section 2.2). We observe that also in these other services increasingly SNS-like functions are added: for instance, Twitter now also offers automatic proposals for other users to follow. Therefore it may be very reasonable to call such services SNS and some of them gradually transform into one.[9] However, in this chapter we focus on SNS in which *profiles of the users are central network nodes*, which can be addressed through various channels.

There are many differences between the various SNS, in particular when it comes to the available communication tools or how users can configure their profiles (cf. Boyd and Ellison 2007). Two core functions are always present: *identity management* and *contact management* (cf. Richter and Koch 2007). The profiles map—more or less in the public domain—the contacts of a person and enable access to further members on various paths, i.e. networking. See Figure 3 below for a screenshot of a profile in ResearchGate, a SNS specialized on academia.

As the technical functionality and target groups vary, we may distinguish different types of SNS: There are variations according to the *intended usage forms*. In some SNS private purposes prevail (e.g. MySpace), in others professional fields of application dominate (e.g. Xing, LinkedIn, ResearchGate); in others private and professional use overlap (e.g. Facebook, Google+). *Requirements for access* also vary: some are open, that is they only require a simple registration which, in principle, can be done by all Internet users (cf. Richter and Koch 2008). This is the case with many popular SNS (e.g. Facebook, MySpace). Other platforms offer limited free access, but charge user fees for the full service (so-called "freemium" services; e.g. Xing). Finally there are specialized networks that are open only for certain

---

9 For example, the SNS "Tencent QQ" (qq.com), popular today in China, started as an instant message service (chatting platform), see Boyd and Ellison (2007).

communities, such as a company or research group (e.g. in Ning, a platform for customizable SNS, it is possible to establish such, mostly small SNS). The *available communication forms* vary according to different needs. For example, to nudge someone online (e.g. "poking" on Facebook or "gruscheln" on StudiVZ) is used in a private context, whereas many professional networks offer additional functions such as bibliographic search (for a detailed description of the various functions see below 2.1.1).

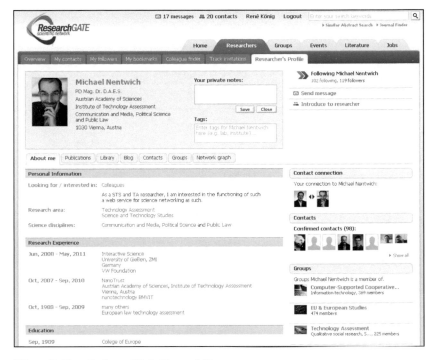

Figure 3: Detail of a profile in ResearchGate

Overview and timeline of SNS

Table 1 gives an overview of a series of relevant SNS with a focus on profiles; the table is not comprehensive and puts particular emphasis on science-related SNS.[10] We distinguish between *general SNS*, characterized by

---

10 See also the category "Social Network Sites" of the Cyberlinks collection, listing a larger number of SNS with short descriptions and Internet addresses: www.oeaw.ac.at/cgi-

Table 1: Overview of SNS

Name	Members	Access	URL
General SNS			
Facebook	800.000.000	Free	facebook.com
MySpace	100.000.000	Free	myspace.com
LinkedIn	135.000.000	Premium	linkedin.com
Google+	40.000.000	Free	plus.google.com
VZ group	16.000.000	Free	www.studivz.net
Xing	11.400.000	Premium	xing.com
Science-specific SNS			
Mendeley	1.392.000	Free	mendeley.com
ResearchGate	1.200.000	Free	researchgate.net
Academia.edu	822.000	Free	academia.edu
Sciencestage	270.000	Free	sciencestage.com
Vivo	40.800	Free	vivo.ufl.edu
Nature Network	25.000	Free	network.nature.com
Epernicus	20.000	Free	epernicus.com
research.iversity	11.500	Free	iversity.org
LabRoots	4.000	Free	labroots.com
Research Cooperative	3.590	Free	researchcooperative.org
myExperiment	3.500	Free	myexperiment.org
arts-humanities.net	1.500	Free	arts-humanities.net
ScholarZ.net	433	Free	scholarz.net
Science 3.0	574	Free	science3point0.com
AtmosPeer	125	Free	atmospeer.net
iAMscientist	>100	Invitation	iamscientist.com
edumeres.net	100	Free	edumeres.net
EPTA Ning	87	Invitation	eptanetwork.ning.com
ScienXe.org	NA	Premium	scienxe.org
SciSpace	NA	Free	scispace.com
Ways.org	NA	Free	ways.org

Sources: For status quo of numbers of members see footnote 11.

---

usr/ita/cyber.pl?cmd=get&cat=64. A comprehensive list of general SNS can be found on Wikipedia: en.wikipedia.org/wiki/List_of_social_networking_websites; see also the list of German sites: netzwertig.com/2008/04/15/zn-aktuelles-ranking-149-social-networks-aus-deutschland.

11 All URLs have been last visited end of November 2011: Facebook: facebook.com/press/info.php?statistics; MySpace: web.archive.org/web/20101104105953/ http://

their rather broad and not specified purpose of usage, and *science-specific SNS*, which have been developed with a view to serving academic purposes. Although only including a subset of existing SNS, the table gives an impression of the heterogeneity and quantity of the observed phenomena. They range from sites with less than hundred members to those serving millions. Note that due to the different available sources and methods the accuracy may vary and not all numbers are up to date. For a further discussion see 2.1.3).

The following Figure 4 shows that the very first SNS appeared as early as by the end of the 1990s, and that the big wave of formation started in 2002/2003. Interestingly, today's largest platform was founded only in 2004—also the year of the foundation of the two first science-specific SNS, Vivo and Ways.org. In the case of Vivo the implementation started at first locally, whereas the supra-regional start only took place in 2010. Summing up, most science-specific SNS have been founded from 2007 onwards; hence it is a relatively new phenomenon.

---

www.myspace.com/pressroom/fact-sheet (November 2010); LinkedIn: press.linkedin. com/about_de; Google+: mygoogleplus.de/2011/10/offizielle-google-plus-nutzerzah-len-40-millionen; VZ-Gruppe: meinvz.net/l/about_us/1/ (July 2010); Xing: corporate. xing.com/no_cache/deutsch/presse/pressemitteilungen; ResearchGate: researchgate. net/researchers; Mendeley: mendeley.com; Sciencestage: geozon.info/ 2010/04/15/ comparison-chart-of-scientific-networks (April 2010); Academia.edu: academia.edu; Vivo: vivo.slis.indiana.edu/images/gallery/activity_poster.pdf (July 2010); Nature Network: network.nature.com; Epernicus: epernicus.com/about/public_site; Research. iversity: iversity.org/pages/digital-campus-opens-its-gates; LabRoots and myExperiment: see Sciencestage; arts-humanities.net; Procter et al. (2010, p. 41; June 2010); ScholarZ: scholarz.net/community_others/search (search for all members within the SNS); Science 3.0: www.science3point0.com/members; AtmosPeer: see Sciencestage; iAMscientist: iamscientist.com/people; Edumeres: according to Andreas L. Fuchs at the conference DigiWiss 2010 in Cologne, Sept. 21, 2010, www.scivee.tv/ node/25099; EPTA Ning: eptanetwork.ning.com/profiles/members (only visible with registration); Research Cooperative: researchcooperative.org/profiles/members.

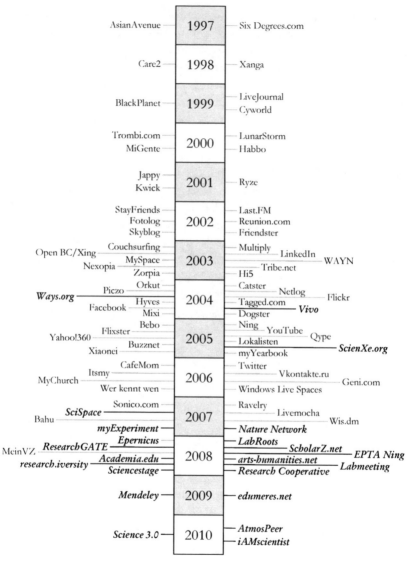

Figure 4: Examples of Foundations of SNS 1997–2010

Source: The figure is based on Heidemann (2010); science-specific SNS in bold and italics; amendments from 2008 onwards only for science-specific SNS. Note that the definition of SNS used by Heidemann partly differs from ours; therefore some not profile-centered platforms might be included here, too.

The economics of SNS

SNS differ with regard to their sources of funding. We observe roughly seven models, which are not mutually exclusive and are often combined:

- *User-specific advertisement:* The substantial data shared by the users gives a comprehensive picture of the interests of persons or groups. This makes them commercially attractive as it is possible to place personalized advertisement and gather valuable knowledge about markets. In order to attract as many people as possible, the network is usually for free in this model, but users have to allow analyzing their data. Therefore this has been labeled the "service-for-profile model" (Elmer 2004; Rogers 2009), as applied e.g. in Facebook, but also in other platforms, such as Google's.
- *Scattered advertisement:* Apart from personalized advertisement, also less targeted, general advertisement may be presented, for example on start pages (e.g. StudiVZ).
- *Fees:* Some SNS charge fees for premium functions (e.g. Xing), such as specific services, or enriched profiles for commercial users. Some of the job exchange services are free for members, but not for those advertising jobs (e.g. Xing).
- *Subsidies:* Some SNS are financed via public money in the form of project grants (e.g. Vivo, research.iversity, ScholarZ.net).
- *Donations:* As the commercial models have often been criticized—in particular with regard to data protection and privacy issues of the service-for-profile model—some users are prepared to donate in favor of non-commercial offers. One trailblazer is Diaspora[12], which is being developed as a future competitor of Facebook. In order to raise donations, the Internet is used in the form of the so-called "crowd funding".
- *Out of the marketing budget:* There are cases where SNS are seen as part of the public relations strategy of an institution or enterprise and is therefore funded from the marketing budget (e.g. NatureNetworks).
- *"Start-up":* Frequently, SNS are set up as start-up companies, which invest first in the infrastructure and in collecting members. Only when the site has a large number of users—the SNS' capital—it may generate earnings (e.g. ResearchGate, Mendeley).

---

12 joindiaspora.com.

In the context of institutional academic usage of SNS it is mainly a policy decision which strategy to choose. Most existing general SNS, such as Facebook, have the advantage of a freely available infrastructure and a high number of users. The drawback is that one is dependent on a commercially oriented enterprise and that one has to accept its terms (this problem is, however, not specific to SNS platforms, but similar to other services, such as Google, see section 2.5). In contrast to commercial SNS, science-specific ones do not have to be conceptualized in terms of financial earnings, as long as they are financed by other sources, such as subsidies, fees or donations. Independently from the issue of sourcing, all SNS have to compete with other providers—unless this market pressure is suspended, for example when universities put pressure on their faculty to join a particular platform (e.g. Vivo). As the value of a SNS is crucially tied to the number and activity level of its members, it is not sufficient to provide an effective and well-financed infrastructure. The well-established incumbents have a considerable advantage presenting a barrier for market entry to all newly founded SNS. One should not underrate this factor given the many providers both on the general and the science-specific SNS market.

2.1.1 Main functions

Despite the differences between the SNS, a number of features can be observed repeatedly. In general, these services provide multiple channels allowing for various types of communication (for a typology of academic communication forms see Nentwich 2003, 30ff.): among users (one-to-one, one-to-many and few-to-few) and between users and machine (searching; proposals based on semantic algorithms). SNS provide for some known communication media (in particular web mail, chat) directly on the platform, others are only offered as links from the profile pages (e.g. Skype). In addition, the exchange of status messages and the integration of external microblogs increase the density of communication among those not present in the same place. In the following, we present the functions and forms of communication that are typical for SNS, though not all of them are necessarily available in each individual SNS (some are only available in certain science-specific SNS).

(1) Profiles: User profiles are digital representations of the users and as such the central nodes of SNS. The following kinds of information can be made available to other members in a pre-structured way:

- Contact information (e.g. address, e-mail, phone, website)
- Personal information (e.g. date of birth, interests)
- Pictures of users and other photos
- Status messages (microblogging on current events etc., indications regarding one's professional and personal relationship status etc.)
- Tracking of user activities (e.g. messages regarding changes of the profile, the joining of groups etc.)
- Record of contacts, affiliation to groups etc.

In some SNS it is also possible to have specific profiles for organizations. In Facebook, for instance, these are called "pages", but their structure and functions are similar to "groups" (see below). Thus profiles are like enhanced calling cards of individuals, organizations and groups. To some extent, it is possible to control the visibility of all or some specified data of the profile, for instance for all members of the SNS, or only for certain contacts/friends).

(2) Communication: Various web-based tools are available in order to communicate with other members:

- *Web-based messaging:* Bilateral sending and receiving of simple text messages between individual members or groups. Some platforms (e.g. Facebook) also offer e-mail addresses, hence allowing even non-members to contact their users.
- *Chatting:* Synchronous instant messaging among individual members (e.g. Facebook, Ning).
- *Discussion forums/groups:* Thematic groups offer a forum-like space for discussion and exchange.
- *Microblogging:* By writing textual status messages one can notify contacts/friends according to the one-to-many principle. Sometimes one can include pictures, videos and external links directly in the message; the messages of others may also be commented on. This can be done either via a platform-specific service or via linking up to other services. In ResearchGate, for example, one can send platform-internal messages to other services, or vice-versa one can integrate platform-external messages (e.g. from Twitter) in ResearchGate (for more information on microblogging and its academic potential, see 2.2).
- *Nudging functions:* Via "poking" (Facebook) one can make other members aware of oneself, without necessarily having any follow-up communication.

- Inclusion of *videoconferencing* tools (e.g. as add-on feature on the Ning platforms).

The integration of different communication channels within one platform is a distinctive feature of SNS, as compared to various other web-based communication tools.

(3) Networking: As networking is one of the basic functions of SNS, all sites offer various tools to promote it:

- *Contacts/friends:* Network members can add other members, represented by their profiles, as "contacts" ("friends" in Facebook) and can administer them in lists and groupings. As a rule, the other member has to confirm the contact request; in some SNS it is possible to unilaterally "follow" another member (e.g. ResearchGate and Academia.edu).
- *Automated propositions:* On the basis of semantic analysis of the information given in profiles and the activities of the members, the SNS produces proposals for new contacts, related groups, interesting publications or events etc.
- *"Manual" propositions:* Other members can trigger requests and recommendations by themselves.
- *Search function:* Users may find members, groups etc. by search terms.
- *Automated search* of potential contacts is supported via the contact lists of one's own e-mail, microblogging or other SNS' account.
- *Invitation:* Users can invite potential new members via external mail (possible with most SNS), also with tracking of invitations (in particular with ResearchGate)
- *Bookmarking* of profiles, in order to keep persons in mind who are no contacts or whom one does not follow (e.g. ResearchGate).
- *Gift service:* User can give presents to other users (e.g. the "Give a gift" button in Ning).
- Automatically generated *requests* to welcome new members or propose something or someone to them (e.g. Ning, Facebook).
- *Network presentation* in various forms: as a list of all contacts or all members like a directory; visualization and analysis of one's own network in form of an interactive picture (e.g. as a wheel with spokes in ResearchGate; as an additional application in Facebook, see Figure 5); in Academia.edu all institutions are presented as directory tree.

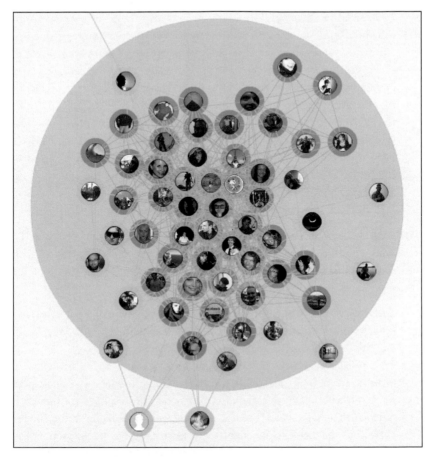

Figure 5: Network visualization by "Social Graph" in Facebook

(4) Directing attention: The great variety of opportunities to communicate and network in SNS suggests further tools to establish the relevance of content and to direct the attention of its members towards particular items. We observed the following:

–   *Start page:* The personal start pages present in structured manner information about the current events within the SNS. They show status messages and further activities of one's contacts as well as news, dates, contact requests, propositions etc.

- *External notifications:* Without being logged into the SNS, users are kept informed via e-mail of all kind of news (contact requests, group information and invitations, uploads, status messages, new events etc.).
- *"Like this" button/ "Share-this" function:* Contributions of other users may get additional attention by clicking on such buttons. This may concern individual comments or status messages, but also certain profiles, links to external offers etc. (e.g. Facebook, Google+, ResearchGate). The trailblazer is Facebook, which makes money by offering such buttons even on web pages outside the platform. These data may be used in the future as indicators for relevance, discussed under the label of *social search* (e.g. Biermann 2010).
- Special tools for *attention direction regarding literature* (see below).

(5) Groups: All users can found thematic groups. By usually offering the following functions, groups enable the detection of and networking with members with similar interests and they provide a digital environment for discussion and collaboration:

- *Discussion forum:* In the forum of a group members can write and read contributions in threads. Moderators with extended rights may facilitate the discussions.
- *File upload:* Users may upload documents, photos and other files in order to make them accessible to other group members. In this respect ResearchGate provides rudimentary version control, i.e. a tool to keep track of successive versions of a document; in ScholarZ.net the file archive has been developed into an information management tool, where users can attribute keywords, notes and projects to items in the archive with a view to integrating them directly in common texts. Ning offers the option to link directly to an external document management system.
- *Collaborative writing environments:* Some SNS offer for example a wiki tool or other collaborative online text editors[13] (e.g. ScholarZ.net, arts-humanities.net, edumeres.net, Ning). In ScholarZ.net this function is implemented with further features, such as using notes to bibliographic quotes in common texts, which may be later exported for instance as a Word document.

---

13 E.g. Zoho writer (writer.zoho.com) or Etherpad (etherpad.org).

- *Teaching and events:* There are special tools to administer participants in events (e.g. research.iversity; see also below).
- *Selective access:* Groups may be open to everyone or made accessible by group members or the administrator only upon invitation or request. Thus it is possible to create protected work and discussion spaces.
- *Passive membership:* Group memberships is usually shown on one's profile; even without one actively participating in the group; this serves as a tool to manifest one's interests or opinions.

(6) Calendar: Some SNS offer their users, in particular members of groups, calendars in order to coordinate dates, plan and market events of all kinds. We observed the following typical functions:

- Publish dates for events, meetings etc.
- Invite members to participate
- Register accept and decline (e.g. Facebook, research.iversity)
- Checking for dates in groups (similar to the service Doodle; e.g. ResearchGate)
- Exporting appointments to other digital calendar systems.

(7) Literature-related functions: Given the central position of publications in academia, science-specific SNS also offer a number of literature-related functions:

- SNS support *searching for academic literature* by giving access to other, external, mainly open access databases (e.g. ResearchGate), as well as internally in the publication lists and database entries of members (this is the main function of Mendeley).
- The platform automatically provides hints to other literature in the database by computing *semantic relationships* to the members' own publications. A special feature is the support of an author's search for publication opportunities based on a so-called "similar abstract search" or keyword search (e.g. ResearchGate).
- *Compiling bibliographies:* Science-specific SNS support the compilation of lists of one's own publications and of reading lists that may be published in one's profile. Mendeley, for example, is specialized in organizing quotes of academic literature for direct use in word processing software, similar to the EndNote plug-in for Microsoft Word.

- *Open access archive:* ResearchGate provides a platform for self-archiving of the full texts of one's publications according to the principle of Green Road Open Access.
- A number of further functions help *direct attention to literature:* one receives notes when new literature in one's area of expertise is published (e.g. Mendeley); there is a "Have read" button to highlight one's reading (e.g. Academia.edu); one can comment on or rate database entries of literature; with the "Share this" function one can post a hint on literature found in the SNS, e.g. via an external microblogging service or in the framework of social bookmarking; some SNS offer access statistics to show what has been most frequently read or downloaded (e.g. ResearchGate, Academia.edu)
- Vivo offers a tool to *visualize networks of co-authors* (see Figure 6).

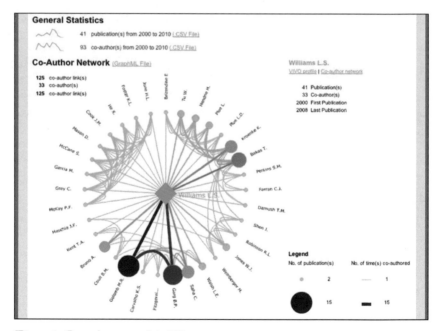

Figure 6: Co-author network in Vivo

Source: vivo.slis.indiana.edu/gallery.html#coauthor

(8) Further services: In addition to these functions, further specialized and target-group-specific services are offered:

- *Job exchange* services help matching offer and demand for open academic positions.
- *Blogging:* Some SNS offer their own blogging platforms and/or have collective blogs, edited by a board on the basis of blog posts on the platform (e.g. ResearchGate).
- *Embedding of services of external providers:* Additional functions may be included in the SNS via so called "apps" (applications), thus creating interfaces between the SNS and other services (e.g. integrating Twitter or Academia.edu in Facebook) or providing additional possibilities. Most prominent are social games such as "Farmville" on Facebook, which also make use of the existing social networks of the platform.
- *Advertisement:* It is partly possible to buy space for advertisement in SNS (e.g. for "pages" in Facebook; see above).

SNS members may also use many of these functions via specialized client software or browsers in mobile devices, thus connecting the members beyond their desktops.

2.1.2 Potential for science and research

Obviously the providers of science-specific SNS see a potential for academic use of these platforms and have consequently developed a series of sophisticated tools serving this very specific and demanding target group. A systematic analysis of the potentials for academic SNS use starts with the four core areas of scientific activity (see above 1.3) and reveals that SNS provide functions for all four areas, namely knowledge production, processing and distribution, as well as institutional settings (cf. Figure 7 below).

Knowledge production: The various functions of directing attention may be helpful in the process of acquiring information, particularly with regard to literature. Shared data archives potentially help working groups to administer their files.

Communication (processing of knowledge): The multiple possibilities for communication are the core of each SNS; thus these platforms are, at least from a technical perspective, functional for academic communication as well. Through the various channels, knowledge can be presented and offered for academic discourse. The group functions may support collaboration. We see a particular potential of integrated text editors to help organizing the collaborative production of texts within working and project groups.

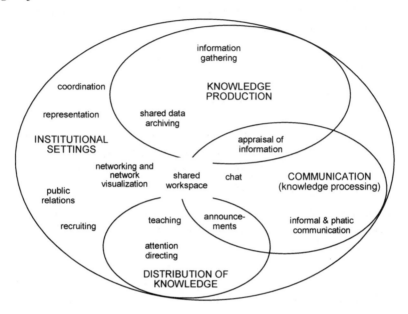

Figure 7: Scholarly activities and social network sites

Distribution of knowledge: SNS are not currently an adequate place for publication, even though in principle documents may be published within the network (e.g. file upload in groups; open access archiving in ResearchGate). However, as it is usually necessary to register, access to documents is hampered. In addition, there is no formalized peer review process in any of the observed SNS, thus the knowledge distributed via this channel will not be reputable and less relevant to many. Hence, publications within SNS seem inappropriate at the moment. By contrast, SNS may be a valuable additional channel for pointing at texts that have been published elsewhere. They provide a number of functions in that respect: profiles, means of internal communication, tools to direct attention, group functions and literature-related services. SNS may also be used as e-learning platforms.

Institutional settings: At the organizational level, SNS are potentially useful as a digital infrastructure. For example, SNS serve as a dynamic list of contacts and as "digital calling cards". Obviously SNS may help to set up

networks of scientists with similar interests as a pool of potential cooperation and communication partners. Using SNS for public relations is another option. In particular academic organizations such as research institutes, universities, scholarly associations and networks, but also individual
researchers may use SNS, in particular the general ones, as a platform for
public outreach and prestige advertising. In this sense, SNS may be considered an additional "window in the ivory tower" (Nentwich 2010a, see also
section 3.2).

Corresponding to these multiple options, different user practices are
conceivable: SNS could serve multilaterally as a discussion forum or as a
platform for exchange of information, similar to other web forums and in
particular e-mail list-servers. Furthermore, they may be used as bilateral
communication channel, asynchronously via web mail or synchronously as
chatting platform. Finally, SNS may serve as platforms for microblogging
to exchange science-related or day-to-day information, and for e-learning.
Thus we note that SNS seem to be functional for a number of essential
academic activities. We may expect that the technical functionality may
increase as these sites mature, in particular when additional functions provided by external suppliers are integrated via the application programming
interface (API).

2.1.3 Usage practices and impact

In the next step of our analysis we investigate how academics actually use
and shape SNS. First, we consider the current diffusion of SNS in academia; second we analyze the usage practices that may be empirically observed, distinguishing between general and science-specific SNS.

The diffusion of SNS in academia and the intensity of usage

A first indication for the diffusion of SNS in the academic world is the
number of members, mostly published by the SNS themselves, and their
growth rates. ResearchGate, for example, had 150.000 members in August
2008, 700.000 in December 2010, and announced on the website a million
by May 2011. We observed similar growth of other SNS (cf. Table 1), but
the figures may not hold in practice, given their origin. The member count,
in any case, does not necessarily correlate with actual use, because there

certainly are some (partly) inactive accounts. Therefore, more differentiated usage studies would be needed.

Nevertheless, some studies provide first insights into the diffusion of SNS among scientists. In an online survey among researchers of German universities (n=2.361) a majority of 64 percent indicated that they use "social networking tools"[14] never or very seldom, and 23 percent answered that they use them often or very often (Koch and Moskaliuk 2009). This study, however, does not give any answers regarding the purpose of the SNS use; the average age of the respondents was rather low (a=30,15) and we may expect that usage is lower among older scientists. SNS use is much more widespread among students, as shown by a representative study for German universities (Kleimann et al. 2008): a majority of 51 percent (n=4.400) uses social communities such as Facebook or StudiVZ frequently or very frequently; among them are 34 percent whose use is study-related. We may expect that the proportion of SNS users among scientists will increase as the younger generations move up in academia. There is an online survey in British universities (n=1.308), of which the authors say it is "reasonably representative", but note a "bias towards social sciences and economics" (Procter et al. 2010, 17). It shows that a significant minority of researches use "social networking services" in a broad sense: Facebook is used by 24 percent. We may, however, assume that most of this usage is not of professional, i.e. academic, but private as Facebook is a general SNS (but see below).

With regard to future studies we propose to differentiate types of activity levels and usage intensities, which we have observed:

–   *"Me-too presence"*: These users just set up a rudimentary profile with only some basic data; they have only occasional contacts and never, or only sporadically, become active. This is probably the most frequent case, also in the science-specific SNS with huge numbers of members, such as ResearchGate and Academia.edu. These users rarely visit the SNS.

–   *"Digital calling card"*: These users set up a more detailed profile with contact data, research interests, possibly a publication list—like a type of additional personal homepage or digital calling card. This type of user also practically never becomes active. This is probably the second

---

14 We cannot disregard the possibility that the study design or the participants referred to platforms that do not correspond to our above definition of SNS.

most frequent case at the moment. These members use the SNS seldom, perhaps only at the occasion of receiving a contact request or a direct message, forwarded by e-mail.

– *"Passive networking"*: In some cases the previous type of user searches the network in the beginning and thereafter in irregular intervals for other members whom she/he knows; or the user reacts to automated suggestions to contact other users. Then she/he either turns them into bilateral contacts or "follows" them unilaterally. This type of user visits the SNS irregularly and rather seldom and has sporadic communication with other members.

– *"Active networking and communication"*: Some SNS members are regularly online, use further services, such as publication search, and participate in group forums. They actively search for potential networking partners, beyond those they know in the offline world, in order to follow their activities or even introduce common ones.

– *"Cyberentrepreneur"*: A few are not only active participants in the network, but also serve as moderators or animators of group forums, they administer groups, are in charge of institutional profiles, or give feedback to the site developers. This is obviously the rarest form of participation of researchers in SNS (cf. Nentwich 2003, 175ff.).

These are certainly ideal types and in practice appear mixed. We observed repeatedly the above usage types, but cannot offer results regarding their precise empirical distribution. In any case we need to consider that the activity levels and usage types vary considerably. Consequently, member counts do not lead to insights into the vitality of a SNS. This is confirmed by the study of Procter et al. (2010, 19) on the scientific use of Web 2.0: only 13 percent of the participants fall into the category "frequent users", 45 percent are "occasional users", and 39 percent do not actively use Web 2.0. A large qualitative study with 160 interviews and focus group discussions with US researchers (Harley et al. 2010) notes that SNS arc not widely used in academia—they investigated archaeology, astrophysics, biology, economics, history, musicology and political science. However, they also report exceptions, for example archaeologists who actively promote SNS in science (ibid., 96). Some interviewees noted that while they would not use SNS themselves, they nevertheless see a need for it; they wished for a "Facebook for researchers" (ibid., 583) or a "Facebook for astronomy" (ibid., 178).

At this point, we may draw the following conclusions: SNS are not yet part of the academic mainstream, but we observe growing numbers of members in science-specific SNS—a trend that will presumably continue in the future. This hypothesis is supported by our analysis of the theoretical potential (see 2.1.2), which is even acknowledged by non-users and by the forceful international trend of SNS in general. The more users SNS have, the greater their potential benefits. It nevertheless remains difficult to assess whether scientific SNS may reach the tipping point, because users may never experience the benefits as long as a certain threshold of users is not reached—despite all theoretical potential (cf. Harley et al. 2010, 686). For a further discussion of this issue, see also section 3.1.

Academic usage practices in general SNS

What is known of academic usage practices in SNS? If researchers decide to deploy SNS for professional purposes, they have multiple options to choose from. We distinguish between general or multi-purpose SNS, which can also be used for academic purposes, and those SNS that have been designed with researchers as the main target group in mind. Both types of SNS differ in what they offer for professional activities and consequently in usage practices, thus we shall analyze them separately, beginning with the general SNS.

Many scientists have become members of multi-purpose SNS, such as Facebook, LinkedIn and Xing, not least because they are widespread and accepted. Usage practices are heterogeneous because these SNS are not particularly focused on academic users. Consequently, academics use these services in a variety of ways, hence it is difficult to separate professional and private identities or roles.[15] There are techniques to enable users to separate their roles; Facebook, for example, allows users to exclude in part or fully other members from otherwise public messages or to make certain content only available to pre-defined groups of contacts. Nonetheless, this is no simple task and there are multiple privacy conflicts as noted by many authors (among others Ferdig et al. 2008; Lehavot 2009; Lewis et al. 2008;

---

15 By "identity" we mean the reference to a real person with its correct name and real attributes; "roles" point at the option that persons may play different social (private, professional, etc.), but also fictitious roles, whereby they are able to delimit these roles from each other in the SNS.

Barnes 2006; Fuchs 2009; Cain et al. 2009; Lack et al. 2009). We shall return to this issue in section 3.5.

We observed the following science-related practices in SNS: communication with colleagues, e-teaching, public relations of research institutes and self-marketing, job exchange:

Communication with colleagues: We found that general SNS are not only used by academics for private or non-professional purposes, but to some extent also for bilateral and multilateral communication among colleagues using the different channels introduced above. In Facebook, for example, there are many thematic groups, in which experts communicate alongside lay people. The experts exchange hints to scientific events or new sources etc. In part, information from other sources, such as specialized news networks, is fed into the forum by automated robots. Analyzing the content of the information exchanged in such open groups, we conclude that they are mostly targeted at the professional communities and may not be considered part of public relations activities (see below). While the members of such groups are rather unspecific and broad, and group discussions are not used intensively by many, one can also find closed science-related groups, in which academics tackle certain research questions in a more shielded environment.

E-teaching: As SNS are widely spread and accepted among students, some teachers experiment with these platforms for e-teaching: an option is to organize group work among students; another is to promote exchange both between the teacher and the students and among the latter. Some report experiments with tutoring at a distance (Griffiths and Brophy 2005, 80). University libraries also attempt to reach students via SNS: "If librarians truly wish to be where students are, Facebook is an effective way to reach them" (Mack et al. 2007). While there are indeed some success stories (Mack et al. 2007; Mathews 2006), others report of students who reject this channel especially because of a perceived threat to their privacy (Connell 2009; Mendez et al. 2009).

Public relations: The wide reach of the big SNS makes them attractive to target a large part of the public. Indeed, many scientific organizations are present in SNS such as Facebook with pages, groups and profiles. We know of one example of an extra-university social science institute in Austria, whose staff have been asked to become members of Xing and a group devoted to this institute.[16] The German-speaking community of technology assessment discussed the necessity not to neglect the new Web 2.0 platforms (including SNS and Wikipedia) because of their potential medial outreach (cf. Nentwich 2010b). Similar to our observations regarding Twitter (see 2.2.3), it is not always clear who is responsible for these Web 2.0 representations. Often they have been founded by students and not on the initiative of the public relations department; hence one does not necessarily find official positions. However, also in this context, we observe a tendency towards formalization. Some SNS allow verifying such offerings; so-called "Edelprofile" ("classy profiles") are, for example, used for official appearances of universities in StudiVZ.[17] As a consequence we have a heterogeneous picture consisting of professional representation handled by public relation departments and unofficial groups in which students exchange information about study-related issues, opinions about university politics, practical advice regarding the university etc. It seems likely that academic organizations will become increasingly aware of the impact of these platforms. Correspondingly, we expect more and more formalized institutional appearances and SNS optimization strategies.

Job exchange: In this context academic job advertisements are communicated. In the professionally-oriented SNS Xing, in particular, these are posted in science-related groups. SNS with a large scope, such as Facebook, may serve as multipliers. As an example, the career portal *academics.de* publishes advertisements and news via Facebook so that they can be further distributed by other members.[18] In addition, job opportunities are also a frequent topic of messages distributed in SNS, apart from these "official" channels. For instance a researcher, interviewed by Harley et al. (2010, 178) stated:

"I think there's a fair amount on MySpace that goes on by kids younger than me… it's not my generation, but I think… I remember being told when students were deciding what department they were going to go to for a Ph.D., other students knew via the MySpace universe."

---

16 Source: Oral communication of a member of the said institute in December 2010.
17 studivz.net/Sitemap/All/category/65/o/desc/c/cnt/p/1; similar "verified accounts" in Twitter, see 2.2.1. In practice, it may, however, be difficult for a scientific institution to control an institutional profile by itself. SNS such as Facebook are not equipped to conduct the verification of identities or handle disputes over trademarks adequately.
18 facebook.com/academics.de.

Self-marketing: Individuals seize the opportunity offered by wide reaching SNS to promote themselves, as a kind of "individualistic public relations". While the accessibility of personal data may be disadvantageous from the point of view of privacy protection (see 3.5), it may also be used in a positive manner. It is possible to generate publicity for oneself and reach a public whose size and effectiveness depends on one's individual network. For example, SNS may be used to make one's latest publication known among colleagues and one may build up a reputation as someone knowledgeable in forum discussions.

In summary, we note that on the basis of present empirical studies and our own observations, general SNS play a minor role in the practice of research communication, even though we may expect it to grow given the overall increase in usage of platforms such as Facebook.

Academic usage practices in science-specific SNS

Since about 2004, and more intensely from 2007, SNS that target specifically research communities have come into existence alongside the general ones. In almost all cases they offer science-specific functions, such as special literature search, job exchange devoted to academia, groupware services to support online cooperation among researchers, for instance with a view to writing texts jointly (see 2.1.1). Today there are a number of such platforms (see Table 1), among them we highlight the following:

- *ResearchGate* started in the life sciences, but is now multidisciplinary in scope, with more than 100.000 social scientists,[19] but still a large majority in the natural sciences. It is, at the time of writing, the science-specific SNS with most members (over a million accounts); it offers inter alia literature search in a number of databases and the typical group functions, but has a few features not implemented by its competitors, such as similar abstract search.
- *Mendeley* specializes in the exchange of scientific articles and offers, in addition to the web platform, desktop bibliographic software to integrate literature as quotes in word processors.

---

19 See the interactive statistical graph on the start page of ResearchGate in June 2011, based on members' self-assignment. We added the figures given for "political science" (10.064), "social sciences" (45.920) and "economics" (47.961), see researchgate.net.

- *Nature Networks*, offered by the publishing house of the same name, provides, among other things, blogs and subject forums.
- *Vivo* is an US-American software-based SNS with (still) a national focus, developed originally at Cornell University and later subsidized by the National Center for Research Resources (NCRR) of the National Institutes of Health (NIH).
- *Academia.edu* started as a worldwide directory of universities, research institutions and researchers, but now offers services similar to Facebook.
- *ScholarZ.net*, developed as a spin-off of a research project at the University of Würzburg (Germany), is much smaller than the others and perceives itself as providing integrated online software for scientific work.

When we observe this young and dynamic market we find, first, that there is indeed a significant market, which supports our hypothesis that SNS are, in principle, functional for academia. Second, the dynamics of the market show that there is no convergence yet towards one single provider—unlike Facebook in the field of general SNS. According to the special intentions and needs, the target group for these types of SNS is much narrower. Market concentration is less likely as long as all workers in a specific field join one particular SNS. However, given the trend towards broad interdisciplinary cooperation encompassing SNS, covering many, if not all, fields may be useful (see 3.4).

The explicit focus on academic needs leads to different usage practices as compared to the general SNS. We observe the following activities in science-specific SNS: limited public relations of research institutions and self-marketing; communication and cooperation with colleagues; job exchange; e-teaching.

Public relations and self-marketing: Because of their limited target group, these SNS are of limited use for public relations, as you can hardly reach larger groups outside the science communities.[20] By contrast it is potentially easier to target workers in particular fields by means of the sophisticated mechanisms for networking that most SNS provide. Similar to general SNS, self-marketing is also possible in science-specific SNS, focused

---

20 Note, however, that the profiles can, at least to some degree, also be visited from outside the network site and often are listed among the first search results in Google. ScienXe.org, for example, advertises the site by promising that the members' pages are ranked high in search engines.

on one's peer group, for example by drawing attention to one's own publications. Based on our observations, this is currently probably the most widely used activity.

Communication and cooperation: One specific strength of science-specific SNS could be their potential to support communication and cooperation among researchers. We did not observe, however, efficient and successful working groups in these SNS. A few self-experiments in our own area have been only modestly successful. They mainly failed because of a lack of potential cooperation partners inside the chosen SNS as we were not able to motivate all relevant colleagues to actively participate in that particular SNS. In contrast to the attraction of large general SNS, the rather young and small science-specific networks suffer of a lack of sufficient numbers of active users.[21] We observed the following further obstacles:

- technical limitations, in particular lacking platform or browser independence of the software, and long response times;
- lacking experience of the participants in exposure to these new platforms;
- skepticism regarding file security and the associated loss of control with regard to the documents uploaded to the SNS;
- the need to develop first a common culture of online collaboration, for instance with regard to the intrinsic value of a common file archive; of having a protocol of the common activities in a forum; discipline when communicating via threaded web forums etc.); and finally notably
- the problem of "multiple channels", i.e. the need to watch over yet another channel besides the usual ones; this problem discourages many users from the outset or after a few first tries because of the additional time effort (more on this in the next sub-section, see also 3.4).

In order to reach a sufficient level of participation, the platforms need to be designed as much as possible according to the practical needs of researchers (on this see in particular: Harley et al. 2010; Procter et al. 2010). This is no guarantee though for broad acceptance, which depends on a number of factors that are not easily controllable. In particular, disciplinary differences (Becher 1989, 95ff.; Nentwich 2003, 168ff.) play an important

---

21 For example, arts-humanities.net counted in June 2010 1.500 members of which only 50 contributed regularly, see Procter et al. (2010, 41).

role. For instance, Harley et al. (2010, 283) cite a biologist who says with science–specific SNS in mind:

"I would ban my students from using Nature Network because they could be saying all sorts of stuff about what we're thinking and working on that I don't really want anyone else to know."

E-teaching: We did not observe that science-specific SNS are used frequently in teaching. There are specific functions to support it, for instance in research.iversity, but there is not much known yet about their actual usage. Obviously, these professional networks do not seem particularly attractive to students, in contrast to Facebook and other general SNS, because they fit less well with their day-to-day needs and more with the workaday life of a scientist. Hence, students are hardly reachable via this channel, except in experimental settings. However, certain effective student-orientated platforms exist, for example Carnets2 Descartes[22] at Paris Descartes University. In any case, SNS may turn out being a good platform for exchange among teaching scientists when they prepare their courses.

Mixing private and professional roles is less of a problem as compared with general SNS and the related privacy conflicts are attenuated: We observed that most researchers reveal only their professional identity. This is usually supported by the set of information one is supposed to enter when setting up one's profile: the form asks for biographical information relevant in academia and less for private facts such as relationship status. Note, however, that even ResearchGate asks for pet books and hobbies, but receives answers only by a few according to our observations (see also 3.5).

Job exchange: These services have the advantage of having a pre-selected target group in science-specific SNS as opposed to general ones. In June 2011, for example, we found more than 1.800 job offers on ResearchGate, mainly from biomedical enterprises, and only very few on Academia.edu. The extent, to which these job exchanges are actually used, is unknown to us.

Assessment of potentials and impacts

On the basis of our description of the functions of SNS (2.1.1), of a theoretical analysis of what may be relevant for academia (2.1.2), and finally of our summary of what is known about the practical usage of SNS by aca-

---

22 carnets.parisdescartes.fr.

demics today (see above), we take the next step by discussing some of the issues that will influence the future development. Will ever more and, perhaps at some point, most academics use SNS—as they use e-mail today? What consequences may this have? In order to answer these questions we will focus on the following puzzles: Is the necessity to observe multiple channels in parallel possibly dysfunctional for science communication? How important are network effects? Will the trend towards multi-functionality and one-stop-services generate the necessary network effects? What potential do SNS have for informal communication among academics, with what effects? What roles play identity, pseudonymity and anonymity in scientific SNS? Will there be important privacy issues?

Observing multiple channels: Together with the more traditional communication channels, such as the telephone and e-mail, SNS are yet another one to keep track of—or indeed multiple channels, if we take into account that SNS include forum discussions, status messages etc. This is indeed a big challenge, which is probably mastered by only a few and by most only insufficiently. Me-too presence or accounts that are not actively used are probably the consequence in many cases. However, even if one tries to tend accounts and profiles actively and conscientiously (as the authors of this study did during the experimental phase), it becomes obvious that the present state of Web 2.0 is suboptimal for professionals under constant time pressure. While there is no doubt that the multitude of communication channels is a value in its own right and may be useful in the workaday life of scientists, we note that tending several SNS profiles is inefficient. However, this is indispensable at this point if one wants to network with one's own scientific community that is distributed over many SNS. As long as not all or a majority of the colleagues in a field communicate via one specific SNS, it cannot be used as a central platform of mutual exchange. Possibly we are only facing a transitional phenomenon, as SNS have existed for a few years only. We could imagine the following development paths:

−   The first is monopolization. It could be that one SNS for all research fields or, more likely, one for each particular field establishes itself as the market leader and produces an irresistible attraction.
−   Alternatively, the providers continue[23] to harmonize the interfaces (APIs) between their sites, which would allow the creation meta-

---

23 It is already possible in many SNS to automatically distribute status messages beyond the

services, so that the individual user may administer his/her multiple profiles via only one interface.

- In parallel to and partly supporting the above two ongoing developments, we observe a trend towards multi-functionality. The SNS constantly develop further; their providers observe each other; take over promising ideas; and implement ever more functions. At the end of the day, some SNS might have become platforms satisfying practically all academic electronic needs for communication, cooperation, search for literature, provision of information etc.—quasi "one-stop-services 2.0" integrating microblogging, groupware, e-mail, calendar etc.[24] This strategy may add to the overall attractiveness of the most successful SNS.

If neither monopolization nor interface harmonization is realized, the problem of multiple channels will persist as a central hurdle for academic use of SNS (for a detailed discussion see section 3.4).

Network effects and informal communication: One of the central functions of all SNS is that they support the maintenance of existing and creating of new social networks. In so doing users expect that SNS may produce surplus value for their scientific work. There is no doubt that effective networking among researchers is desirable and SNS offer an infrastructure to do so. Whether this infrastructure is actually fulfilling its promises, mainly depends on the activity levels of the members, on individual networks and on the individual's ability to cope with them. As noted above, we cannot observe as yet that many researchers are active in the SNS, even though we expect the level to rise. Thus we need to mark time and explore empirically if any and which of these effects may be realized on a larger scale.

By offering multiple electronic paths to reach and chat with members of the research community, SNS may increase the possibility and likelihood of informal communication. It will be interesting to see what impact this may have on the structure of the science system. We may also ask whether the SNS may contribute to formalize the informal by making social networks of researchers—the so-called "invisible colleges" (Crane 1972)—more transparent.

---

borders of one SNS; many allow registering simply by using an existing Facebook account; finally SNS usually offer the option to find new contacts in the networks by uploading automatically contacts from other networks.

24 Google is obviously striving to offer such a one-stop-service, integrating webmail, group functionality, the new SNS Google+, shared documents etc.

Identity, pseudonymity and anonymity: With regard to private use of SNS, pseudonymity instead of having a profile with one's real identity is frequently practiced, though discouraged, for example, by Facebook and Google+. Thus it is possible to differentiate between different roles. Anonymous accounts are not usually possible. By contrast, in professional SNS, which also serve as public calling card directories, pseudonymity would be counter-productive, because the users need to get in touch with or hire "real" people. Similarly, pseudonymity is dysfunctional in academia. Science communication rests on the premise that you communicate, whatever the medium, with actual persons in order to be able to cooperate or co-author. In other words, merits need to be attributable: researchers definitely expect that behind a profile in a SNS is another researcher who has actually written the papers listed in the publications attached to the profile. Some SNS try to guarantee this by verifying the identity on registration (e.g. BestThinking).

However, there are two cases where temporal or functional anonymity is in the interest of academia: In many fields, the peer review process is usually double-blind. We may conceive that also the various rating systems within SNS, most of which are not anonymous as yet, may be implemented in a way allowing anonymous rating. The other case is when it comes to testing new ideas in a creative forum space or during collective brainstorming. Here it may fuel creativity when the relation between callow thoughts and the originator would not be registered permanently in a written archive. (For a more in-depth and comparative discussion of these issues see section 3.5.)

Privacy issues: People using SNS leave their digital marks and traces, and so do researchers. There is currently an intensive discussion about privacy concerns in the general SNS, such as Facebook. At least some of researchers' reluctance to join SNS may be explained by fear of losing control over their privacy. In science-specific SNS, the data needed to enable efficient networking based on automatically generated suggestions, is to a very large extent professional in nature, such as curriculum vitae, publications, research interests, office contact, etc. Nonetheless, if researchers are very active on various Web 2.0 platforms, they create significant digital traces that can be analyzed by data-mining tools (see section 3.5).

Identity theft (OECD 2008) is another salient issue. Profiles may be hacked with the intention of damaging somebody's reputation or false identity may be pretended in order to gain some benefits. On the big platforms, such as MySpace and Facebook, there is a broad discussion about this.[25]

2.1.4 Interim conclusions

Social network sites, in particular those specializing in academia, are a moving target, as there are many different providers and the various sites still experiment with new functions targeting academic needs. As researchers are distributed across many platforms, potential benefits are not fully realized and hence activity is not very high in any particular site. The platform per se, that is without communication, upload of publications or exchange of information taking place, is not too attractive for academia; it is after all not much more than a directory of people. It all depends on the diffusion among relevant scientific communities and on what the researchers actually do or will do with it.

The few empirical studies focusing on the academic usage practices, coupled with our own systematic observations, show that academics' use of SNS is steadily increasing, but not widespread yet; practice is often experimental and hardly institutionalized, as exemplified by a lack of systematic SNS policies by higher education institutions and low-key reflection on the privacy issues involved, in particular as related to the general SNS. There are, however, already first examples of learning effects and the evolution of good practice. Whether the potential of SNS for academia will be realized in practice will not only depend on technical improvements alone. We assume that even a technically less advanced site may be successful, if it manages to mobilize enough researchers to break through and when it chooses a sustainable model of financing.

When assessing the potential of science-specific SNS, we need to take into account competition with the established general SNS, which are standard applications of the current web and exercise an enormous attraction. Their sheer size has already attracted many researchers and will attract even more in the future, at least for private reasons. One possible scenario may be that add-ons to the general SNS provide more and more of those functions that are now mainly typical for the science-specific SNS and so become even more attractive. Two serious issues speak, however, in favor of separation between the two worlds. First, concerns regarding data protection, misuse and privacy infringements are a main reason for many not to use Facebook et al. (Initiative D21 and TNS Infratest 2010, 25). These concerns are particularly pertinent where private data and messages are part of everyday practice and the provider's business model is based on interpreting and utilizing them commercially. Here the advantages of the solely professional and in particular the academic network sites are obvious, as they do not rely on private data and are usually funded without the exploitation of user data. Furthermore, it seems likely that academics will want to separate their private and professional roles with a view to avoiding conflicts and distraction by mixing both. We face, however, a dynamic development, which is not restricted to the academic world, but encompasses our societies at large. We simply do not know yet, in which direction the knowledge society will evolve, when it comes to the separation of identities and the perception of privacy.

Both the general and the specific SNS line up to change practices in a, technically speaking, more or less well functioning academic communication and information space. Researchers who are able to satisfy their main communication needs well with cyberscience 1.0 tools would rather not switch to another communication channel unless they detect a convincing surplus value of that new channel. E-mail is a strong competitor in this respect as practically all academics are "on e-mail", but only a small fraction is "on SNS". Thus, finding a substantial majority of all potential communication partners on a new platform may be essential for the last to switch, but there has to be something else to convince the majority in the first place. Even when we take into account that most science-specific SNS have had only a very short time to collect enough members, it seems that none of the current platforms has as yet found the essential lever, the convincing unique selling point (USP) or "killer application", to make itself indispensable in the eyes of a majority of researchers in any particular field.[26] It is difficult to speculate what such a USP might be. It needs to be something that researchers have difficulty to get elsewhere or that they have access to within the platforms much more readily; it may also be solutions to current problems of the academic information and communication space. There are a few candidates: structured and well managed access to scientific literature and to everything which is available on open

---

26 We are convinced that even the impressively high numbers of members of some science-specific SNS are no sign of a break-through. As analyzed above, a majority of all accounts is of the "me-too" type and hence not active.

access, but currently scattered; encompassing groupware tools for project groups that are very easy to handle and need no further set-up; discipline-wide interactive calendars of scientific conferences and workshops; transparent solutions to the current peer-review system; strong incentives for interdisciplinary and cooperative research; etc.

One particular factor that could promote the diffusion of SNS far beyond the current path of a bottom-up construction of these networks would be top-down initiatives by relevant institutions. One such example is the fast growing Vivo (Gewin 2010), which is heavily supported and promoted by a few large US universities. This approach would have the advantage that the problems of financing and data security were attenuated. The obvious disadvantage is that enforcement and even indirect pressure is not very welcome in academic circles and may possibly lead to passive resistance.

In summary, our case study of SNS shows that they are, in principle, functional for academic communication and that they have a serious potential in academia, despite some hurdles and as yet rather cautious use by researchers. Whether the potential will be realized depends on many complex factors, which need to be researched further in more detail, in particular as there are, up to date, only limited large-scale empirical studies. In particular, we encourage detailed studies on the concrete impact of SNS on the daily practices of academics (some relevant hypotheses will be discussed throughout chapter 3).

2.2 Microblogging

"Blogging" is the writing of a "blog", which is a usually public webpage that is comparable to a diary or journal as it can be assigned to the author(s) of that webpage and is in reverse chronological order. The term "blog" is short for "weblog", derived from "web log book". "Microblogging" is a form of blogging with the characteristic feature that the entries in the diary are not small articles, but short textual messages—hence the prefix "micro". In other words, the term microblogging is used to refer to those services which make it possible for Internet users to send short messages in real time, i.e. with no more than a brief delay, to anybody who is interested. The content of these messages ranges from what is known as status updates ("Where am I?", "What am I doing?"), and links to other Internet sources ("Have you seen this?"), to commentaries on whatever is happening in the world, in one's own immediate surroundings, in politics, and so on. As with the "macro" version of blogs, the sequence of messages is represented chronologically (in reverse order, i.e. most recent on top).

There are a number of such services,[27] some of which are integrated into more comprehensive social network sites (SNS, see also 2.1) such as Facebook, ResearchGate and Academia.edu. So far, there is one microblogging service specializing on science, namely ScienceFeed[28], but it is not very large yet. In contrast, Twitter, which went online in 2006, is clearly the best known and most widely used one. Therefore, most of this chapter will refer to this service and occasionally point to others. Messages on Twitter—the so-called *tweets*—are limited to only 140 characters. While some other services offer slightly more space (ResearchGate and Facebook, for instance, allow for so-called "updates" of 420 characters, but most users nevertheless do not write long texts), this restriction is constitutive of microblogging. It leads to the use of an abbreviated form of language,[29] and sometimes to the extreme condensation of the ideas being communicated (on the linguistic characteristics of microblogs, see e.g. Honeycutt and Herring 2009). It is not the usual practice to cut a message up into a number of tweets. In addition to sending text messages, it is also possible to integrate small images, audio messages or even videos by linking to them.

2.2.1 Main functions

To start, one needs to set up a personal account in order to have access to a microblogging service as a reader or writer. This is done via a web interface[30]. In Twitter, for instance, minimum information is a "full name" (though one can use a pseudonym), a "user name" (under which one ap-

---

27 For example: twitter.com; identi.ca; jaiku.com; yammer.com; plurk.com; for an overview of alternative platforms, see Herwig et al. (2009, section 1.5).

28 sciencefeed.com.

29 There are a number of services one can use to shorten URLs—a typical ingredient of such messages—in order to be able to comment on them in only a few characters (e.g. snurl.com, bit.ly, tinyurl.com). In 2011 Twitter included its own a platform-specific URL shortening service.

30 There are also applications for mobile devices, which provide access from any location where there is either mobile phone or, preferably, Internet reception.

pears on the platform), a password, and an e-mail address. Users can, but do not have to, add a limited "profile"[31] with a photo, a location, a URL to a website, and a very short description. Whether the information is correct or not, is not normally verified; only in case of an "impersonation problem"[32], i.e. if someone pretends to be someone else, a "verified account" can be assigned.

Unless one explicitly chooses to "protect" the account, one's messages can be seen by people not registered on Twitter. Depending on the settings chosen by the sender, messages can be sent to a selected group of other users of the platform or, and this is more frequently the case, to all those who have said they want to "follow" an individual user. Most users apply the standard practice of effectively subscribing to the self-selected group of "friends" or "contacts". On Twitter one can also follow the "public timeline", which means reading all tweets sent by all users anywhere in the world.[33] Twitter offers the additional option to follow the timeline of those users who have been added to so-called "lists", selected either by oneself or by other users according to thematic, geographical or other criteria. Moreover, logged in users can choose to see the personal feeds of others. There is also the option to search for certain keywords explicitly identified by Twitter authors. These are known as "hashtags" (i.e. words with the prefix "#", like "#cyberscience"), and in this way one can read messages relating to certain topics. Approximately five percent of all tweets include hashtags (Beus 2009a).

In principle, microblogging is an asynchronous communication channel (Herring 2007) as it is not necessary for communication partners to use it at the same time (as is the case with "chatting", a text-based form of dialogue) and one can read the messages and reply to them later. However, despite the, technically speaking, asynchronous nature of microblogging, an "advertency field" is generated, if people who follow each other use it more or less simultaneously, including from mobile devices. They participate collectively in a flow of information and, potentially also, of communication with the effect that they feel quite near to each other although not physically present in the same place. Because of providing fast (as opposed

---

31 For the notion of "profiles", see section 2.1 on social network sites.
32 twitter.com/help/verified.
33 twitter.com/public_timeline has, however, approximately 95 million tweets per day, says Twitter on its website: twitter.com/about (as of April 2011).

to permanent) access to published content, microblogging is part of the so-called "real-time web" (Kirkpatrick 2008).

Over time, microblogging users, in particular those using Twitter, have developed a specific communication practice, based on the functions offered by the service. For instance, it is possible to reply publicly to another user by using the "@" sign, followed by a username (called @-reply or @-response). A study estimated that approximately 21 percent of all tweets are of this type (Beus 2009a), another study found this proportion even as high as 30 percent (Honeycutt and Herring 2009). It is also possible to send direct messages to only one of one's followers. Some emergent functions[34] were not originally implemented in Twitter, like for instance, the use of "hashtags" (see above) or "retweeting" (Boyd et al. 2010). Users retweet other users' messages, i.e. they forward it to their own group of followers by copying the message and quoting the original sender. This practice has been originally developed by the users and later also implemented as a functionality of Twitter. According to the estimate of Beus (2009a) only one percent of all tweets are retweets; academics, however, seem to forward others' tweets much more than the average Twitter user (Weller et al. 2011, treat them in the context of the culture of citation). As tweets soon get displaced by newer messages in the timeline, the time span in which a tweet might be read can be prolonged by retweeting. Other reasons for retweeting are the wish to comment a message (which is, however, not possible in the automated retweeting function), to support or oppose the content of a message or to maximise its readership (Boyd et al. 2010).

Although text and URLs are the main content of microblogs, some users also integrate small images, audio messages or even videos. To do so in Twitter one has to subscribe to separate services[35]; in case microblogging is included in social network sites, such as ResearchGate or Academia.edu, this is sometimes included in the platform.

It is possible to publish messages either via the web interface of the microblogging service, via SMS, via smartphones, or via special microblogging clients. The latter use an *application programming interface* (API), which allows other programs to access and use the data generated in the source

---

34 Herwig (2009) distinguishes in this context between "default" and "emerging social mechanisms".

35 For pictures, e.g. twitpic.com, flickr.com, twitvid.com; for audio, e.g. twitsay.com; for slides, slideshare.com.

program. There are a number of microblogging clients for smartphones or clients that allow the users to manage several microblogging accounts at once[36]. Furthermore, a multitude of further programs use the API to offer special services, which make microblogging and in particular Twitter more useful or easier to use;[37] there are also a few applications targeting the research community (see next section).

Microblogging servers usually do not offer unlimited easy access to older messages: for Twitter older tweets can only be retrieved approximately a mere ten days via the search function; they are not deleted, but can only be accessed via the exact URL, which includes a ten-digit code. Therefore, microblogging services like Twitter as such do not seem to be suitable for immediate use in research, in particular not for a traceable and comprehensive documentation. However, a number of specialized web applications (using the API) try to fill this gap[38] and some media companies or libraries started to archive microblogs.[39] However, later Twitter even forbade the forwarding of Twitter data-sets and now sells the data via re-sellers such as Gnip.[40]

2.2.2 Potentials for academia

Although, at first sight, messages that are only a few characters long and not properly archived do not seem to be particularly functional in science and research, a second look reveals that an increasing number of scholars frequently use microblogging for a variety of research-related purposes. We shall come back to the actual usage practices below and focus here on the overall potential (for an overview see Figure 8).

---

36 E.g. TweetDeck.com.
37 See, for instance, the listings on the TwitterFanWiki at twitter.pbworks.com.
38 E.g. Friendfeed.com, Twapperkeeper.com, Snapbird.org.
39 E.g. apa-defacto.at; the US Library of Congress acquired the Twitter archive in 2010: blogs.loc.gov/loc/2010/04/how-tweet-it-is-library-acquires-entire-twitter-archive.
40 See blog.ynada.com/628, and allthingsd.com/20101117/gnip-becomes-twitters-first-authorized-data-reseller.

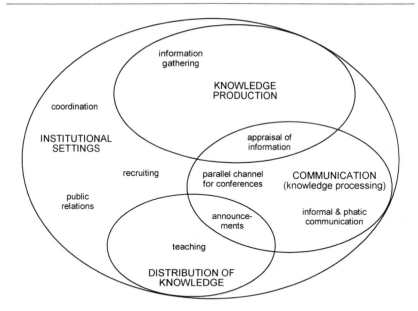

Figure 8: Scholarly activities and microblogging

Knowledge production: Obviously, microblogs cannot be used in the production of knowledge, at least not per se. For most purposes microblogs are too short to conduct serious work on texts; one cannot discuss issues or formulate hypotheses that are anything more than ideas expressed as briefly as possible and which will therefore need to be properly worked out in another medium. They may, however, play a role in the process of information gathering and exchange of information about the objects of research. Depending on the field, empirical facts, or at least hints to sources where these empirical facts may be found, can be communicated in microblogs and hence contribute to the efficiency of the research process. These hints are "loaded with context", that is they usually convey descriptive clues and they originate from people explicitly chosen to follow because their messages have proven to be particularly relevant.

Communication: Although a very specific type of communication channel, microblogging can be used in knowledge processing and internal scientific communication. If we assume that groups of researchers, whether local or dispersed, agree to use microblogging as a medium of communication, it may be well suited to the targeted exchange of information. However, because the messages that can be sent have to be very short, this exchange can only function within narrow limits. Besides its potential role in the exchange of factual information on the objects of research (see above), it can be used to make announcements of all sorts, for instance in relation to scientific events, institutional matters, and new publications. We would, however, classify microblogs themselves (as opposed to blogs) not as genuine publications. Because microblogging can be used in a synchronous way, they may also serve as a parallel channel to conferences by which the conference participants exchange additional information and comments on the topic presented in the current lecture. Finally, science is not just a matter of specialized work on substantive issues. It also consists of social relations which are established and maintained through informal and phatic communication, as also Honeycutt and Herring (2009) pointed out with regard to informal collaboration. Conversations around the institute's coffee machine or in the corridor or during a conference break could take a kind of virtual form for dispersed research groups in the shape of a close-meshed network of microblogs, which also go beyond work on the substantive issues as such. Microblogging thus can be seen as part of an emerging culture of phatic digital communication, filling the time span between meetings in person. In any case, the potential advantage of the medium is that it allows rapid and uncomplicated casual communication.

Distribution of knowledge: Microblogs can be used to distribute information regarding the processes and outcomes of research, both internally, i.e. targeted towards fellow researchers, and externally, i.e. targeted at the interested public, stakeholders, and politics. The more people use microblogging services and follow, among others, researchers or their institutions, the more efficient it may be to use this new channel for the purpose of scientific marketing and public relations. In addition, microblogs may play a role in university teaching as this channel of communication can be applied both for organizational matters and for commenting or collecting questions during a seminar or lecture.

Institutional settings: Apart from scientific marketing, the processes of recruiting researchers and other science-related staff may be supported by this new channel of distribution of information. Furthermore, microblogging may contribute to individual and institutional reputation management. The entirety of one's messages and also the size and composition of the group of one's followers build up a certain reputation or online persona, which may possibly be useful for "offline" purposes, too.

2.2.3 Usage practices and impact

Today, microblogging is one of the most prevalent Internet activities. Twitter "took off" in 2009 (Beus 2009b), has now more than 100 million registered users all over the world and seems to be still growing.[41] Microblogging within the various social network sites such as Facebook is an increasingly frequent activity, as shown by the impressive and growing number of accounts of these sites (see section 2.1). The number of registered users or accounts, however, only partly correlates with user activity. The latest Sysomos study (Evans 2010; Sysomos Inc. 2010) reports that 22.5 percent of all users have accounted for about 90 percent of all activity, and there are many who hardly send messages themselves, but mainly follow others.

Among the growing microblogging community, there are many academics—or "scientwists" (Bradley 2009). Apart from those who send status messages within the science-specific social network sites, such as ResearchGate or Academia.edu (see 2.1), there are a number of lists of scientists or scientific institutions using for instance Twitter.[42] These lists though are inevitably incomplete, because there is no need to declare oneself, so they are based on self-description and partly self-assignment, and they are necessarily fuzzy: While in general microblogs posted in professional platforms like Academia.edu or ScienceFeed are of a professional (here: research-related) nature, general purpose platforms such as Facebook or Twitter are often used for both professional and private use. It is unclear whom to count as a scientwist (e.g. students or only senior researchers) and how to find out about this status anyway (cf. Schmirmund in Herwig et al. 2009, 23f.). Despite this fuzziness and although there seems to be no comprehensive systematic study on the genuine academic population of Twitter yet, we estimate that there are at present thousands of academic users of Twitter and many more using microblogging services

---

41 The latest official figure is from Sept. 2011: 100 million users, cf. blog.twitter.com.
42 In April 2011, the site sciencepond.com, for instance, lists approximately 200 scientists twittering in English; "Scientwists" at twitter.com/Philaeus/scientwists follows more than 300; "scientwitters" at twitter.com/sciencebase/scientwitters (see Figure 9) follows a bit less than 500 (as there is a limit set to number of profiles a list can follow); in 2009, David Bradley had already found more than 600 (cf. www.sciencebase.com/science-blog/100-scientific-twitter-friends, not updated anymore)—and estimates the actual figure ten times higher (in a personal tweet on 7 April 2011). See also Scheloske's collection: www.wissenswerkstatt.net/2011/12/01/wissenschaftler-bei-twitter-eine-studie-zur -wissenschaftlichen-twitternutzung.

within social network sites, both for purely professional and partly private purposes.

Figure 9: Screenshot of a public Twitter list of twittering scientists (April 28, 2011)

Typical content of science-related microblogs

Investigating the actual usage practices, it turns out that the standard questions on top of the input box—"What are you doing?" (e.g. Facebook) or "What's happening?" (e.g. Twitter)—are being answered in a creative way and answers are going well beyond them. The input boxes of the microblogging services in professionally oriented social network sites are more general, for example "Ask a question"/"Update Status" (Academia.edu) and "Post Question/Publication/Link/Image/File" (ResearchGate). A number of researchers proposed empirical categories of microblogs. For instance, Java et al. (2007, 62f.) distinguish between daily chatter (largest and most common use); conversations; sharing information/URLs; and reporting news. Mischaud (2007, 18f.) differentiates, based on content analysis, between "What are you doing?"; personal; family & friends; work; popular culture; news and information; food; technology; weather; activity; and miscellaneous (there are even more categories in Honeycutt and Herring 2009, 4; see also Smith and Rainie 2010).

Turning to scientific use, we observed that academics are quite creative when using microblogging platforms. We found the following typical content in science-related microblogs and reformulated it as new questions (Herwig et al. 2009, 13f., including examples):

- *"Which event do you wish to draw attention to?"* Hints to scientific events or calls, such as conferences or workshops, are typical microblogging content; they usually contain a short summary and a link to further information; occasionally, the author adds a personal note regarding the significance of the event. This type of message enlarges the potential reach of a conference announcement.
- *"Which publication do you wish to draw attention to?"* Similarly, people with related interests suggest new publications or presentations to each other. This may be about their own publications (i.e. a form of self-marketing), but is more frequently about other authors' work. Often, the microblogs refer to (longer) blogs reviewing publications. Special "overlay" services may use this information and, for instance, rank publications according to references made to them on Twitter.[43]
- *"What are you currently reading?"* Some academics inform their followers occasionally about what they are just reading. In this way others come to know about current interests of each other, which may potentially lead to co-operations. There is certainly an individual limit to what one wants to reveal. In any case, these hints to current reading may lead to fruitful discussions outside microblogging about the literature processed in parallel by the communication partners. Finally, this kind of microblog provides an indication what others perceive as relevant.
- *"Do you have a short question?"* Similar to "old-fashioned" e-mail discussion lists, but certainly with serious limits for the level of sophistication of both the question and the answer, microblogging is often used to ask colleagues for help, somehow complementing the research process. This function is mostly used by those who have already a sub-

---

43 Such a service existed for a while in 2009/2010, named Tweprint, which aggregated hints to working papers in the physicists' working paper "arXiv", but is not online any more.

stantive number of followers (Dvorak 2009), who most likely have
quite similar interests and possibly complementary expertise.
- *"Would you like to coordinate common activities?"* Many microblogs are devoted to coordinative purposes, such as agreeing on a rendezvous, e.g.
in a conference break, or regarding the next step in a common project.

In summary, scientists seem to be quite creative when it comes to using
microblogging tools for their professional purposes, but there are more
than pure work-related reasons for microblogging, as we shall see.

Informal communication—microblogging as a virtual café

In addition to the various microblogs with the above questions in mind, we
also observed that a considerable portion of scientwists not only microblogs professionally in the strict sense—that is goal-oriented information
exchange and communication—but also uses the same account (identity)
for informal communication. They send private or semi-private messages
making, for instance, political observations or simply commenting a late
arrival of a train. In other words, these are answers to the questions *"What
is affecting you right now?"*. Often short written dialogues develop, which
could be compared to conversations in the kitchen of a research institute.
Despite or just because of its informal character this kind of communication is important for research or working groups as a sort of "social lubri-
cant". For instance, the cafeteria of CERN is a well-known and well-
researched example for the importance of informal exchange of thoughts
among CERN researchers (e.g. Merz 1998; Nentwich 2003, 198ff). Emrich
and Flatau (2004) describe a number of social functions of the café,
kitchen or tearoom: it is easier to start a conversation; status clues are
weaker; they may serve as a forum for cooling down heated debates; it is
more convenient to provide personal background information in this
framework; and it might the best place to get sensitive information, hence
be a place where particularly newer or younger staff members are being
socialized. In contrast, virtual teams could suffer from not having this kind
of meeting place and we may ask whether a microblogging culture might
take over functions of the café culture?

Obviously there are some similarities between the communicative space
of a microblogging forum and a real tearoom in a research institute: Messages are equally coincidental, as they are not usually directed towards
specific persons, but rather to groups; it is not easy to control whom one

will meet and communicate with, because it is at random which followers will react. Microblogs disappear in most clients after a certain period, so the time slot in which communication is possible is narrow—similar to the café in which there is not always someone to talk to. As an easy entry to informal communication, microblogging is convenient. Microblogs using the @-sign, i.e. those addressed at a specific person, are public and can be read by others (unless they are sent as direct, private messages); similar to the café, the occasional passer-by can join it or just "listen". As microbloggers also exchange information not always directly related to work, a feeling of social closeness may be produced, like in a break. Based on a series of interviews with staff in an IT firm Zhao and Rosson (2009) distinguish between the following effects of microblogging at the level of social relationships: it may change the perception of other persons; establish a common ground; and a feeling of connectedness. Similarly, Miller (2008) describes Twitter as "phatic" communication: not the essence or meaning of the messages may be decisive, but it is simply the fact *that* they communicate, which produces or sustains a social relation.

Comparable to the café, communication via Twitter is in general not considered as particularly compulsory or binding. It is, however, hardly possible to take back or deny a written statement: users may delete a message, but others may already have saved or forwarded it; with Twitter, even deleted messages can be retrieved for ten days via the standard search box. So the real café is obviously a better place to exchange sensitive information. It is yet open whether microblogging may actually have an impact on social differentiation. While being prepared to disclose personal background information may level out status differences, but—in contrast to a real coffee break situation—there is no time limit in which social relationship patterns may prevail that differ from normal circumstances. Microblogging might turn out like e-mail, a medium which also did not alter much regarding the social distance—despite earlier expectations (Matzat 2004; Nentwich 2003, 254ff.). Furthermore, while it may serve as a means to let off steam bilaterally, microblogging does not seem adequate for conflict management in groups. This is difficult in any electronic medium, but particularly so when there is only space for a few characters at a time and the communication is public. However, the increased knowledge of personal background information and the development of what we have called social closeness may help to avoid conflicts in the first place. Microblogging certainly contributes to building cliques: once you follow another person you have to actively take the decision to break the connection, whereas in the real tearoom you may just walk away. In this sense, microblogging may be even better suited to self-stabilizing groups than shared breaks (Herwig et al. 2009, 16).

For informal communication in the café, the mélange of professionally interesting and semi-private personal content seems essential. Closed, professional microblogging platforms for departments or institutes would not be attractive, if only professional content is exchanged, as they would be similar to E-mail lists. Furthermore, if one microblogs only in one's own professional team, it is less likely to stumble across new information and ideas because of the close common frame of reference. At the end of the day, it will be less the new technical subtleties, but the evolving usage culture that will or will not make microblogging interesting for academics. Similarly, the department's kitchen is rather uninteresting if used only to percolate coffee.

Accompanying conferences

A good deal of academic microblogging now goes on around some conferences (and also in connection with other cultural and social events).[44] Why is this so? Both, for large conferences and lectures, the following situation is typical: one person speaks, many listen. Direct communicative interaction is limited to a short period of time after the speech. From a technology enhanced learning perspective, Anderson et al. (2003, 119f.) identified the following challenges that could be met by parallel, computer-supported feedback:

- *Feedback lag:* Questions are temporarily suppressed, waiting for a better opportunity, but may be discarded if that opportunity does not arrive;
- *Student apprehension:* Younger scholars often do not have the courage to put questions because of the size or atmosphere in the room;
- *Single-speaker paradigm:* Only one person speaks at a time, which excludes from the outset the majority, given large audiences and restricted time.

---

44 One can find examples of collected tweets sent during a conference at: friendfeed.com/
   lindaunobel; delicious.com/J_SCH/solo09; Saunders et al. (2009) cover similar Twitter-
   Friendfeed reporting from another conference.

Based on these observations, Reinhardt et al. (2009) explored how Twitter is used around academic conferences. They distinguished between various roles, in particular the organizers and the attendees, and between before, during and after the conference. Their framework can be put into Table 2 below (see also Herwig et al. 2009, 18). In addition to a conference management agency's recommendations (Lisa 2007), the respondents in Reinhardt's et al. study used Twitter for commenting and discussing the presentations taking notes, putting questions, and referring to related resources. Furthermore, microblogging (direct mailing) is used for bilateral communication during a session; respondents also mentioned the possibility to get at least online presence during the event.

Table 2: Typical uses of microblogging during conferences

	By organizers	By attendees
Before the conference	announce dates and deadlines, special events, give reminders, organizational hints	organize the trip, exchange information on accommodation and travel
During the conference	updates, hints to venues, animate participants, post links to blogs and pictures	discuss papers, ask questions make notes, give feedback, post links to related resources
After the conference	thank participants, encourage feedback and writing of conference reports, document the conference	post links to blogs and pictures, stay in contact beyond the conference, document the conference

Source: Based and expanding on Herwig et al. (2009, 18) and Reinhardt et al. (2009)

Around conferences, the practice of including a conference-specific hashtag (see 2.2.1) in each related message evolved: as soon as the current hashtag is agreed upon or set in advance by the organizers, it allows all interested Twitter users to set up an automated search for that particular hashtag thus creating a conference-specific timeline which lists all messages related to this event in real-time. This option is open even for nonparticipants who can in this manner follow synchronously or review later what is or was going on at the conference. For those present and even for those who are not microblogging themselves, there is sometimes an additional option: a so-called "twitterwall", i.e. a real time projection of relevant tweets in the conference room with an overhead beamer or a large computer screen. Special websites may be used to present Twitter messages in an optimal way on a twitterwall (better readability, automated updating).[45]

With a conference-specific hashtag and even more so with a twitterwall, microblogging may contribute to better communication and collaboration related to the conference: participants finding out who is present in the lecture room or participates at a distance. This improves the chances for follow-up communication on the microblogging platform, but also during the breaks, as one may identify other microbloggers via their profile pictures and one can easily start or continue a dialogue with reference to an earlier electronic comment. Analyzing conference tweets recently became a vibrant topic of research (e.g. Dröge et al. 2011).

Another important field of application is the *documentation* of a conference. One problem which arises, however, is that Twitter itself restricts searches for past hashtags[46], even though they are still in the archive. Thus Twitter is a good medium for real time communication, but not very good at maintaining archives. However, other services such as Friendfeed and Twapperkeeper[47] can serve this purpose. In fact, many of the archives on Twapperkeeper consist of tweets from conferences, so there does seem to be a demand for this service. Friendfeed allows not only for collecting and archiving microblogs, but also for comments to individual messages and for creating groups. Groups can be used to enable parallel electronic conversations around a common topic. A typical example for using a collection of microblogs for a conference report is the paper by Saunders et al. (2009) who compiled their report on the International Conference on Intelligent Systems for Molecular Biology (ISBM) 2008 using Friendfeed. All comments and conversations around that conference built up an ad-hoc documentation[48], which formed the basis for Saunders and his colleagues to write their report. In addition, they analyzed on a meta-level what they were experimenting with and came to a surprisingly positive assessment:

"We found that it enhanced our note-taking skills, allowed us to compile notes from parallel sessions, attracted wider interest from non-attendees, and, in addition

---

45 E.g. twitterwallr.com, twitterwall.me or twittbee.de.
46 For example, the tweets relating to a conference organized by the Interactive Science research project in early September 2009 (twitter.com/#search?q=#Insi09) could no longer be found only a few weeks later.
47 friendfeed.com; twapperkeeper.com.
48 friendfeed.com/ismb-2008.

to the 'live' aspect, generated a permanent archive of the meeting." (Saunders et al. 2009, 5)

So on the one hand, the emergence of an additional level of written communication and even reflection parallel to the actual conference is considered useful by a growing number of academics as it enables both participants and non-participants to follow and digest the arguments being presented. On the other hand, there have been instances of conference organizers banning live blogging and tweeting to protect the confidentiality of closed conference sessions, for example to ensure that journalists only report when presenters have given their consent (Bonetta 2009). Others may deliberately choose not to actively microblog during conferences in order to keep focused on the speaker and avoid distraction.[49] We will discuss this general problem of information overload in a larger context in section 3.4.

A channel for scientific marketing and communication

As the Internet in general, and Web 2.0 applications in particular, have gained ever more users over the past few years, it also becomes ever more attractive for the purpose of public relations (Nentwich 2010a). Web 2.0 is characterized by the fact that the majority of activities, and hence of content, is provided by the users—posing new challenges and opportunities for public relations activities. Users act in different roles: they author, comment, criticize, rate, add keywords, or multiply the impact by forwarding links. Although providing only very little space at a time, we observe that microblogging also plays a role in public relations of academia. Presumably this is a form of scientific marketing that makes it possible to reach a target group which one would not reach by using the usual channels of press releases, newsletters, or mass e-mails.

While traditional public relations work was characterized by specialists, in the digital social network non-specialist staff is also involved and often acts informally for an enterprise or institution. Consequently, the borderlines between the personal and the professional spheres are being renegotiated: on the one hand, the expectations regarding the communication style are changing (for instance, a blog is expected to have a more personal

---

49 This was e.g. the practice of the symposium "'Slow Down, You Move Too Fast': Rethinking the Culture of Busyness and IT", Seattle, WA, May 5-7, 2011.

touch than a press release); on the other hand, the question arises who owns the social capital generated in digital social networks by collecting professional contacts. In the context of external science communication, i.e. the transfer of research results to a broader, mainly non-scientific public, similar questions arise: What communication style to choose, is Twitter an adequate means? Are scientwists recognizable as researchers and/or representatives of their home institution? How should they deal with the likely overlaps of their private and professional spheres? We will consider all of these aspects, first from the point of view of the research and teaching institutions (1), and second from the perspective of the individual researcher (2).

(1) *Institutions:* Whether or not microblogging is used is primarily dependent on the institutional culture. We observed two variants: It is either applied to distribute information and serves as an additional channel of one-way science marketing, or it is an element of an interactive dialogue with a broader or more specific public. An example for the first variant is the Richard Dawkins Foundation for Reason and Science (RDFRS): new articles published on their website richarddawkins.net are being automatically posted on Twitter; the message consists of the title and a short URL linking to the article. Potentially, dialogue in the form of feedback and comments may appear on the website, but no microblogging dialogue is intended there.

By contrast, if dialogue is intended, the question arises who communicates in the name of the institution. Is the profile one of the whole institution, or of only a subunit, e.g. the public relations department or a research project? Is it one specific person or a group who is taking care of the profile? It has been suggested to have communication guidelines in order to develop a recognizable microblogging style over time (Herwig et al. 2009, 20f.). One such example is the good practice guideline of the Institut National des Sciences Appliquées (INSA) de Toulouse (France) regarding the use of the institution's Facebook and Twitter accounts.[50]

An example of a heavily twittering and dialogue-seeking institution is Johns Hopkins University (JHU) in Baltimore/USA[51]: The profile picture

---

50 netpublic.fr/2011/04/charte-d-utilisation-des-reseaux-sociaux-facebook-et-twitter-de-l-insa-de-toulouse-bonne-pratique.

51 twitter.com/JohnsHopkins; in addition, many other sub-units of this university microblog, like the the Peabody Institute announcing events, the news department of Johns Hopkins Medicine with health-related tips, the Milton S. Eisenhower Library announc-

is the one of the university's founder, so it is not recognizable who exactly is behind the account; the messages usually deal with references to the house gazette, current seminar offers, invitations, links to other media, but also retweets (from staff, students, and sub-units) and answers to other users' messages—indicating that someone is following a timeline and manually, hence time-consuming, providing the service. Academic publishers[52] and scientific journals[53] started using this fast communication channel to arouse interest for their latest publications. So far, they seem to consider microblogging as an additional distribution channel only; one could, however, imagine a more interactive, dialogue-oriented way, involving authors and potential readers with a view to building-up a community around certain topics.

(2) *Individuals:* Reinhardt et al. (2009, 151) found that about two thirds use microblogging both for professional and private purposes, 15 percent only for private, and a quarter only for professional purposes. Correspondingly, microblogging is also used to communicate about one's personal research work. Academics circulate to their followers information about their own work, typically announcing their latest article or an upcoming conference they organized or where they will have a presentation (Bonetta 2009 provides some examples of this). This activity is not only an altruistic contribution to the flow of information among fellow researchers, but is obviously aimed at self-marketing. This may possibly lead to higher credibility if scholarly and personal tweets are mixed (Johnson 2011).

How much researchers microblog, and if at all, depends not only on personal preferences and needs, but also on the organizational culture in which the researcher is embedded, and on the subject matter of the research. For instance, if you are interested in patenting your research later on, you are not likely to twitter much about it beforehand (see Nentwich 2003, 162f. for a discussion of the influence of the degree of competitiveness on a research field's level of "cyberness"). It is conceivable that individual, public statements are not welcomed by the mother institu-

---

ing new collections or the university publisher JHU Press and many others. For an extensive list of twittering universities see the special category of the Twitter Fan Wiki at twitter.phworkm.com/Universities.

52 E.g. Random House twitter.com/randomhouse, Addison-Wesley twitter.com/Addison Wesley.

53 See, for example, these lists: scholarship20.blogspot.com/2009/07/twitter-journals-journals-that-tweet.html and mobile-libraries.blogspot.com/2009/05/scitechmed-journals-publications-on.html.

tion. An early and much debated example, though outside academia, are the social media guidelines of the Washington Post. They have been developed after a conflict over a top journalist' microblog, which was considered to be not in line with the newspaper's policy of strict objectivity (Alexander 2009). According to these guidelines, all social media activities of journalists are considered part of their professional sphere (Kramer 2009). It seems however debatable whether relinquishing some of one's personal privileges as a private citizen can be contracted-out. The situation of journalists and academics are certainly similarly sensitive in this respect. In any case, when individual scholars act for their research institutions or if this is expected, the separation between the professional and personal spheres is non-trivial. New communication cultures and practices are evolving.

Teaching aid

Microblogging is also used in university teaching, although as yet only seldom and rather experimentally (e.g. Grosseck and Holotescu 2008; Ebner and Maurer 2009). There are quite a number of motivations and ways to include this channel in the class room, as students usually react positively to additions and alternatives to the traditional lecture, and they are both inspired by and used to Web 2.0 tools. To arouse their active collaboration and motivation is often the main reason for such experiments (Aspden and Thorpe 2009; Rankin 2009). We found the following functions of microblogging in teaching environments:

– *Administrative purposes:* University administrators and lecturers are using Twitter to communicate more directly and efficiently with students by circulating organizational information via this service. Access to and of students is easier than with e-learning software, as they may use various paths, including the web and mobile devices.
– *Enabling discussion:* With large numbers of students in a class, microblogging may help to organize discussions as Rankin (2009) reports: students separated in discussion groups collect questions and comments, which are sorted by teaching assistants and answered towards the end of the teaching unit.
– *Parallel feedback channel:* Even without proper group or plenary discussion, students may contribute to the class by posting questions, com-

ments, links etc.—which could be particularly attractive for shy students (Holotescu and Grosseck 2008, 8).

– *Learning diary and networking:* Microblogs may also be used by students to make notes in-between sessions and for communication among themselves (Aspden and Thorpe 2009).
– *Evaluation tool:* Stieger and Burger (2009) used Twitter for what they called formative evaluation, i.e. students are asked to send feedback (possibly with anonymous profiles) immediately after each class so that the teacher may react immediately, as opposed to ex-post feedback.

While Johnson (2011) argues that microblogging may contribute to the teachers credibility and hence to positive learning outcomes, using microblogging platforms for teaching may be problematic. To begin with, the low limit of characters does not allow for sophisticated or extended communication. In addition, one needs to be aware of the sensitive change between a non-public, be it bilateral or restricted to the group of students in a classroom, to a more or less public communication situation (Kerres and Preussler 2009). While it may be convenient to use one's usual private Twitter account in the classroom, not everyone would like to do that, and in this case needs to set up a second account. Furthermore, it may be necessary to authenticate anonymous accounts when used for participating in a class and for evaluating—not an easy task. In any case, it seems that it may only be one additional element among many tools potentially used in teaching environments.

Microblogging as a research tool

Apart from the above mentioned possibility to use microblogging as an unsystematic tool to get answers to empirical questions or queries for literature etc., hence indirectly contributing to knowledge production, it is also conceivable to use it to collect data systematically. One such example has been reported by Dambeck (2009): Twitter should play a role as a swift information channel for reports on earthquakes in California and so contributes to a research-based early-warning system (USGS-TED or U.S. Geological Society Survey Twitter Earthquake Detector). Many also use social media via their PDAs/smartphones (which increasingly provide location data, e.g. via GPS), allowing applications in further contexts, where quick data gathering coupled with qualitative information would be useful, ranging from natural disasters, pandemics, to weather or traffic conditions etc. By contrast, it does not seem to be particularly suited for surveys because both the question and the answer would have to be very short. However, microblogging occasionally plays a role in recruiting respondents, who are redirected to online survey websites.

Finally, Twitter is an interesting object of research in itself and, as a digital platform, generates huge amounts of data that may be useful in network analysis, for linguistic purposes, historical research or political science analysis (e.g. on social movements). However, Twitters restrictive policy regarding the use of Twitter data (see above) partly hinders such practices.

2.2.4 Interim conclusions

We may ask whether typical cyberscientists will soon become "scientwists" (Bradley 2009)? We observe that microblogging is used by an increasing number of scientists for a growing diversity of purposes. The main application fields for microblogging in science are in context-augmented searching and publishing and in reputation management. In teaching and at conferences, microblogging is becoming more and more established as a parallel communication channel as the social components of open and informal communication gain importance. Whether this trend will persist and further develop depends on a number of factors, such as individual usage patterns and disciplinary or subject-related variables (see above chapter 1.3). In other words, the question is, whether and how microblogging is functional in academic practices? Is it in line with the framework conditions of modern research? The following factors play a role in this assessment (Nentwich 2009, 17ff.):

Lack of time, a general issue for all activities of academics, may work against widespread use of microblogging: updating one's microblog, reading the timeline of others, and identifying useful contacts needs time. Having said that, receiving up-to-date information, which is already filtered by one's personal network, may also *save* time. Furthermore, microblogging can be seen as an "in-between" activity, filling the gaps between phases of more in-depth research work (in a break, while travelling, after having read an article). This may possibly be quite efficient. The personal balance of each academic will probably be different in this respect.

Information overload (see also 3.4) may be the result of yet another channel through which additional information is perceived by scientists— depending on individual information seeking and media usage behavior.

While some prefer to receive scientific information through the standard channels (journals, databases), others prefer to rely on their personal information networks. Within the latter, microblogs may play the role of a filter, thus contributing to avoiding overload. It certainly also depends on the type of information a researcher seeks in a particular phase, so that microblogging use may both increase and attenuate overload.

Incentive system (see also 3.3.4): Analogous to the early days of e-journals, which were not prestigious enough and thus academics only hesitantly started to publish in them, the incentive for using microblogging is currently not very strong. It is rather unlikely that posting microblogs will soon be included in scientific evaluation schemes. A number of web platforms emerged, which try to evaluate the influence of microblogging profiles. Typical parameters are: how communicative they are (measured in reactions to and conversations with other microbloggers), how often one's microblogs get retweeted, and the number of followers, including journalists. The aim is to enhance the visibility of the researcher and the research. However, as yet, the visibility that counts is not necessarily within the scientific community, but rather outside it.

Quality (see also 3.3) Because of their brevity, microblogs in the academic context usually do not stand on their own, but refer to other sources. The latter then need to meet scientific standards in order to play a valuable role in the professional practice of scientists. There seems to be only few studies on the scientific quality of the data and information distributed via microblogging as yet (Weller et al. 2011; Dröge et al. 2011). Retweeting—the equivalent of scientific quoting—alone is certainly no guarantee for factual accuracy.

Benefits of using the information fragments received via microblogging in a research context depend on the specific context. Scholars specializing in Internet research find many microbloggers in their field of expertise; in other areas, a sufficiently attractive number of experts may not yet be actively microblogging. The various forms of using Twitter & Co. for asking questions, giving feedback and comments during conferences, in teaching etc. (see above 2.2.3) may generate benefits in those contexts.

Being online permanently is not essential for microblogging, as it can be used as an asynchronous medium, but the short-lived nature of individual messages and the option to react immediately suggests checking the microblogging account frequently. While some purposes may be achieved by infrequent use (e.g. reviewing what happened during a conference), it would be necessary to be online constantly in other cases (e.g. actively participating in a conference). Ubiquitous and permanent microblogging—via mobile devices and/or with clients that automatically update the timeline—is probably not everybody's choice.

Competition among researchers is prevalent in many fields, open cooperation and a culture of information sharing is not the rule. Premature disclosure of interim results or exciting hypotheses may be counterproductive, as others may profit and publish faster (Nentwich 2009). This is an important factor for non-adoption in some fields. To protect microblogging messages selectively and to make them accessible only for some of one's followers is only possible by using multiple accounts—which enhances the personal administrative burden. In very competitive fields, microblogging would therefore tend to broadcast only less sensitive information, such as conference announcements.

Authorship: Although each microblog is always directly related to an account, the latter are often anonymous and one cannot guarantee that the names are not false, corresponding to other persons in the offline-world. In addition, the proof of authorship is difficult in the long run, as microblogs are usually not properly archived. In this sense, microblogging is similar to oral transmission, where the attribution to a specific person also blurs over time. This unclear situation makes microblogging unsuited for all kinds of research-related activities.

In conclusion we hold that microblogging is still a dynamic and fast developing new communication medium, which is not only offered by the market champion Twitter, but is also increasingly embedded in other social media platforms. Consequently we reckon that—whatever the future of Twitter may be—microblogging will continue to function as a platform-independent communication principle. This principle, i.e. a short, fast, and ubiquitous written communication channel, is appealing to many, not least in academia.

2.3 Collaborative Knowledge Production—The Case of Wikimedia

Collaborative knowledge production in the form of co-authoring academic papers is a core activity of most academic fields. While the age of cyberscience added some easy ways to exchange digital files, the age of cyber-science 2.0 added a novel infrastructure for authors to co-write, practically simultaneously, texts stored on Internet servers. Recently this became a growing market, with even the "big players" offering such services (e.g. Google Docs[54]), but with many alternative formats. The free software Etherpad, for example, focuses on the co-production of short texts by many authors in "real time".[55] In this section we shall focus on wiki software which enables simple, quick and reliable editing of complex and inter-linked hypertexts (see below 2.3.1).

The online encyclopedia Wikipedia is probably the best known collaborative writing project in the Internet and at the same time, one of the most popular websites worldwide.[56] Early 2001 its predecessor *Nupedia*, which was peer reviewed and expert-based, introduced it as "a fun project loosely associated with Nupedia"[57]. Obviously, the developers themselves regarded it as rather "wild-and-woolly" in contrast to their main project, which they characterized as "much more rigorous and serious."[58] Today most people have not heard of Nupedia. Wikipedia has not only pushed its predecessor aside, but also seriously challenges traditional, well-institutionalized competitors such as the Encyclopædia Britannica. Apart from the enormous pace of Wikipedia's success, this development is especially remarkable when we consider the revolutionary organization of the encyclopedia: Instead of relying on trusted experts and a rigorous peer review system, the encyclopedia seems to be built on a principle that is often euphemistically associated with a "wisdom of crowds" (Surowiecki 2004), allowing basically everybody to produce and edit content.

Wiki software is the driver of Wikipedia's success, which in turn became the spark for many other projects: many different language versions of Wikipedia have been established, as well as a number of related wiki projects, for example Wiktionary (a dictionary), Wikibooks (a platform for collaborative book projects; see below), Wikinews (for general news), Wik-

---

54 docs.google.com.

55 In an "etherpad" (see etherpad.org) all users can see what others write at the same time in, possibly colored differently, as if there were multiple cursors active in the very same text.

56 In May 2011 wikipedia.org was ranked seven on Alexa's list of global top sites (alexa.com/topsites).

57 web.archive.org/web/20010118225800/http://www.nupedia.com.

58 web.archive.org/web/20010406105416/www.wikipedia.com/wiki/Welcome,
_newcomers.

isource (a collection of original sources), Wikiversity (an e-learning platform; see below) and many more; additionally, countless independent wiki
platforms in very different fields have emerged.

Since 2003, Wikipedia and its sister projects have been operated by the
US-based *Wikimedia Foundation*, a nonprofit organization that takes care of
global strategies, such as improving the overall quality, fund-raising, public
relations, legal affairs, maintenance of the technical infrastructure etc. Furthermore, local independent chapters support the foundation internation-
ally. Although the umbrella organization and its head, Wikipedia founder
Jimmy Wales, have certain extraordinary rights for governing the projects,
Wikimedia describes itself as a bottom-up organization: "Normally Wikipedia is a self-governing project run by its community. Its policies and
guidelines are intended to reflect the consensus of the community"
(Wikimedia 2011k). Its mission reads:

"The mission of the Wikimedia Foundation is to empower and engage people
around the world to collect and develop educational content under a free license or
in the public domain, and to disseminate it effectively and globally. In collaboration with a network of chapters, the Foundation provides the essential infrastructure and an organizational framework for the support and development of
multilingual wiki projects and other endeavors which serve this mission. The
Foundation will make and keep useful information from its projects available on
the Internet free of charge, in perpetuity." (Wikimedia 2011c)

Indeed, at first glance the obstacles for contributing seem rather low: most
articles can be created and edited even without being registered. However,
logged users (accounts are free) have more rights and, since every change
can quickly be reversed, edits usually "survive" only when they are in line
with the policies of the projects, which will be outlined in the next section.
We will particularly focus on those three Wikimedia projects we regard as
most relevant for academia: the encyclopedia Wikipedia, the e-book writing
project Wikibooks and the e-learning platform Wikiversity.

2.3.1 Main functions and core principles

The main function of Wikimedia projects is collaborative text production:
pages cannot only be read, but they also come with options for editing,
discussing and following the revision history. The latter records every single edit made and allows for undoing changes quickly by reloading older
versions (Figure 10). This way, no serious "harm" can be done to the con-

tent, which is why Wikimedia projects encourage everybody to participate actively.

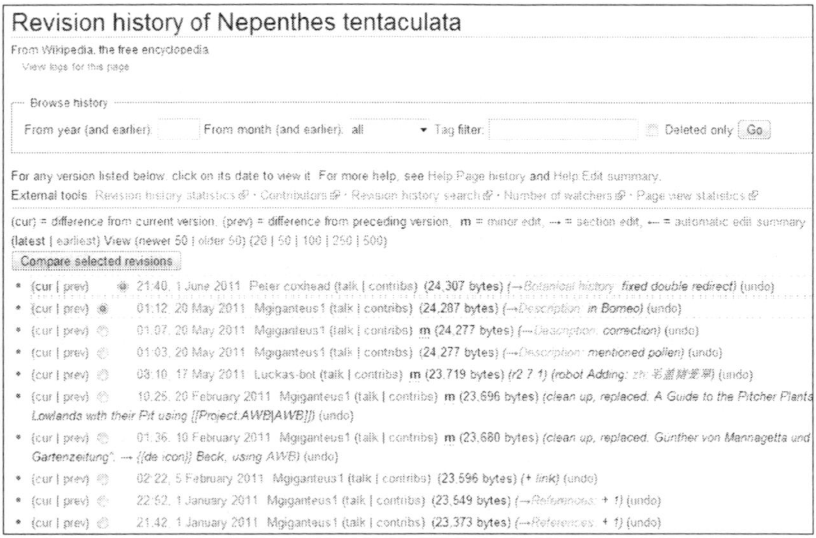

Figure 10: Revision history of a Wikipedia article

One of Wikipedia's fundamental principles says that "Wikipedia does not have firm rules" and suggests to be "bold (but not reckless) in updating articles and do not worry about making mistakes" (Wikimedia 2011j). This openness is also reflected in the overall founding principle stating that Wikimedia content in general is supposed to be in the public domain (Wikimedia 2011b).[59] Although the participatory structure allows constant change of most of the content (including administrative pages such as rules), changes ("edits") are only sustainable when they are in line with the community's consensus and its policies. Wikimedia's platforms provide various tools for communication in order to enable discussion between contributors and decision-makers. These debates take place mainly on *discussion pages*, which are attached to each article; here directly related aspects can be debated. Besides these forums specialized on individual articles, there are initiatives with broader scopes, such as *WikiProjects* focusing on specific thematic fields and aspects, as well as options for communica-

---

59 Still, because of the participatory architecture, copyrighted material is uploaded occasionally.

tion at the micro level, such as user-to-user messages. In this vein, these platforms are not pure collaborative writing tools, but the nucleus of digital social networks, in which users have profiles, follow each other, and gather around topics. Additionally, members can use external channels like mailing lists and offline meetings.

Despite Wikimedia's general preference of transparency and flat hierarchies, there are experienced users who have been entrusted with certain additional rights and access to administrative tools. While the Wikimedia Foundation serves as the ultimate instance, there are *administrators* who are able to (temporarily) ban users or pages from further editing, *stewards* who can perform administrative action across different Wikimedia projects, *editorial boards* who supervise projects on Wikibooks etc. (for more details see e.g. Wikimedia 2011m). For outsiders it is difficult to understand the complex power structure of Wikimedia and its ways of decision-making. Community members described it as "a mix of anarchic, despotic, democratic, republican, meritocratic, plutocratic, technocratic, and bureaucratic elements" (Wikimedia 2011g). The technocratic elements refer to frames attributed by the software and its developers: they structure user behavior, for example, by *templates* which standardize content production to a certain degree, but also by applying *bots*—small programs that automatically perform defined actions such as correcting common mistakes (for a study on the influence of bots see Geiger 2011).

For readers, the platforms provide various ways to access the open content, for instance: internal search engines; topic-related portals; featured articles (respectively books, courses); and categories that can be browsed from multiple perspectives. Moreover, much of the material is linked across the different platforms. Since the steps of content production are publicly documented to a large extent, for example on discussion pages, readers may get insights into the construction process of the platforms. In the case of Wikipedia and Wikibooks, this is particularly remarkable because consumers of traditional encyclopedias and books usually do not have such opportunities. Also Wikiversity's transparency is rather uncommon if compared to most other e-learning projects.

Apart from shared technical structures, goals and ideas, the projects differ depending on their intended outcomes. Table 3 gives an overview of the breadth and impact of the selected Wikimedia projects by listing the number of articles, views per hour and active users for the English version of each project and the estimated global web rank for the domains. We will go on by focusing on further peculiarities of the different platforms.

Table 3: Breadth and impact of the selected Wikimedia projects

	Articles	Views/hour	Active users	Web Rank
Wikipedia (en)	3.649.867	9.401.602	142.865	7
Wikibooks (en)	35.219	16.085	457	2.988
Wikiversity (en)	15.718	4.068	398	19.189

For Sources and methodological information see footnote 60.

Wikipedia

Wikipedia clearly serves as a role model for the other Wikimedia projects, not only because it was the first one historically, but also because it is by far the most successful in terms of breadth, usage and societal impact. Regardless of possible methodological issues, Table 3 illustrates this beyond doubt.[60]

Over 250 language versions exist, though the English version clearly is most extensive (over 3.8 million articles) and grew exponentially, whereas the others grew in a linear fashion. The English version is followed by the German (1.3 million articles) and French (over 1.2) versions, and the Dutch, Italian, Polish and Spanish versions with over 800.000 articles each[61]. Figure 11 gives an overview of the growth of the largest Wikipedias. The English version alone has more than 14 million registered users,

---

60 Statistics for Articles and Views/hr have been taken from stats.wikimedia.org (for April 30, 2011) for the English version of each project. Active users show the number of users who have performed an action in the last 30 days on the English versions, taken from en.wikipedia.org/wiki/Special:Statistics, en.wikibooks.org/wiki/Special:Statistics, en.wikiversity.org/wiki/Special:Statistics (on June 10, 2011). The Wikipedia statistics page refers explicitly to "registered users" (unlike Wikibooks and Wikiversity). Web Rank describes the estimated rank among global websites by alexa.com (for June 6, 2011) and refers to the general domains, including all language versions. Note that the reliability of Alexa Web Rank can be questioned, among other issues, because certain browsers are not included. Still, due to the very significant variations we believe the given data is solid enough to prove the obvious differences between the projects. Also note the slightly different dates.

61 As of December 2011; data source: stats.wikimedia.org/EN/TablesArticlesTotal.htm.

of which approximately 142.000 are considered to be active, which means
that they have performed at least one action within the last 30 days).[62]

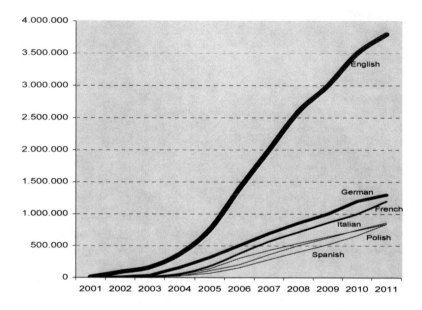

Figure 11: Article growth of the six largest Wikipedias[61]

As an encyclopedia, its scope is relatively limited, shaping the content allowed along three core content policies (Wikimedia 2011i):

-   All Wikipedia articles and other encyclopedic content must respect a
    neutral point of view (NPOV), that is, they have to represent significant
    views fairly, proportionately and without bias.
-   Material challenged or likely to be challenged, as well as all quotations,
    must be attributed to a reliable, published source. The threshold for
    inclusion in Wikipedia is *verifiability*, not truth. By this, Wikipedia
    means, whether readers are able to check that the material added to
    Wikipedia has already been published by any reliable source, not
    whether an author or the majority considers it to be true.

---

62 Source: en.wikipedia.org/wiki/Special:Statistics (retrieved June 5, 2011). We are not sure
   what exactly is counted here as a "user" as it is possible to log in also with other Wikimedia accounts.

- Wikipedia does *not publish original research*, that is, all material in Wikipedia has to be attributable to a reliable, published source and articles must not contain any new analysis or synthesis of published material that serves to advance a position not clearly advanced by the sources.

As parsimonious and univocal as these three core rules may seem, a closer look at Wikipedia policies reveals that many additional explanations are required (Butler et al. 2008); not surprisingly, there are constant debates about their concrete interpretation, especially in controversial contexts. One may, for example, ask what is "neutral" or what source can be considered as "reliable", and so on. Arguments between "deletionists", who tend to exclude questionable content, versus "inclusionists", who follow a rather liberal interpretation of the policies, occur frequently. Due to Wikipedia's massive popularity and its significant position in modern societies, encyclopedic articles defining and constructing realities often have a political notion, too. In combination with the participatory architecture, this often leads to so-called *edit wars*, in which users quickly undo changes made by others and vice versa. Consequently, the Wikipedia community is very active in order to protect and productively develop its content. Rigorous actions, however, are rather exceptional: On May 5, 2011, for example, just 0.05 percent of the articles of the English Wikipedia were restricted to edits by administrators only and 0.16 percent by registered users only.[63] We conclude that contributing to Wikipedia successfully, i.e. without risking that one's contribution is deleted by others, is much more difficult than the interface suggests. Profound knowledge of this special community and its social dynamics is needed to become a successful author.

Wikibooks

Founded in 2003 by Wikipedia users, Wikibooks is deeply rooted in the encyclopedia project and can be seen as a reaction to Wikipedia's limited scope and specific form. Although it shares many functional principles and ideas with Wikipedia, the major differences are obvious: First, the intention of "collaboratively writing open-content textbooks" (Wikimedia 2011e) leads to a different form of content, second, its breadth and impact is much smaller than Wikipedia's (see also Table 3, p. 77). Dozens of language versions were created, but only a few of them contain a notable

---

63 Source: toolserver.org/~avatar/sperrungen.php?wiki=en.

number of articles—or "modules" as these sections are called here with reference to the different format. Again the English and the German language versions are the largest (over 35.000 respectively 16.000 modules[64]).

On the one hand, Wikibooks are no typical books. The term "books" might be misleading because the specific wiki format comes with distinct attributes:

"Wikibooks is not paper. Thus, Wikibooks has no size limits, can include links, etc. It also means that the style and length of writing appropriate for paper may not be appropriate here. The authors of a Wikibook module don't worry about an event occurring tomorrow that makes all the large, expensive paper copies outdated, as the Wikibook will change as well." (Wikimedia 2011f)

Thus, as in Wikipedia, the content is dynamic and in that sense never completed. Another major difference to regular books results from the collaborative nature of the platform, leading to unclear authorship. For instance, Speakman (2008) simply refers to himself and "anonymous authors". Wikibooks are similar to "regular" books in some respect. It is common to "dewikify" content at some point by removing internal hyperlinks because "each book should be self-contained" (Wikimedia 2011d). Consequently, the text becomes linear as in standard books. Indeed, sometimes Wikibooks even get published as regular books (e.g. Speakman 2008) and many are available in book-like PDF-/print-versions.

Again, despite Wikibooks' open architecture, edits can only be sustainable when they meet the rules of the project. In the first place, this means that they have to be in line with a rather narrow policy of inclusion allowing only specific books:

"Wikibooks is for textbooks, annotated texts, instructional guides, and manuals. These materials can be used in a traditional classroom, an accredited or respected institution, a home-school environment, as part of a Wikiversity course or for self-learning. As a general rule only instructional books are suitable for inclusion. Most types of books, both fiction and non-fiction, are not allowed on Wikibooks, unless they are instructional. The use of literary elements, such as allegory or fables as instructional tools can be permitted in some situations." (Wikimedia 2011f)

As in Wikipedia, primary research is not allowed and the community explicitly excludes "proposing new theories and solutions, presenting original ideas, defining new terms, and coining new words" and instead suggests it

---

64 As of December 2011; source: wikibooks.org.

"should be published elsewhere, such as [in] a peer-reviewed journal, or our sister project Wikiversity" (ibid.).

Wikiversity

The learning platform Wikiversity emerged from Wikibooks in 2006. It is not only the youngest Wikimedia project we analyzed, but also the smallest: The English version again stands out as the largest (with over 15.000 articles), this time not followed by the German version (which has only around 1.800 articles), but by the French version (over 8.200 articles) and the Russian Wikiversity (over 2.200 articles).[65] According to the project's self-description it is "devoted to learning resources, learning projects, and research for use in all levels, types, and styles of education from pre-school to university, including professional training and informal learning." (Wikimedia 2011n)

Thus, the platform welcomes what Wikipedia and Wikibooks (and in fact all other Wikimedia projects) explicitly forbid—original research. However, it "is limited to research activities that promote learning in the spirit of the Wikimedia Foundation's goals" (Wikimedia 2011p) and it is suggested that small language versions might better follow the usual rule of excluding original research (ibid.). Wikiversity also occasionally allows moving away from the neutral point of view policy, "as long as biases are disclosed and high standards of scholarship are adhered to" (ibid.), but as stated on the English Wikiversity policies page, "[m]ost Wikiversity pages adhere to NPOV" (Wikimedia 2011o). Due to the relatively early and experimental stage of the platform, the rules are not yet as established and settled compared to the other projects. Since it lacks public attention and the number of contributors is rather low, regulating the content is also apparently less urgent than in Wikipedia.

The main principle that basically everyone can edit everything is applied in Wikiversity as well, thus unlike in common universities there are no distinct set roles as "professor" or "student". Users can take over the teaching role by creating or editing content or they can become learners, mainly by browsing through the articles that are often organized in courses with very different structures. Sometimes additional interactive elements are used, for example questionnaires which include answers (Figure 12), in

---

65 As of April 30, 2011, source: stats.wikimedia.org/wikiversity/EN/Sitemap.htm; see also Table 3, p. 77.

other cases no questions are given except by request on the discussion pages or by contacting other users. Research projects can equally draw on multiple ways of non-hierarchical communication, mostly within the common wiki software framework of collaborative text production. Pages like the *Research discussion forum*[66] may serve as additional space for broader collaboration beyond projects and disciplines.

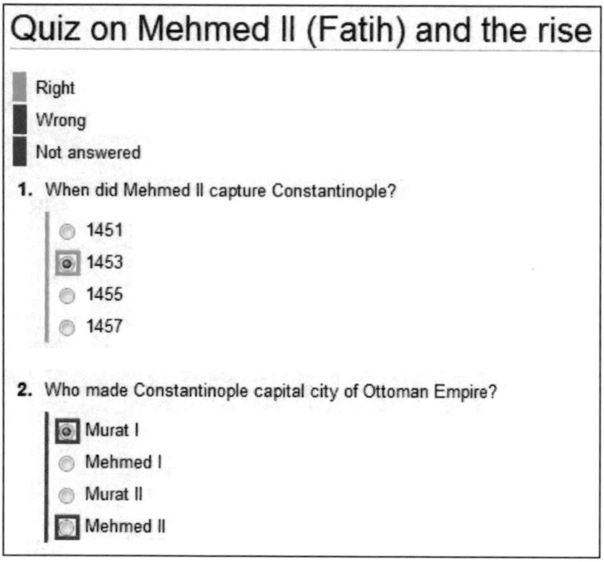

Quiz on Mehmed II (Fatih) and the rise

▌ Right

▌ Wrong

▌ Not answered

1. When did Mehmed II capture Constantinople?

⊙ 1451

◉ 1453

⊙ 1455

⊙ 1457

2. Who made Constantinople capital city of Ottoman Empire?

◉ Murat I

⊙ Mehmed I

⊙ Murat II

▣ Mehmed II

Figure 12: Interactive questionnaire in Wikiversity

Source: en.wikiversity.org/wiki/Quiz_on_Mehmed_II_(Fatih)_and_the_rise_of_the_Ottoman_
Empire#quiz0

2.3.2 Potentials for academia

As mentioned above the global mission of the Wikimedia Foundation is defined as: "to empower and engage people around the world to collect and develop educational content under a free license or in the public domain, and to disseminate it effectively and globally" (Wikimedia 2011c). Considering this mission and the main functions of the available platforms, potential points of intersection between academia and Wikimedia projects

---

66 en.wikiversity.org/wiki/Research_discussion_forum.

come into focus. These potentials are outlined in the following (see also Figure 13) and will be put in relation to the actual user practices in the next subsection.

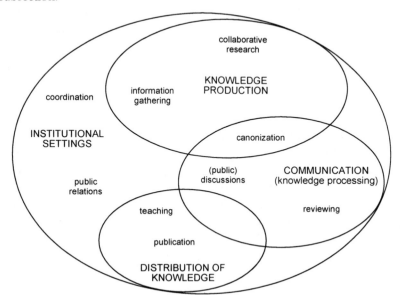

Figure 13: Scholarly activities and Wikimedia projects

Knowledge production: Obviously, all three projects can be used to gather information. As a general encyclopedia, Wikipedia provides a wide-ranging body of short articles that may be relevant for scholarly purposes. Due to its wide scope and rather strict criteria for inclusion, they might appear as insufficient and only suitable for initial fast and sketchy information gathering. In contrast, Wikibooks and Wikiversity potentially allow more profound content but their limited size limits their breadth. Since all three projects lack traditional peer review procedures (albeit other forms of peer review are applied; see below) and since their method of content production does not follow common practices in academia, their content may seem questionable as a scholarly source. Because of the explicit exclusion of original research in the policies of Wikipedia and Wikibooks, these platforms do not seem appropriate for this purpose. However, such collaborative text production can potentially lead to a form of canonization, for example when experts write articles on topics that are the subject of professional research. This is in particular likely in the case of Wikipedia, since its impact is high. Wikiversity allows original research but lacks popularity as an attraction factor.

Communication: All platforms provide opportunities for science-related communication, for instance via discussion pages or on the pages of Wiki-Projects within the specific focus of each project. Due to the Wikimedia policy of openness and transparency, most communication will be public and inclusive, regardless of formal hierarchies (of course users might draw back on side-channels, such as e-mail). Nevertheless, hierarchies might evolve from reputation and roles within the wiki communities or by giving credible references on one's user page. Although formal *ex ante* peer review is not performed, content is reviewed *ex post* by the communities of all projects. Since all levels of participation, including reviewing, largely rely on the dedication of volunteers, it depends on the individual context whether this type of quality control is applied, how and by whom. Wikiversity's relatively liberal content policy, which also allows original research, particularly challenges this procedure, since it cannot always draw on the reputation of external sources, which are used as obligatory references in the other projects. Therefore, more formal and expert-orientated review boards have been discussed and may be established in the future (Wikimedia 2011p).

Distribution of knowledge: Scholarly knowledge can be distributed by all platforms, but only within their specific scopes. As discussed above, this is in particular narrow in Wikipedia, which only allows encyclopedic articles following strictly defined rules. Wikibooks is broader, yet limiting it to instructional "books" of a certain kind. Wikiversity seems most suitable for the distribution of scholarly knowledge because it has the least limitations and is more focused on an academic audience. Thus, Wikiversity may be used as a publication platform for journal-like articles, as well. However, these forms of knowledge distribution are of course not in line with common academic practices, since they lack established standards such as attributable authorship and formalized quality control. Especially Wikiversity could serve as a source/platform for teaching, although technically speaking, all three platforms can be used for this purpose to a certain extent.

Institutional settings: Wikiversity, in particular, embraces a number of scholarly activities and might serve as a free alternative to other services, therefore lowering costs for software. It can moreover potentially serve as a platform connecting institutions and scholars—also across disciplines.

Wikipedia's popularity and impact gives it some significance for public relations. Scholars and their institutions may be represented here, if they fulfill the criteria for inclusion. Note that—in contrast to the traditional channels of public relations—these activities are bound by the Wikimedia principles, which means that the content can be changed by everybody anytime and has to follow the community's rules. Consequently, institutions and individuals have only limited possibilities of interference. Whether or not one is present in a Wikipedia article may be desired or unwanted, but is in any case publicly relevant. Given the public relevance of Wikipedia as a whole, academics may also be interested in the way their fields and related content are represented in this context.

2.3.3 Usage practices and impact

The rise of Wikipedia to one of the most popular websites worldwide makes it difficult to ignore. This holds true in particular for academia as we noted above when discussing its potential. At the same time, Wikimedia's functional principles conflict with those of academia to a large extent. Thus, the striking question is how Wikimedia projects deal with this conflict—or rather the other way round—how academia tackles it? This question is also to be addressed with regard to Wikibooks and Wikiversity, which are under less public pressure. In the following, we analyze this especially with regard to content production, to teaching, and to collaborative research; finally, we shall reflect on the platforms' impact on the institutional framework of academia.

Writing the wiki way

The participatory open writing environment of Wikimedia projects is probably one of the most challenging aspects for academia. As the editors of *Nature* once put it: "To those familiar with the peer-review process, the premise behind the new publication seemed crazy: any user, regardless of expertise, can edit the entries." (NPG 2005) Therefore, especially in the early stage, skepticism towards these projects was high. Many researchers did not believe that, under these circumstances, something could evolve which would meet the high quality standards of science. Indeed, many without formal qualifications contribute to the platforms, including scientific content. Contrary to skeptic voices, this fact is not necessarily unproductive. For example, a young Hungarian student set up a WikiProject on genetics, became administrator in Wikipedia and was later labeled as "prominent medical voice" by *Nature* (Keim 2007, 231). There are also examples of established scholars contributing to the encyclopedia:

- A group of researchers transferred content from a gene database to Wikipedia (Huss et al. 2008).
- The Journal *RNA Biology* publishes abstracts of their articles on the platform (Butler 2008).
- The German *Netzwerk Technikfolgenabschätzung (NTA)*, a group of scholars from the field of technology assessment, started an initiative for improving Wikipedia content related to their field and created a WikiProject for this purpose and also organized offline-meetings.
- The *Association for Psychological Science (APS)* tries to enhance psychological content in Wikipedia with an own initiative (APS 2011).

One could easily add more examples of this kind. Still, such involvement of professionals does not change the fact that formal qualifications are not required to contribute effectively in Wikimedia projects. This also works the other way round—formal qualifications are no guarantee for successful participation. Although "Wikipedians" gain their reputation mostly by their work within the platform(s), it is well imaginable that external factors are considered here, too. For instance, *The New Yorker* referred to a very active "user known as Essjay, who holds a Ph.D. in theology and a degree in canon law" and stated that he was a "tenured professor of religion at a private university" (Schiff 2006). Later, an editor's note was added, correcting this statement:

"At the time of publication, neither we nor Wikipedia knew Essjay's real name. Essjay's entire Wikipedia life was conducted with only a user name; anonymity is common for Wikipedia administrators and contributors, and he says that he feared personal retribution from those he had ruled against online. Essjay now says that his real name is Ryan Jordan, that he is twenty-four and holds no advanced degrees, and that he has never taught." (ibid.)

On the one hand, this shows the irrelevance of formal qualifications in Wikimedia projects. On the other hand, one might argue that he became successful partly *because* he claimed such qualifications. Moreover, this incident points at problems resulting from such anonymity (or rather pseudonymity), which conflicts with practices in academia. However, this does not mean that contributors can anarchically add random content regardless of its quality, as Wikimedia projects use a quite sophisticated system of ex post reviewing (see above). Since verifiability via reliable sources is an important factor for inclusion, (academic) reputation may be more relevant than the "everyone can edit" policy suggests. Indeed, a closer empirical look at how the rules of inclusion are debated and applied concretely during the construction of an article, reveals the significance of this factor, so one of us has concluded that "the lack of a predefined role of experts within Wikipedia leads to an *externalization* of this role to sources outside of the community" (König 2011, 5).

In any case, the review process depends on the level of participation, which varies widely. Thus, it is reasonable to say that Wikimedia builds on a culture that Reagle portrayed as "good faith collaboration" (2010). Academia's recent advance towards the encyclopedia, such as the initiatives cited above, may be taken as a sign of acknowledging that this principle works better than critics of the platforms would guess. Hypothetically, we could even interpret this as a first sign of a paradigm shift regarding academia's relation to Wikimedia, albeit probably not generalizable. At least, it is a very different approach than a simple "ban" of Wikipedia, as it was imposed for example by Vermont's Middlebury College (Jaschik 2007).

Research on the quality of Wikipedia mostly does not draw a too dark picture of the encyclopedia. A study conducted by *Nature* received much attention when it found that Wikipedia's accuracy is comparable to that of the renowned Encyclopædia Britannica (Giles 2005). The study's methodology was criticized, and others followed (Hammwöhner 2007), partly with contradictory conclusions. An analysis comparing Wikipedia's quality in the field of history with articles from Encyclopædia Britannica, the Dictionary of American History and American National Biography Online found:

"While Wikipedia provides a wealth of information and is a model for non-proprietary peer-production of reference materials, it does not fare as favourably as do other reference resources under scrutiny for accuracy, comprehensiveness and reliability. Academics may question students' or colleagues' use of Wikipedia as a scholarly resource." (Rector 2008, 20)

Regardless of discrepancies resulting from varying methodological approaches, studies focusing on different realms or points in time have a high chance of coming to dissenting conclusions—for a simple reason: the content is, at least potentially, dynamic and it always depends on the contributors who are often volunteering amateurs. Hence, the content also

varies according to their interests as Halavais and Lackaff argue with regard
to their empirical analysis of Wikipedia's topical coverage:

"As articles on Wikipedia are created and develop according to the interest of
contributors, some topics expand rapidly (popular culture and physical science)
while other topics are developed more slowly (national poetries and prosodies)."
(Halavais and Lackaff 2008, 436)

Moreover, they noticed that "Wikipedia remains particularly strong in
some of the sciences, among other areas, but not as strong in the humanities or social sciences" (ibid., p. 431). Scholarly initiatives (as mentioned
above) potentially lead to increasing professionalization of Wikipedia. This
will apparently be the case as we will assume in 2.3.4. It is actively encouraged by the Wikimedia Foundation which tries to recruit scholars to contribute. Events like the *Wikipedia Academy* are "designed to coach academics and other experts in how to contribute to Wikipedia, and to foster a
positive impression of Wikipedia", with the main goal "to increase the
quality and—to a lesser extent—the quantity of articles in Wikipedia"
(Wikimedia 2011h).

Professional initiatives may have a major impact because Wikipedia is
apparently less "crowd-driven" than it is often perceived. A comprehensive
quantitative analysis of the largest Wikipedia versions found that not even
ten percent of the authors are responsible for over ninety percent of all
contributions (Soto 2009, 106). Moreover, "an extraordinary[ly] high mor-
tality rate in all languages" (ibid., p. 157) was observed, meaning that a
"significant proportion of authors (more than 50% in all versions) aban-
dons the project after more than 200 days" (ibid.). This observation also
means that a loss of relatively few active authors could have drastic negative effects and it indicates that the obstacles to becoming a successful
active contributor are rather high.

Currently, Wikipedia definitely profits from its wide public attention,
which obviously also attracts researchers. This is much less the case for the
other two platforms under review, Wikibooks and Wikiversity. As outlined
above, the breadth and impact of these projects is much lower. This might
be a relevant factor for scholarly engagement, as these projects also receive
a much quieter echo in academia—although their main functions and core
principles might be better suited for scientific usage. Both projects are
related, not only because Wikiversity emerged from Wikibooks, but also
because the content of the latter is now partly used as material for courses
in Wikiversity.

One can find many science-related articles on Wikibooks, which can be ordered by subjects and also by reading level. According to Wikibooks' mission, a large part of the content is addressed to non-academic or under-graduate audiences, but there are also a number of articles labeled for an "advanced" or "professional reading level". It has to be stressed that they are often "stubs" (Wikimedia jargon for short incomplete articles), which do not have much in common with typical books. In June 2011 only 132 books within the English version were categorized as "completed books".[67]

The study by Sajjapanroj et al. (2008) based on interviews with 80 Wikibooks contributors revealed remarkable insights about their demographics, showing that they are disproportionately often male (97,5 percent) and young (83 percent under 35 years, 58 percent under 26 years). A glimpse at their education levels (Figure 14 below) characterizes them as "educationally-oriented individuals" (ibid., 42) who are probably often still on their way to an academic degree (given their relatively young age).

According to our earlier observations (König and Nentwich 2009), many of the contributors have limited expertise and are therefore rather atypical authors of academic literature. This is understandable since the platform probably does not appear very attractive to renowned scholars: The collaborative authorship hardly allows for gaining reputation, ideas may undergo unwanted changes and Wikibooks is neither a renowned publisher nor does it pay royalties. In contrast to Wikipedia, not even public relevance can currently serve as a driving force for academic engagement in this platform. To our knowledge, there is no systematic study of the quality of Wikibooks, but assuming these factors, it seems unlikely that it is very high on average. Similar statements can be made for the even smaller Wikiversity. Following its focus on learning/teaching and research, we will deal with it in the next sections.

---

67 The full list (so-called "category") can be found under this link: en.wikibooks.org/ wiki/Category:Completed_books (June 2011).

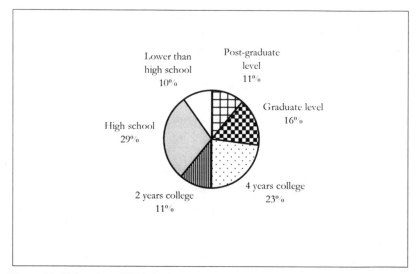

Figure 14: Education of Wikibooks authors

Source: Sajjapanroj et al. 2008, p. 42

Teaching the wiki way

Looking at these platforms from a teaching and learning perspective we may differentiate student-initiated and teacher-initiated practices: On the one hand, especially Wikipedia is commonly used by students for learning, no matter whether this is approved by their universities. On the other hand, some teachers actively decide to use the platforms for educational purposes, partly even with the purpose of adding new or enhance existing content.

Again, in both cases Wikipedia's popularity and visibility may serve as an important factor, especially among students. Kuhlen (2005) remarked already four years after Wikipedia was founded that it is hardly possible to prevent students from using it. Haber and Hodel (2007) later pointed out that the encyclopedia gains its popularity not only from the fact that it is easy and free to use, but also because articles are often highly-ranked in Google. Indeed, this corresponds with our observations regarding this search engine: it is indeed widely-used among students and ranking of the content plays an important role (see 2.5). These statements are somewhat supported by a study among 4.400 students in Germany (Kleimann et al. 2008). Sixty percent of them claimed that they use Wikipedia often—the top rank among the other suggested Web 2.0 platforms in the study. Moreover, students expressed high trust in this source, but only a minority actively contributed themselves.

Considering the unconventional way content is contributed to Wikimedia projects, it is understandable that such student practices are often not appreciated, as noted above. Apart of the debatable quality, teachers frequently report it is used as a source for plagiarism (cf. Wannemacher 2008; Haber and Hodel 2009). While the latter problem can potentially be solved by applying software against plagiarism, quality-related issues remain the main concern, especially because usage of Wikipedia simply cannot be effectively avoided. Therefore, a more constructive way to deal with this seems to actually embrace the platforms in class—a practice that is explicitly encouraged by the Wikimedia community:

"Everyone is welcome here. If you're a professor, teacher, or student within the college community, we encourage you to use Wikipedia in your course to demonstrate how an open content website works. Many of these projects have resulted in both advancing the students' knowledge and useful content being added to Wikipedia." (Wikimedia 2011l)

In fact, the specific wiki technology seems suitable in particular for constructivist views on knowledge production. For example, it can be used to demonstrate how historical "facts" are created (Miller 2007; Haber and Hodel 2007). Of course, this still has to be in line with the community's rules and the given technical structure, which is not always easy. Students and teachers may have troubles with the software, students sometimes do not agree with the publication of their material, or teachers may have difficulties to identify individual work. In some cases, the student's efforts are simply deleted because they are found to be against applied policies, such as the "no original research" rule (Timmer 2007).

Such problems are less immanent in the other Wikimedia projects due to their rules which are more appropriate for teaching, because they are, to a large extent, designed exactly for this purpose. As a matter of fact, much of the content in Wikibooks has been established in the context of higher education.[68] For example, undergraduate and graduate students at three Israeli universities cooperated in a project across multiple courses and departments (Ravid et al. 2008); the participatory architecture was per-

---

68 A list of such projects is presented in:
en.wikibooks.org/wiki/Wikibooks:List_of_class_projects.

ceived rather positively, as a way for empowerment. A project at the University of Cape Town called *Free High School Science Texts (FHSST)* also made use of Wikibook's possibilities for collaborative writing and Wikimedia's policy for open content. In this case, however, the participatory architecture became a pitfall, since it led to undesired edits, and the project finally withdrew from Wikibooks (Petrides and Jimes 2008). Thus—as in Wikipedia—the dependence on the platform's tools and policies can be seen as an obstacle for wider application in teaching. At this point, we are not aware of systematic studies assessing the overall quality of Wikibooks' content or its general usage for learning activities outside of single projects—so we cannot finally assess this. Nevertheless, the relatively low number of completed books in Wikibooks on a level suitable for higher education limits its overall usefulness. In conclusion, Wikibooks apparently still plays a minor role in teaching and learning, especially in comparison to Wikipedia.

Similar observations were made for Wikiversity. Due to its participatory architecture and no limitation to academia, it contains various courses that are not scholarly relevant. Although a number of courses address scientific topics, many of them are incomplete and not necessarily meant for teaching in an institutionalized manner. This is partly because Wikiversity also distinguishes itself from regular universities:

"Wikiversity is devoted to individuals and individuality. Conventional 'bricks and mortar' universities are constrained by the expense of existing in physical space. Conventional universities tend to clump students together in to groups for a coordinated 'factory' approach to 'assembly line' education. Wikiversity exists in a virtual learning space where the individual interests and needs of learners can be respected." (Wikimedia 2011q)

Nonetheless, one can find a number of examples for its application in the classroom. In June 2011 a list regarding the English version showed 35 past projects, mostly affiliated to courses at US universities.[69] A list of courses in the German version[70] is apparently not continually maintained (no updates since more than two years), therefore there may be more completed courses than the two on that list (June 2011). So although such lists are apparently incomplete, the rather low number of articles, page views and active users (see Table 3, p. 77) point in the same direction:

---

69 en.wikiversity.org/wiki/Wikiversity:School_and_university_projects#Projects.
70 de.wikiversity.org/wiki/Wikiversity:Fertige_Kurse.

Wikiversity is not widely used in academia. Some statistics report even less activity: According to data of all language versions collected by Zachte, only 216 users contributed five times or more in September 2010 (later figures were not available at the time of this study)—almost half of them contributed in the English version.[71] We cannot discuss the methodological details of such data in this context, but our own qualitative observations also find that the activity level in Wikiversity is rather low. In general, many of the articles resemble sketchy drafts, including the platforms' policies and discussion spaces.

This lack of institutionalization and the relatively open and less actively controlled policies, result in very different teaching practices. They are often experimental and not yet routinized; in fact, such exploratory usage is one of the intentions of the platform: "The Wikiversity community is participating in an experiment in education. Just what can be done with wiki technology as a tool for education?" (Wikimedia 2011q)

Nevertheless, we also found examples of "everyday" teaching with Wikiversity. One regular course is conducted by H. Brenner, a mathematician at the University of Osnabrück in Germany. He is the most active user of the German version of Wikiversity (user name: "Bocardodarapti")[72] and offers courses in Algebra and other topics for his students. In an interview[73] given to us, he likes, on the whole, the idea that the content is freely available even outside of the institutional learning context. However, he reports that feedback from users other than his students is rarely recorded. The participatory architecture is also hardly used, since other users only made few orthographical corrections, but no substantial edits of his content. Although this example is not necessarily representative, it corresponds to our other observations regarding the low participation at Wikiversity. It would appear that the platform simply has, as yet, not reached the necessary level of maturity and participation to live up to its potential (cf. Wannemacher 2008, 155). Because of its open and not strictly regulated policy, we may also observe practices that are rather outside of Wikiversity's intention of a virtual learning platform that reaches beyond the

---

71 stats.wikimedia.org/wikiversity/EN/TablesWikipediansEditsGt5.htm (retrieved June 8, 2011).

72 According to statistics at
    stats.wikimedia.org/wikiversity/EN/TablesWikipediaDE.htm (retrieved June 7, 2011).

73 The interview was conducted on March 16, 2009. On June 10, 2011 Brenner replied to our inquiry via e-mail, that his teaching engagement at Wikiversity is still maintained and nothing has fundamentally changed.

boundaries of physical universities. For example, some teachers use it mainly to interact with their students (e.g. as a feedback channel, to organize appointments etc.), as reported by another teacher we interviewed, C. Spannagel, a mathematician at the University of Education, Heidelberg.[74] Nevertheless, he also pointed out that occasionally an external user joined a methodological discussion. Thus, the interactivity of the platform is certainly used in some cases, but obviously not on a large scale.

Researching and collaborating the wiki way

As we asserted above, Wikipedia's and Wikiversity's narrow policies more or less exclude research, making it unlikely that they are used for this purpose. Moreover, the technical boundaries reduce the potential usage mainly to textual communication. Still, there are certain opportunities to engage and collaborate. Scholars are often already contributing to the platform (see above), which more or less forces them to interact with each other and the rest of the wiki community, as edits often need to be discussed to avoid edit wars. Consequently researchers are practically using Wikipedia to collaborate in some way. Although the creation of new knowledge is per se excluded by the "no original research" policy, we can assume that these collaborations lead to new forms of knowledge, as they often involve numerous people with varying educational background from different fields. This is of course a challenging task as it is sometimes difficult to reach a common ground under these peculiar circumstances, including the use of pseudonyms and the need to debate in writing. In cases of constant dispute, administrators may restrict editing possibilities. Indeed, one can find a number of science-related articles in the list of protected pages (e.g. the one on aluminum) as well as biographical articles which might be of interest for historians (e.g. on Che Guevara); in particular, many articles dealing with political issues are protected, which could be looked at from a social science perspective (Wikimedia 2011a). From a more optimistic point of view, such intersections may be seen as a chance for productive collaboration between scholars, students and the public (cf. Haber and Hodel 2009), hence a new form of science communication. Still, we must not forget that only few scientists voluntarily invest their time in Wikipedia.[75] An interview

---

74 The interview was conducted on March 17, 2009.
75 And they do so for good reasons, since its functional principles are somehow contradictory to academia, as discussed above.

partner in a study on the future landscape of scholarly communication stated:

"I'm 55…email is high-tech enough for me. I use Wikipedia, but the idea of using a wiki would require me to learn more stuff and I don't have time to slow down and figure it out. So no, I've not been involved in anything regularly that is more high-tech than a conference call." (Harley et al. 2010, 297)

Since many relevant scholars still do not participate in Wikipedia and seem obviously unwilling to do so, it is questionable whether it can reach its potential of contributing to canonizing a subject field. Although interesting collaboration takes place, we should recall that most encounters between scientists and the public typically occur in the context of heated debates with a lot of public attention. Articles connected to remote fields of highly specialized expertise will hardly experience such consequences. Rather, they suffer from a lack of participation, hence not many people who could critically review the content. In such contexts, the wiki principle of depending on volunteers reaches its limits. To speak with Surowiecki's (2004) rhetoric—no matter whether the crowd is wise or not, there is simply no crowd in these fields.

Given the much lower level of participation, this issue is particularly problematic in the cases of Wikibooks and Wikiversity. Furthermore, the latter also allows original research, thereby lowering the chance to control content by its verifiability. The idea of installing a *Review Board* directly reflects on this issue:

"Some misguided and deceptive research practices may be difficult to detect. The Wikiversity community relies on the participation of people with expertise in good research practices and who can help the community recognize and correct bogus and unethical research practices. The Review Board will be active in guiding the entire Wikiversity community in examination of all Wikiversity research projects and identifying and correcting any problems that breach the Wikiversity research guidelines." (Wikimedia 2011p)

While such ideas reflect the problems connected to a lack of peer review, one could also argue that quality control is less urgent, simply because of the low number of contributions. Evidently, this argument can also be turned upside down: the lack of quality control may in fact be a reason in itself for the low participation. From this perspective, Wikiversity would be caught in a sort of vicious circle that keeps the platform on its current low activity level. In any case, we may conclude that this experiment of applying the wiki principles to research and teaching does barely work as well as it did for its role model Wikipedia. Although some examples of successful collaboration seem to contradict this statement, it is obvious that the other platforms do not enjoy the self-reinforcing power of attraction which Wikipedia feeds on. Hence, such collaboration mostly needs an external driving force and can hardly draw on the Wikiversity community alone.[76]

Finally, we need to highlight another aspect relevant in research contexts, namely consulting Wikimedia content as a scholarly source. As discussed above, this practice is usually associated with students. But one can hardly doubt that it is also happening in proper research on a significant scale. A survey conducted by the Wikimedia Foundation and the Public Library of Science (PLoS) among 1.743 scholars showed the following results:

"In general, respondents expressed a very favorable (58.98%) and somewhat favorable (32.19%) opinion of Wikipedia, and 87.73% indicated they used Wikipedia frequently or occasionally as part of their professional work." (Möller 2009)

Although the survey is probably not representative and to a certain extent biased pro Wikipedia, these numbers are remarkable. Contrariwise, in a qualitative study by Harley et al. (2010), many academics expressed skepticism toward the encyclopedia and often use it only for quick superficial fact checks. This appears logical because the encyclopedic format can hardly provide much deeper information for the highly-specialized needs of researchers. However, cases of more intense usage do exist. The journal *Nature* (2011) even reported on a publication that was removed from a statistics journal because it plagiarized text from Wikipedia.

Wikis in institutional settings

While Wikiversity offers opportunities that can potentially be used to set up a free e-learning, and partly a research infrastructure, this does not happen widely, as we pointed out above. Developing countries which may benefit from such a strategy are practically non-existent on this platform as yet, at least they did not have their own versions by the time of writing. Among the reasons for this state of affairs may be problems related to their functional principles discussed above. Additionally, people in charge

---

76 The need to initiate engagement from outside was also mentioned by one of our interview partners.

might simply not know about the platform or prefer others perhaps because they are easier to use.

On the opposite side, academic institutions or individuals may easily be affected by Wikipedia because it may contain articles about them and has a prominent position in today's information landscape (cf. 2.3.2). This is reinforced by the fact that Wikipedia articles are often highly ranked in search engine results (see also 2.5.3). Indeed, countless academic institutions are described in the encyclopedia. To use a random example, the category for institutions in the field of political science in the German version links to 45 articles.[77] While some institutions may be striving for being mentioned here, but fail because of Wikipedia's inclusion policy, others would prefer to have such content removed. The Wikipedia article on the California Miramar University was, for example, protected against deletion in June 2011—because of heated debates regarding criticism towards this institution.

On a more general level, institutions are of course also affected by the way their disciplines are represented in this important medium. Correspondingly, the above observations regarding scientific content and its production process are also relevant for science communication and public relations (Nentwich 2010a).

2.3.4 Interim conclusions

The closer look at Wikimedia's collaborative writing platforms revealed insights into two main aspects: Their dependence on participation and its connected dynamics, and their relationship with academia.

Conflicts with academia

Examining the functional principles of the Wikimedia platforms, it is possible to identify major contradictions with those of academia. In the first place, they result evidently from the open participatory architecture, but also from the mostly unclear authorship and the format of dynamic content: these principles simply contradict established practices in academia. This leads to concerns on two levels: regarding the quality of science-

---

77 de.wikipedia.org/wiki/Kategorie:Politikwissenschaftliches_Forschungsinstitut (retrieved June 9, 2011).

related information in the encyclopedia; and vice versa, the potential impact of the characteristics of Wikipedia, including the quality of the information on academia. Thus, different scholarly activities are affected by these developments. While the most cited concerns probably refer to students' careless handling of the platforms, we can also observe researchers and institutions being engaged in various ways, including teaching, collaborating, and shaping their public relations. Such activities necessarily need to accept the platform's rules, thus depending on them.

A forced marriage

Given the functional conflicts between academia and Wikimedia projects, a combination of both would seem fairly implausible. However, Wikipedia has become a major provider of information on the web, with an encompassing breadth and extremely high popularity. This can hardly be ignored by academia because many scholarly relevant topics are also tackled in the encyclopedia. Even if researchers decided to disregard this platform, their students would probably still use them, and the public anyway—in either case it will affect scholarly practices. At the same time, Wikipedia can hardly ignore science either. In order to reach its goal of producing a high quality encyclopedia, it has to draw on academic expertise. Therefore, both are intertwined in a kind of "forced marriage". We observe that both parties become increasingly aware of this status of a "forced marriage". The relevance of Wikipedia is obviously recognized by academia to a certain extent, as it has gradually become a subject of academic interest (Figure 15).

Numerous publications and conferences have dealt with different aspects of Wikipedia, for example in the context of the Critical Point Of View initiative (Lovink and Tkacz 2011). A number of practical and theoretical issues regarding the relationship of academia and Wikipedia have been addressed (e.g. Haber and Hodel 2009). At the same time, we can see attempts from Wikimedia to close ranks with science, for example help pages dedicated to this relationship, as well as dedicated events and studies (Möller 2009). Eventually, this may result in a deeper mutual understanding and thereby also in a kind of "wiki literacy": making scholarly users aware of the underlying principles of the platform (see also 3.3, 4.3) would be required to understand its inner dynamics and impacts.

Growth of Academic Interest in Wikipedia

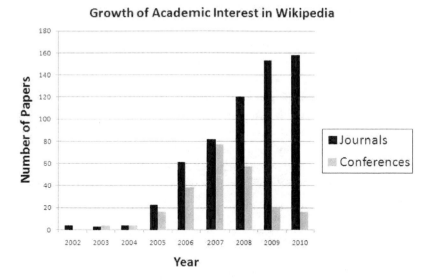

Figure 15: Growth of academic interest in Wikipedia

Source: en.wikipedia.org/wiki/File:Academic_Wikipedia_05_2011.jpg (retrieved June 10, 2011).

Limits to voluntary participation and future perspectives

We identify participation as a crucial factor for all Wikimedia projects: the content largely depends on the contributors—not only in expanding, but also in reviewing. Since the projects are built on volunteers' work, they depend on their good will and engagement (cf. Reagle 2010). As noted above, it is a rather small number of Wikipedia volunteers responsible for most of the content; this is why potentially a small, but very active core group may have a substantial impact. Therefore a well-supported initiative by professionals might lead to significant changes in the encyclopedia. Whether these changes would be improvements is a matter of perspective and depends on the actual practices. The current core group of the community may feel threatened by such attempts of professionalization, which could lead to new conflicts.

By contrast, Wikibooks and especially Wikiversity may be taken as examples for lacking participation. Thus these projects fall short of their potentials. This impression did not significantly change after our first analysis of the platforms (König and Nentwich 2009) about two years ago, so we are inclined to be doubtful whether they ever will. In any case, neither Wikiversity nor Wikibooks seem to trigger "revolutionary" changes as they were perceived for Wikipedia (Möller 2005). Wikipedia will presumably maintain its status as an important information source at least in the medium term. It seems to go be a little early to predict a paradigm change towards "Publish in Wikipedia or Perish" (Butler 2008), but we expect increasing interaction with academia. As these projects strongly depend on participation, the related dynamics have to be watched closely. Future research in this area may focus on other wiki-style platforms, especially those specializing in academic teaching and research (e.g. Büffel et al. 2007) and alternative web-based collaborative writing tools (an example for this is given in 3.3.3).

2.4 Virtual Worlds—The Case of Second Life

Depending on the definition, different platforms can be categorized as virtual worlds and they might also be labeled with varying, often synonymously used terms, e.g. "virtual realities".[78] For our purpose, we are interested in platforms that provide an Internet-based 3D environment allowing for social interaction and user generated content that potentially can be used for scholarly needs. Currently, there are several platforms that meet these criteria but we decided to concentrate our case study on the flagship, Second Life.

Although the hype about Second Life is clearly over, still no competitor took over its place: a large Internet-based virtual world which allows users to create their own content, including 3D models. After a test period in 2002 the US-based company Linden Lab launched it officially in 2003. Users can navigate through the virtual world, with their *avatar*, a designable mostly human-looking figure. In order to access Second Life, a software application needs to be installed on a not too slow computer.[79]

---

78 For a discussion of these terms and definitions see e.g. Steuer (1992), Moskaliuk et al. (2011).

79 The exact system requirements can be found here: secondlife.com/support/system-requirements. There are also a number of alternative third party clients that enable users to access Second Life. Additionally, a web based client is currently being developed and tested.

Users register with a free *basic account* or a *premium* membership, which, among other features, allows for the purchase of "land" in Second Life and costs between 6 and 9.95 US Dollars per month (March 2011). Moreover, it is possible to purchase virtual money, the so-called *Linden Dollar*, so that one can make use of additional services within the virtual world. Since it can be exchanged back into US Dollars, the "virtual" economy is connected to "real" economies, which attracted private investors.

This commercial element makes it difficult to get objective and comparable statistics on the usage of Second Life because the companies involved are of course interested in letting them look good. Linden Lab is publishing quarterly reports with various figures that usually show a positive or at least not clearly negative trend. At the same time, these numbers are harshly criticized by the community that seems to perceive a rather negative tendency[80], in line with numerous commentators who declare that "Second Life is dead".[81] Linden Lab counts almost 26 million "residents" (December 2011)[82], which means registered accounts. This does not, of course, tell much about actual activity of the users (see below).

Regardless of Second Life's popularity and commercial success, it is worth asking whether the application is useful for specific scholarly purposes. To answer this question, we first introduce basic technical functions before we focus on empirical examples of academic usage of Second Life and their impact.

2.4.1 Main functions

The name itself implies the promise of a "second life", a sort of virtual simulation of the "real" world. Beside theoretical debates revealing the problems of this dichotomy between "real" and "virtual" (Bittarello 2008; Boellstorff 2008; Lehdonvirta 2008), a closer look into the platform imme-

---

80 See e.g. comments related to the fourth quarterly report 2010: blogs.secondlife. com/
community/features/blog/2011/01/26/the-second-life-economy-in-q4-2010.
81 testfreaks.com/blog/information/second-life-is-dead;　mediabistro.com/prnewser/its-
official-second-life-is-dead-for-pr-at-least　b378?;
zdnet.com/blog/education/even-with-adult-content-regulated-second-life-is-dead-in-
ed/2445.
82 Linden Lab provides apparently automatically generated real-time statistics via secon-
dlife. com/xmlhttp/secondlife.php. See the field "signups" for the number of registered
accounts. The accuracy of these numbers is unknown to us.

diately shows why it cannot keep its promise of providing a "second life": It simply does not much resemble the world we know, neither its physical design, nor in the possibilities we have to interact with it (including the interaction with other people represented in that environment). Trivial as this may seem, it is important to note this fact because it is the base of a widely perceived crucial misunderstanding. Second Life does not provide a second life or a second world. Instead, it can be described as an Internet-based 3D environment with certain limited options to contribute and interact with it. After registration users can enter the virtual world of Second Life with one of the existing clients, i.e. with special software installed on one's desktop that give access to this world. It is organized in *Regions* (sometimes referred to as "simulator" or "sim") with a size of 256 times 256 "meters" that are simulated by various servers and can host up to 100 avatars. Large parts of Second Life's world are island-shaped, but Linden Lab also runs a larger coherent area called *Main Land*. There are different types of regions that mainly differ in prices, performance (e.g. the number of avatars that can access it simultaneously) and accessibility. "Jumping" from region to region is possible by "teleporting" and locations can be reached directly via specific Second Life web addresses (*SURLs*). Moreover, a search option makes possible finding particular content and locations.

Most communication is done in a synchronous manner via public or private chats, additionally video-chats and a set of non-verbal gestures (e.g. "clapping hands", "hugging", "nodding", "pointing") are available and can be extended by the users. In addition, users can connect to each other with "friendships" and in topic-specific groups. Groups offer sophisticated options for regulating members' access and rights, so that landowners can for example control who can access or edit certain parts of their land. Access to groups can be limited in various ways, including enrollment fees. For founding groups one has to pay 100 Linden Dollars and needs at least two members (April 2011).[83]

Many 3D objects within Second Life provide further interactive options, e.g. audio-visual streams, texts, hyperlinks etc. What distinguishes Second Life from many other virtual worlds, especially games, is the users' possibility to create such objects themselves. This is also why it falls under the label of Web 2.0 as it gives many options to design the virtual world for

---

83 www.wiki.secondlife.com/wiki/Group.

individual needs. Therefore, one can find a very broad range of content with different designs and purposes, from city models where users can randomly chat with each other, shops where one can buy e.g. new avatar outfits, places with games, pornographic content etc., to regions with educational purposes.

2.4.2 Potentials for science and research

Academic usage of Second Life has to respect the limitations mentioned above, of course. It is therefore unlikely to observe a replacement of "real" universities by "virtual" universities as the rhetoric suggests. However, the platform gives researchers a number of interesting possibilities for their different typical activities (see Figure 16).

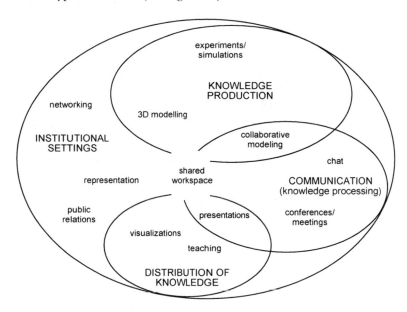

Figure 16: Scholarly activities in Second Life

These typical functions will shortly be explored in the following, and further developed in the next section (2.4.3).

Knowledge production: Obviously, Second Life's most remarkable function (in contrast to other Internet platforms) is the option of editing and displaying 3D objects, which is potentially useful for a number of disciplines.

Due to the large variety of possibilities, we can think of multiple applications for scholarly purposes, reaching from e.g. models of molecules to conceptual designs for architects and engineers, models of archeological excavations, etc. Moreover, these objects can be created collaboratively. As a further step, one can also imagine simulations and virtual experiments.

Communication: Second Life's typical functions, such as chat and groups, can of course be potentially applied for scholarly purposes. But there are many Internet platforms that provide these possibilities much more simply, which is why they probably are not primary motivations for using Second Life. What seems rather interesting is the option to hold virtual meetings and even conferences.

Distribution of knowledge: Again, particularly the virtual 3D-related functions are obviously the most striking ones. They enable researchers to give online presentations, including 2D or 3D illustrations, audio and video streams etc. These options can also be used for teaching activities, e.g. in "virtual classrooms".

Institutional settings: Especially during its boom years, Second Life appeared as an additional channel for public relations. Virtual booths can provide institution-related information and even representations like 3D-models of campuses. Potentially, one can also think of using Second Life for social networking, but other platforms seem more promising for this purpose (see in particular 2.1).

A closer look at the user practices will give further insights into the potentials of this platform, beyond the bare rhetoric of a "second life".

2.4.3 Usage practices and impact

During Second Life's blossoming a few years ago, it appeared as a highly innovative platform attracting people for various reasons. It was considered by many the next "big thing" in the emerging Internet and so it seemed desirable to be on board, especially for people and institutions who would like to be perceived as innovative themselves.

Institutional representation

Against this background, it is not surprising that we can, or could, find dozens of academic institutions represented in Second Life, including renowned universities such as Harvard, Stanford or Princeton.[84] Some of them took "representation" literally by creating models resembling their campuses (see Figure 17), others use completely different images. They usually include objects with further information regarding their institutions—virtual booths with texts, hyperlinks, and multimedia elements.

Figure 17: Representation of Princeton University campus in Second Life

Source: flickr.com/photos/22660321@N02/2377638656/in/pool-664960@N25

However, unlike "real" university campuses, most of the places we visited during our study were rather orphaned and one hardly came across other avatars (visitors). As a result, these institutional representations themselves do not give us any insights into actual user practices, other than their mere existence. In addition, many institutions have withdrawn from Second Life since our initial study in 2008 (König and Nentwich 2008), e.g. Princeton University shut down their virtual campus shown in Figure 17.[85] This observation seems to rather support the claim of Second Life's general de-

---

84 Many more could be listed, e.g. California State University; RWTH University, Aachen; University of Hamburg; Derby University, Derbyshire; Technical University Graz; Heinrich-Heine-Universität Düsseldorf. For a more comprehensive list see: simteach.com/wiki/index.php?title=Institutions_and_Organizations_in_SL.

85 Not all who left Second Life did it voluntarily; e.g. Woodbury University has been thrown out by Linden Labs, see chronicle.com/article/The-Death-of-a-Virtual-Campus/12732.

cline for the academic field as well. It might be partly due to a change of Linden Lab's policy vis-à-vis the academic sector. After supporting Second Life's scholarly usage by providing a discount to academic institutions, the company finally cut this privilege, which led to heavy criticism (Chapman 2010). However, exceptions from this downwards trend exist. For instance, the Meta Institute for Computational Astrophysics (MICA), "a professional scientific and educational, non-profit organization based in virtual worlds" currently exists only in Second Life.[86]

Knowledge distribution

Apart from pure institutional representations, most of the scholarly user practices within Second Life seem to be devoted to knowledge distribution, either for public or student education. Many of these activities try to take advantage of the platform's 3D environment in various ways. Here are some illustrative examples:

– The *Nanotechnology Island*, financed by the British National Physical Laboratory (NPL), informs about nanoscience and -technology, e.g. by exhibiting nanoparticles in relation to other objects.
– NASA runs the relatively extensive *CoLab Island* as well as *Explorer Island*, which focus mostly on the demonstration of NASA's work. It gained some public attention because of a partial simulation of the Mars surface that is supposed to make it possible to experience virtually the planet within Second Life's technical limits. Charles White, manager of the Island, stresses the innovativeness of this way of representing scientific data: "[T]he historic first is that it's based on real science data from the Mars Reconnaissance Orbiter, including real photo and elevation data" (Noyes 2008).
– National Oceanic and Atmospheric Administration (NOAA) demonstrates for example various weather phenomena and shows real-time weather data on a walk-on map. Looking at Figure 18 below it becomes obvious, however, that this type of visualization is less than convincing as yet.
– The American Chemical Society Island offered space that allowed researchers to exhibit their work (Lang and Bradley 2009).

---

86 mica-vw.org.

Figure 18: "Tsunami" on NOAA's island

Teaching

Although often on an experimental level, the usage of Second Life as an E-learning tool appears to be the most established scholarly usage of the platform. There are numerous examples for the usage of Second Life for teaching in various ways. Experiences, pros, cons, best practices etc. are debated vividly on mailing lists[87], on various websites[88], in numerous papers[89] and during conferences, including events such as the Annual Virtual Worlds Best Practices in Education Conference[90], which was held in Second Life in March 2011, or the Second Life Education Workshop (L'Amorcaux et al. 2007). We cannot discuss the different arguments and experiences of these practices in detail here, but it is obvious that educators are interested in the didactic potential that comes with the "novel" techni-

---

87 E.g. https://lists.secondlife.com/cgi-bin/mailman/listinfo/educators.
88 E.g. simteach.com (also includes links to many additional resources).
89 See e.g. Bignell and Parson (2010) and many more within the Annotated Bibliography of Second Life Educational Online Resources at web.ics.purdue.edu/~mpepper/slbib.
90 vwbpe11.vwbpe.org.

cal possibilities of Second Life. Various issues are addressed, reaching from technical difficulties and required user skills to economical questions and of course the actual effectiveness of teaching in this environment. From our perspective, most of the teaching in Second Life pursues explorative purposes, experimenting with the technology. However, we did not find everyday teaching routines, in Second Life, at least not on a large scale (see however Kemp et al. 2009).

Meetings and conferences

Similar conclusions can be drawn from our observations of communicative and collaborative practices of researchers within the platform. There are numerous examples for presentations, meetings and conferences in Second Life. Notably, Nature Publishing Group used to offer virtual space for these purposes and organized over 50 events from 2006 to 2009 before it withdrew from the platform.[91] Lang and Bradley (2009) refer to experiences with conferences in Second Life and conclude:

"While Second Life conferences cannot give the full experience of a real-life conference, they have been shown to continue some of the benefits of real life conferences, including effective teamworking, networking, collaboration, innovation, and socializing."

NASA experimented with "mixed reality broadcasts" (Smith 2008) in which offline conferences were broadcasted in Second Life and online conferences mirrored in a real conference room, partly even at the same time in both directions (see Figure 19).

The concept of "dual reality" takes this approach even further by creating "an environment resulting from the interplay between the real world and the virtual world, as mediated by networks of sensors and actuators" (Lifton and Paradiso 2009). Innovative and interesting as such ideas may be, they are still on a very experimental level and far from being established. This applies even more in the case of simply designed conferences in Second Life, which cannot be regarded as a serious and widely-accepted alternative to ordinary offline events at the time of this study—although we found a few examples in which this was the case (e.g. the above mentioned Annual Virtual Worlds Best Practices in Education Conference).

---

91 nature.com/secondnature/events.html.

Figure 19: NASA conference with "mixed reality" elements

Source: globehoppin.files.wordpress.com/2008/02/davidian_in_sl.jpg

Collaboration

There obviously is a demand for virtual worlds across various disciplines, for instance with regard to collaborative work on 3D objects and data visualization—which seems especially desirable in fields such as engineering and design (Rosenman et al. 2007). Different shortcomings of other platforms with such options have been addresses e.g. by Bourke (2008a, 1):

"The software tools available for visualisation very rarely support any form of remote collaborative experience. There have been some attempts at this [...] but they have either not escaped the research/exploratory stage, have depended on proprietary hardware/software, are high cost commercial products, are only available for a limited range of hardware platforms and operating systems, or are rather difficult to install and operate. As a result, collaborative visualisation has been relegated to experiences based upon the sharing of images and movies. Even these 2D projections generally do not form a real-time collaborative experience but a delayed in time file exchange through email and web servers."

Bourke introduces Second Life as "an interesting environment that satisfies many of the requirements for collaborative visualisation in the sciences" while also referring to "clear limitations" (ibid., p. 7) when it comes to more complex applications, especially because the volume of data that can be hosted in a unit area is limited (see also Bourke 2008b). McConaghy likewise concludes that Second Life "isn't good for complex simulations or 3D modeling" (2007, 7).

In addition to types of communication and collaboration that use of Second Life's 3D nature, academics may use various other communicative tools offered by the platform. These also allow for social networking, as Lang and Bradley describe:

"By simply spending some time on Second Life to create content or assist students, one often accidentally meets people who may ultimately end up as collaborators at some point. People that one meets can be added to a friends list very easily by clicking on their avatar. Whenever one logs in the list of friends currently online is highlighted and any of these people can be contacted by IM or teleported over to interact with a group. The ease with which this can happen in Second Life enables rapid growth of contacts via friend-of-a-friend networks. The authors of this paper represent an excellent example of a collaboration originating from Second Life and evolving to include work in drug discovery, solubility and data visualization, both in Second Life [...] and on the bench [...]." (Lang and Bradley 2009)

Furthermore, Lang and Bradley refer to a "vibrant community of scientists" (ibid.) in Second Life, which is obviously needed for such experiences. However, according to our less specific and broader view on the platform, this might be the case for a few special fields, whereas we cannot observe a widespread involvement of scholars within Second Life. We believe that other applications (especially Twitter and Social Network Sites, see 2.1 and 2.2) might be more useful for purposes such as social networking, especially as they require fewer technical skills and are more likely to attract a large number of people.

Knowledge production and research

Second Life is also used for knowledge production and research. In particular, one can find examples of research focusing on the platform itself and is in part conducted within it.

- Due to Second Life's commercial character, much of its use and content comes from the field of market research, for instance: The US-based Social Research Foundation (SRF) allegedly draws on the "largest consumer research panel in Second Life with 13,000 members from newbies to the most active and involved 'residents' of Second Life".[92] The French institute Reperes conducts qualitative and quantitative research among 10.000 avatars[93] and Market Truths is a company active in several countries that conducts market research and provides reports on different aspects of Second Life.[94] Some commercial projects might also include fundamental research, e.g. People Path follows an ethnographical approach, focusing on the specific culture within Second Life.[95] And eLab City is a project by University of California's Sloan Center for Internet Retailing, which studies consumer behavior in Second Life by analyzing e.g. avatar movements and their interaction with objects (Novak 2007).[96] As part of her dissertation project on socio-psychological aspects of Second Life, Krotoski created the Social Simulation Research Lab in Second Life, which mainly consisted of a "library" with hyperlinks to resources related to Internet research. However, this was mainly established to "present a trustworthy and credible persona" (Krotoski 2009, 72) within the community.

– There are a number of ambitious research projects that were terminated or did not lead to publications worth mentioning yet. University of Derby's SL-Labs were for instance focusing on researching/treating autism by simulating social situations in Second Life (Parsons 2008) and another project looked at attitudes regarding environmental issues with the help of Second Life[97]. University of Surrey's "Norm Watch"[98] was supposed to study social norms in Second Life but failed because of a lack of participants and university support.[99] Many research projects seem to concentrate on the explorative experimental usage of Second Life itself, rather than using Second Life as an established tool for research. Usually, exploring Second Life is at least one of the main purposes in such projects, often combined with the purpose of reaching new (public) audiences. Prattichizzo, for example, explains the ac-

---

92 socialresearchfoundation.org.
93 reperes-secondlife.com.
94 sl.markettruths.com
95 people-path.com.
96 www.elabcity.com
97 previewpsych.org.
98 cfpm.org/sl/normwatch.
99 Source: e-mail correspondence with project leader Bruce Edmonds, April 2011.

tivities of IEEE Robotics and Automation Society (RAS) thus: "The aim of this project is to use SL [Second Life], or similar systems, as a means to spread robotics culture as well as a platform to investigate the social interaction in heterogeneous communities of robots and humans." (Prattichizzo 2009, 100)

2.4.4 Interim conclusions

Our observations show that academia is engaged in Second Life in various ways. Rhetoric referring to these activities often implies misleading expectations, for instance when it euphemistically suggests that "Virtual Space Travel" or "Surfing to Mars" (Noyes 2008) would be possible here. Instead we find a 3D world that allows for numerous interactions with it and other users, including the creation of user-generated content within certain technical limits. Unpretentious as this statement may seem, it appears very necessary to bring expectations down to a realistic level instead of painting the colorful but simply wrong picture of a platform that simulates and expends the reality we live in.

This picture is not only painted by the provider Linden Lab and other commercial actors to promote their products, but also by journalists who use it to write entertaining articles. Even many researchers tend to euphemistic descriptions of their work with the platform. This has obvious reasons: Since engagements in Second Life often require notable investments for their establishment as well as for their maintenance, the decision of staying on the platform or leaving it is of political/strategic significance because prior or future expenses have to be justified. Consequently, especially auto-evaluations tend to give an over-optimistic picture of Second Life experiences. Critics have followed an opposite but often equally biased agenda. Combined with a lack of objective and independent research on the matter, it is challenging to formulate a valid assessment of Second Life's potential for scholarly use.

However, it is obvious that there is considerable interest in virtual worlds, especially among educators, but also in some academic disciplines, which would particularly profit from possibilities such as collaborative working on 3D objects. Activities such as virtual conferences and combinations with "multi/dual reality" seem interesting and potentially useful, as well as certain approaches that make use of the platform for research.

From our perspective, it seems fair to conclude that most of these activities are still on an experimental level with often undefined goals and unclear utility. This does not necessarily need to be regarded negatively because experimentation is precisely the intention of some actors[100] and can of course lead to useful insights. However, we do not see a widespread use of Second Life for everyday academic work as yet.

Some of the constraints seem to result from technical limitations and difficulties described by many authors (Kumar et al. 2008; Smith 2008). While some of them might be solved in the future, we must not underestimate the fact that interacting in virtual worlds requires certain skills that are not readily available, as reported frequently (Penfold and Yeung 2008; Everts 2007). Moreover, the financial and personal effort that is required to maintain projects in Second Life is certainly an obstacle. Nature Publishing Group, for instance, explained the termination of their engagement in Second Life thus: "We found that the resource needed to support these Second Life activities was substantial and, at least at the present time, was not financially sustainable."[101] This assessment also goes for platforms other than Second Life that might become interesting alternatives. Especially *OpenSimulator* appears to be promising as its open source architecture allows integrating and enhancing various worlds (including Second Life).

To sum up, our case study revealed that this "early" virtual world Second Life was no long-term success, certainly not in academic circles. We see, however, a potential for virtual worlds in general, especially if the technology is further developed and adapted for academic needs.

2.5 Search Engines—The Case of Google

Soon after the evolvement of the World Wide Web search engines became important tools for bringing order to the rapidly increasing number of web pages. Although Web 2.0 platforms certainly gained importance for the way knowledge is communicated (as discussed in this book), search engines still have to be considered as central actors who strongly influence these practices. They often serve as gatekeepers, not only making the vast

---

100 See e.g. Nature's engagement within Second Life (nature.com/secondnature).
101 Source: e-mail correspondence with Louise Woodley, Communities Specialist, Nature Publishing Group, April 2011.

amount of web information quickly accessible via search terms, but also by ordering these data in their results. Most modern algorithmic search engines use hyperlink networks as important indicators to determine websites' relevance and to arrange them hierarchically in their search results. Thus, despite their automated functionality, search engines significantly shape digital social networks by connecting and mediating between them and of course, by making them accessible to users. The role of search engines for the web can hardly be overemphasized. Given today's societal importance of the Internet, they also can be seen as central actors in certain fields[102] as well as on a global societal level. Halavais (2009) even speaks of a "search engine society" to emphasize this development (similar: Lehmann and Schetsche 2007)

When the economic background is taken into account, this is particularly striking: The search engine market is dominated by only a few providers, among which Google is the clear leader on a global scale. Google.com is the most frequented website worldwide[103] and various other Google domains are close to this top position. In some countries Google's position even comes close to a monopoly, for instance in Germany, where it holds a stable market share of around 90 percent[104].

According to the company's ambitious self-description, "Google's mission is to organize the world's information and make it universally accessible and useful." (Google Inc. 2011c) This goal may seem bold, but considering Google's encompassing activities, it actually can be taken seriously to some extent. Apart from the well-known web search engine, Google developed and/or acquired a large number of information-related services, ranging from more specific search engines and platforms for videos (Google Video, YouTube), for academic publications (Google Scholar), books (Google Books) or locations (Google Maps, Google Earth, Google Streetview) to services for (collaborative) knowledge production (Knol, Google Docs, Google Wave), communication (Gmail, Google+, Buzz), mobile applications (Google Latitude, Orkut) and many more, including operating systems and even hardware.[105]

---

102 See for example Mager (2010, 2009) for an analysis of their impact on health information and Hindman et al. (2003) for their influence on political issues.

103 alexa.com/topsites, December 2011.

104 webhits.de/artwork/ws_engines_historical_druck.png.

105 In some cases these products are no longer actively promoted and/or integrated into other services (e.g. Google Video, Google Wave).

Obviously, the company has left its initial path of merely providing a tool to search the web, as it was when Google was developed by Sergey Brin and Larry Page at Stanford University. Since its beginning in 1998 in California, Google has undoubtedly become one of the most influential Internet companies. Some rate it as the most expensive brand (Brand-Finance 2011) and it is leading the global online advertising market, which is also Google's main revenue. The company takes advantage of the large amount of information that it can access itself and that it receives from its users. With *AdWords*, for example, customers can place advertisements close to related search results, depending on specific keywords that they "buy".

Basically, the more intensively Google products are used, the more information about the user can be collected and applied to produce more sophisticated search results and highly individualized advertisements. Thus although the usage of Google products is usually free of charge, customers "pay" by providing information about themselves, which is why this model has been described and criticized as "service for profile" (Elmer 2004; Rogers 2009; Röhle 2009). Privacy-related issues resulting from these practices have become a major concern in public debates about Google.

However, such criticism has not been able to seriously hamper the company's success. With projects such as Google Books, aiming at making "all books in all languages" (Google Inc. 2011d) accessible online within the frame of Google's functional logic, the company influences the cultural foundation of modern societies. As "googling" (a word that can nowadays be found in numerous dictionaries) for all kinds of information has become a daily routine in many people's life, it is not surprising that alarms about a "googlization of everything" (Vaidhyanathan 2011) have been raised and even the "google society" (Lehmann and Schetsche 2007) has been postulated. Since working with information is also a core task of academia, it comes as no surprise that Google is significantly affecting this part of society too, as we are going to show.

We focus our case study on three examples of text-based search products, namely the well-known Google Web Search, but also Google Scholar, designed in particular for academic purposes, and Google Books, the book search engine connected to a massive book digitalization project. Before proceeding with the analysis of their impact on academia, we introduce these platforms and their main functions.

2.5.1 Main functions

Due to their wide popularity, most readers are probably familiar with the basic functions of the outlined services, at least with Google Web Search: A plain surface shows a field that allows entering any keywords which will lead the user very quickly to a hierarchically-ordered list of clickable search results. Experienced users might also know about the various options for specifying searches, for example searching for groups of words in exact word orders (instead of just keywords), limiting searches to certain geographical regions, languages, dates etc. Furthermore, they might be aware of additional options within the search results, such as downloading cached versions of HTML documents in Google Web Search; browsing texts which cite an article shown in Google Scholar; looking up items in local libraries in Google Books and Google Scholar. Recently, Google added an algorithm to some of its platforms which makes suggestions for search terms while the user is typing; these propositions are based on typical or frequent search items.

Even beginners will quickly understand some major differences between the platforms. Most obviously, Google Books needs to draw on data that cannot be reached by an ordinary web search engine. This banal insight leads us to a crucial issue of search engines: They can only access a certain set of information within their individual technical limits. At the same time, they are confronted with a vast amount of data that has to be distributed quickly in a form that is helpful for users. The less specific a query is, the more a search engine has to intervene by reducing or ordering the processed information. Considering this, we become aware that behind the simple-looking façade of search engines in general, and Google products in particular, a sophisticated and complex technology is at work.

In the following section we explain how the analyzed platforms are dealing with these issues, after a brief introduction to each.

Google Web Search

Web Search is the oldest Google platform and at the heart of the company's success. The developers Sergey Brin and Larry Page recognized a fundamental problem of search engines in the late 1990s: The sheer size of the rapidly growing web had become a challenge, particularly because commercial content increasingly corrupted the search results by spam, making them ineffective and frustrating for users. PageRank, named after

Google co-founder Larry Page, was introduced as a key to handle this problem (Brin and Page 1998; Page et al. 1998). Until today, it is a crucial functional principle that was taken over by many other search engines. Its basic idea is to estimate a website's relevance by measuring the references it received, similar to citation analysis in academia:

"Academic citation literature has been applied to the web, largely by counting citations or backlinks to a given page. This gives some approximation of a page's importance or quality. PageRank extends this idea by not counting links from all pages equally, and by normalizing by the number of links on a page." (Brin and Page 1998, 4)

Thus, well-interlinked websites get a better PageRank and are higher ranked in Google results than websites with fewer links—especially when the linking websites have a high PageRank themselves. However, Page-Rank is just one of about 200 factors (Google Inc. 2011g) which lead to the order of Google's search results with the help of an underlying algorithm. Since it is secret and permanently adapted, it is hardly possible to give precise information about the logic of this algorithm. The new marketing field of search engine optimization (SEO) aims to do so, but by methods that are largely based on "trial and error". Information retrieval research gives some insights into the functional principles of search engines (e.g. Lewandowski 2005). Thus it is known that apart from factors independently estimating a website's relevance (like the PageRank), many factors relate to the actual queries. For example a website is more likely to be ranked high if the search term appears in its title or more often on the site. Also geographical and various interpretative factors may play a role in the ranking. "Googling" for "pizza" will, for example, most probably bring up local restaurants serving this dish at the top of the results. Thus, Google is assuming we want to order a Pizza from the place where the query was entered (instead of, for example, information about the history of Pizza, recipes etc.). This is possible because a computer's individual IP-address provides information about its approximate location. Users who are logged in with a Google account send additional information that can be analyzed, allowing for more interpretative ordering of search results. The underlying strategy was described in an official blog, outlining "The future of search":

"Maybe the search engines of the future will know where you are located, maybe they will know what you know already or what you learned earlier today, or maybe they will fully understand your preferences because you have chosen to share that information with us. We aren't sure which personal signals will be most valuable, but we're investing in research and experimentation on personalized search now because we think this will be very important later." (Google Inc. 2008)

Already today, search results might not only vary depending on the location, but possibly also depending on the individual/the computer. In this way, Google is actively and profoundly shaping the distribution of information.

Before websites can even appear in search results they have to be found. Web search engines like Google apply so-called *crawlers* (also spiders, robots) which follow hyperlinks to identify a large number of websites. These are indexed in a compressed form so that they can be searched very quickly. Google users do not search the web itself but the Google index. This is important to note because the act of crawling the web is anything but simple as the Google founders pointed out:

"Running a web crawler is a challenging task. There are tricky performance and reliability issues and even more importantly, there are social issues. Crawling is the most fragile application since it involves interacting with hundreds of thousands of web servers and various name servers which are all beyond the control of the system." (Brin and Page 1998, 10)

Content not captured by the crawlers is part of the so-called *deep web* (also *hidden, invisible or dark web*). Bergman explains the issue with the metaphor of "dragging a net across the surface of the ocean" and adds: "While a great deal may be caught in the net, there is still a wealth of information that is deep, and therefore, missed" (Bergman 2001). Crawlers are struggling with all kinds of obstacles. Some are simply of a technical nature and possibly removable (e.g. PDF files are no longer a problem for Google's machines), others are man-made, for example when webmasters exclude crawlers by protecting their content with passwords or commands in the source code. Bergman (2001) initially estimated the dark web might be about 500 times larger than the "visible" web. Other researchers pointed out methodological issues of Bergman's study, for example Lewandowski and Mayr (2006, 5ff.), who suggested to count the number of documents, rather than the size of data because large parts of the dark web consist of extraordinarily big files (e.g. satellite pictures). Besides, the boundary between the dark and the searchable webs is not easy to define due to the constantly changing web and its technical dynamics:

"A definition of what constitutes a truly invisible resource must necessarily be somewhat fluid, since the engines are constantly improving and adapting their methods to embrace new types of content." (Sherman and Price 2003, 297)

Without elaborating on this issue in more detail, we may assume that during the process of crawling Google probably misses significant parts of the web. Further sources are voluntarily excluded by Google itself, partly because they are classified as spam or as very similar content, but also as an act of censorship.[106]

Together with the unclear ranking methods, "googling" has to be regarded as a highly obscure way of information retrieval, especially because these processes remain mostly hidden to average users. The simple surface of the search engine hides the underlying complexity. Yet, Google's success shows that it is apparently doing a good job, at least for the majority of its users. One might even argue that the lack of transparency and the oversimplified surface are crucial factors not against but *in favor of* Google's success. Users need neither special skills for a query nor for the interpretation of the rapidly produced results—at least it seems so. It comes with a promise: "Web search engines suggest that all information available can be searched within just one system" (Lewandowski and Mayr 2006, 1). Although this promise cannot be kept on a technical or theoretical level, it seems to be kept on a pragmatic level. Google simply often enough guides users efficiently to the answers they are looking for. The very expression "to google something" implies that "the something" can be found via Google, making it rather a *finding* than a *search* engine (cf. Schetsche et al. 2007, 30).

The broad coverage is extended even beyond the conventional web by drawing on other Google platforms.[107] Two of them (Google Scholar and Google Books) are part of our case study and will be introduced in the following pages. Afterwards we will discuss the academic potential and user practices related to these platforms.

Google Scholar

Google Scholar was founded in 2004 to address some of the issues of web search outlined above and to provide an information service that is better

---

106 An often mentioned example was the Google version for China, see Google Inc. (2006).
    Also illegal content such as child pornography is supposed to be excluded.
107 Google deployed this feature called *Universal Search* in 2007.

adapted to scholarly needs. Unlike traditional academic databases, Google Scholar is able to access many full texts, as well. The targeted coverage is relatively wide, as stated in the company's description of the platform:

"Google Scholar provides a simple way to broadly search for scholarly literature. From one place, you can search across many disciplines and sources: articles, theses, books, abstracts and court opinions, from academic publishers, professional societies, online repositories, universities and other web sites. Google Scholar helps you find relevant work across the world of scholarly research." (Google Inc. 2011b)

At first glance, users will recognize many similarities to Google Web Search: The start page is designed equally simple and the results also appear quickly in a hierarchical list. However, a second look reveals details indicating functional differences: The search options vary, so one can for instance look for publications by particular authors (instead of domains) or focus queries on specific subject areas. The search results (Figure 20 below) contain additional features, such as links to other text versions or to articles citing an item. If possible, the results indicate the type of publication (e.g. "Book") or file type (e.g. "PDF"), or whether the item is a quotation.

The latter function indicates a ranking principle with a similar logic, but a different database than the PageRank: Instead of counting hyperlinks to estimate relevance, Google Scholar uses citations. Again, little is known about the various ranking factors and their weight. The company provides this vague description:

"Google Scholar aims to rank documents the way researchers do, weighing the full text of each document, where it was published, who it was written by, as well as how often and how recently it has been cited in other scholarly literature." (Google Inc. 2011b)

However, experiments indicate citations play a major role, so that highly cited articles have a good chance to gain a top position in search results (Beel and Gipp 2009). Google Scholar runs its own system to extract and analyze citations—a tricky operation since it mainly relies on automatic identification of bibliographic data within texts. That means Google's algorithms need to decide which words are names, titles or the body of the text, which numbers are publication dates and which are pages etc. Unsurprisingly, errors occur frequently during this process. They can lead to bizarre results, for instance when "Password", "P Login", "Subscribe" or

"Ltd" appear as extremely productive and highly cited authors (cf. Jacsó 2008, 2009). At the same time, actual authors might not be identified; other versions of a text are often counted as completely different publications; etc.

[BOOK] Modern **information retrieval**
R Baeza-Yates, B Ribeiro-Neto - 1999 - simmons.edu
Copyright © 1999 by the ACM press, A Division of the Association for Computing Machinary, Inc. (ACM). Addison Wesley Longman Limited Edinburgh Gate Harlow Essex CM20 2JE England and Associated Companies throughout the World. The rights of the authors of this Work ...
Cited by 8172 - Related articles - Library Search - All 25 versions

Information retrieval: data structures and algorithms
WB Frakes... - 1992 - citeulike.org
Information retrieval is a sub-field of computer science that deals with the automated storage and retrieval of documents. Providing the latest **information retrieval** techniques, this guide discusses **Information Retrieval** data structures and algorithms, including implementations in C. ...
Cited by 1912 - Related articles - Cached - Library Search - All 3 versions

Relevance feedback in **information retrieval**
JJ Rocchio - 1971 - citeulike.org
... CiteULike is a free online bibliography manager. Register and you can start organising your references online. Tags. Relevance feedback in **information retrieval**. by: JJ Rocchio. edited by: G. Salton. RIS. Export as RIS which can be imported into most citation managers. ...
Cited by 2077 - Related articles - Cached - All 3 versions

Figure 20: Google Scholar search results

Source: Screenshot of the first three results for the query "information retrieval", April 27, 2011

One of the features impeding the extraction of citations is Google Scholar's large and diverse data base. In order to reach beyond regular web crawling and to access the "academic invisible web" (Lewandowski and Mayr 2006), Google Scholar cooperates with libraries and publishers who share their data to get it indexed in the search engine. To our knowledge, Google never published a complete list of its cooperation partners, which is why the exact coverage of the search engine is unknown. Early studies on this matter (Jacsó 2005; Lewandowski 2007; Mayr and Walter 2007; Neuhaus et al. 2006) noticed gaps in certain fields, for example because important publishers such as Elsevier did not cooperate at first. However, more and more publishers joined and correspondingly the coverage increased. Jacsó (2008, 106) later stressed the "broad content coverage of Google Scholar", while pointing out remaining flaws. Until recently Google itself declared the imperfection of its service by keeping labeling it as "beta" on the start page (April 2011), but has now removed this label. Given the wide and constantly changing database (including private websites and a lot of grey literature), ranking items and extracting metadata automatically remains a challenging task in practice.

Apart from the basic function of searching a large corpus of academic literature, Google Scholar offers additional features, such as exporting items to reference management software (e.g. BibTex, EndNote, RefMan) and looking them up in local cooperating libraries (via an OPAC—an online public access catalogue).

Google Books

The Google Books website, allowing the searching of full texts of books and many magazines, was launched in 2005. The roots of the most comprehensive book digitalization project (formerly known as *Google Print*) reach back to the very beginning of the company, so that "one can certainly argue that the project is as old as Google itself" (Google Inc. 2011a). As mentioned above, the company's aims seem rather bold:

"Our ultimate goal is to work with publishers and libraries to create a comprehensive, searchable, virtual card catalog of all books in all languages that helps users discover new books and publishers discover new readers." (Google Inc. 2011d)

To do this, Google scans books and converts them to digital text using its own optical character recognition (OCR) method. The books come from two sources: On the one hand, there is the *Partner Program*, which receives them directly from publishers[108] and authors. On the other hand, in the *Library Project*, Google cooperates with a number of significant large libraries,[109] which (partly) opened their shelves for the company.

---

108 As far as we know, there is no complete public list of the cooperating publishers. However Google mentions the following publishers as their initial partners in 2004: Blackwell, Cambridge University Press, University of Chicago Press, Houghton Mifflin, Hyperion, McGraw-Hill, Oxford University Press, Pearson, Penguin, Perseus, Princeton University Press, Springer, Taylor & Francis, Thomson Delmar and Warner Books; see Google Inc. (2011h).

109 Austrian National Library, Bavarian State Library, Columbia Univ., Committee on Institutional Cooperation (CIC), Cornell Univ. Library, Harvard Univ., Ghent Univ. Library, Keio Univ. Library, Lyon Municipal Library, The National Library of Catalonia, The New York Public Library, Oxford Univ., Princeton Univ., Stanford Univ., Univ. of California, Complutense Univ. of Madrid, Univ. Library of Lausanne, Univ. of Michigan, Univ. of Texas at Austin, Univ. of Virginia, Univ. of Wisconsin–Madison; see Google Inc. (2011f) for the current list and further details on the collaborations.

Since authors and publishers were not involved in the latter project, it provoked major controversies, including several law suits. These were mainly focusing on copyright conflicts, which were still not settled by the time of writing this book (see also 2.5.3). Thus, the basic functions described in this section might not only undergo the usual changes aiming at an enhancement of the service, but they could also experience further restrictions, reduced content or even a total shutdown of the project. Moreover, Google is of course still far from reaching its "ultimate goal" of scanning all books while items are constantly added.

Currently, one of Google Books' ways of dealing with copyright issues is to display the results differently, depending on the copyright status of a book: full view; limited preview; snippet view; or no preview at all, as explained on the website:

– *"Full View:* You can see books in Full View if the book is out of copyright, or if the publisher or author has asked to make the book fully viewable. The Full View allows you to view any page from the book, and if the book is in the public domain, you can download, save and print a PDF version to read at your own pace.
– *Limited Preview:* If the publisher or author has given us permission, you can see a limited number of pages from the book as a preview.
– *Snippet View:* The Snippet View, like a card catalog, shows information about the book plus a few snippets—a few sentences to display your search term in context [see Figure 21].
– *No Preview Available:* Like a card catalog, you're able to see basic information about the book." (Google Inc. 2011h)

Basic bibliographic data such as author, title and links to online book stores where items can be purchased are provided for every book. Needless to say, displaying search results differs a lot from Google Web Search. Still, the familiar Google principles can be recognized: search requests are processed equally quickly and results appear in a hierarchically ordered list. Again, the ranking mechanisms remain obscure and critics argue that they would "make no sense at all" (Nunberg 2009). The developers envisioned a ranking method similar to the PageRank:

"[I]n a future world in which vast collections of books are digitized, people would use a 'web crawler' to index the books' content and analyze the connections between them, determining any given book's relevance and usefulness by tracking the number and quality of citations from other books." (Google Inc. 2011a)

Yet, the PageRank cannot simply be applied to books for palpable reasons:

"The printed volumes represented on Google Books form a completely different kind of problem. Google's famous algorithm can't be deployed to search through books because they don't link to each other in the way that webpages do. There is no perfect BookRank corollary for PageRank." (Madrigal 2010)

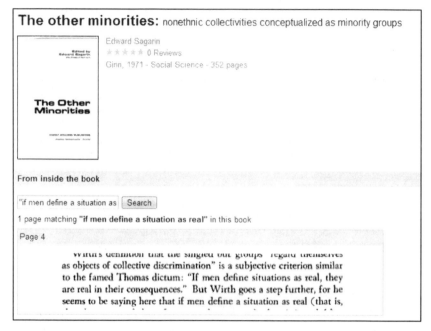

Figure 21: Snippet view in Google Books (detail)

Comparable to Google Scholar, many issues connected to wrong metadata have been reported (Baksik 2006; Duguid 2007; Nunberg 2009). For example, Nunberg (2009) pointed out that many books were incorrectly attributed to the publishing year 1899, including Stephen King's "Christine", or Robert Shelton's Bob Dylan biography. Google later explained the reason for this error, giving insights into how such issues arise and are dealt with:

"[W]e recently began incorporating metadata from a Brazilian metadata provider that, unbeknownst to us, used 1899 as the default date when they had no other…. We've special cased this provider so that their 1899 dates—and theirs alone—are ignored." (Oder 2009)

Nunberg (2009) highlights more metadata-related problems affecting the functionality of Google Books. For example, he questions the reliability of the categories, which can be used for topical browsing. As he claims, the cited errors are not rare cases, but rather "endemic", which was later accepted by Google: "Geoff refers to us having hundreds of thousands of errors. I wish it were so. We have millions" (Oder 2009).

Inaccurate as they might be, categories offer new ways of approaching a topic, in comparison to the more search term based Google Web Search and Google Scholar. Another new access to content can be made via user-generated virtual bookshelves available in the *My library* function. Here, logged-in users can also write their own reviews that appear alongside books (the example used in Figure 21 above shows it was not reviewed yet). In this way, Google also applies typical Web 2.0 features to its platform.

Apart from these main functions, Google Books provides several additional services, for example looking up an item in a local library's OPAC, PDF downloads of fully available books, linking to user-defined text sections, etc.

2.5.2 Potential for academia

Strong ties between Google and academia can hardly be denied: Being itself based on university research, the company is not only rooted in academia, but also has partly overlapping goals as "Google's mission is to organize the world's information and make it universally accessible and useful" (Google Inc. 2011c). Regardless of the company's intentions, its deep impact on knowledge societies is evident. Thus, one can easily imagine potential applications of Google products for scholarly activities, as shown in Figure 22 and explained below. Due to their very nature as search platforms, direct usage is mostly limited to information gathering. However, given Google's dominant status in this field, scholars pointed out that it may serve as an "obligatory passage point" (Mager 2010; Röhle 2010; Mager 2009), connecting but also crucially shaping different actors, website providers and users in particular. Thus, the analyzed Google platforms can be used indirectly beyond mere search.

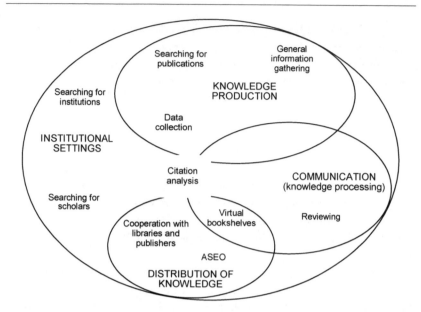

Figure 22: Scholarly activities and Google, Google Scholar, and Google Books

Knowledge production: Most obviously, all three platforms can be used to find various kinds of scholarly relevant information. Of course, Google Scholar is particularly useful to find academic publications since it was designed for this purpose, whereas Google Books enables searching a large corpus of printed (scholarly) literature. Both are largely indexed in full text (unlike traditional keyword-based databases), which enables data collection from these sources for research purposes. The general Google Web Search seems less suitable for finding publications but can be utilized to retrieve all kinds of other information needed in scholarly work.

Communication: The three Google platforms rarely provide possibilities for direct communication to process knowledge. However, some functions could be indirectly used for this purpose. In particular, users may set up so-called virtual individual bookshelves and share items placed in them with other users. Furthermore, Google Books offers the opportunity to add personal reviews of books, which are then visible to others. In this way, new forms of knowledge distribution may arise.

Distribution of knowledge: On the one hand, academic libraries and publishers actively distribute knowledge to Google Scholar and Google Books by partially or completely providing their literature and its metadata. Millions of books from these sources have been digitalized for Google Books—leading both to better access to knowledge and to major controversies. Moreover, some features such as connection to OPACs can help to access local works. On the other hand, individual scholars can hardly influence how their content is being distributed via these platforms. Scholars can only try to upload their content to the web in a form that conforms to the technical algorithms of search engines in order to increase the chance of being indexed and ranked highly in search results—as the concept of Academic Search Engine Optimization (ASEO) suggests (Beel et al. 2010).

Institutional settings: All three platforms can be used to find academic institutions and individuals and detailed information about them, such as contact details, curricula vitae, or project descriptions. Again, the institutions and individuals have only little influence on their representation in Google results, except when using ASEO techniques.

Furthermore, Google Scholar may be used as an alternative citation analysis tool, which also includes—unlike the traditional citation indices—citations of working papers and books.

2.5.3 User practices and impact

In this chapter we discuss the various academic user practices connected to the three Google platforms in our focus and their impact on academia. We start with the most obvious application, the search function in academic contexts. We shall then briefly discuss the opportunities for indirect communication delivered by Google Books, before we elaborate further on the way knowledge is distributed by the three platforms. In doing so, we differentiate between the active distribution of knowledge—academic institutions and publishers co-operate with Google—and passive knowledge distribution—knowledge is distributed to the platforms with little control by its authors. Finally, we focus on the way Google may be used in institutional settings, for example for searching scholars and organizations.

"Googling" In academic contexts

Many, if not all researchers and students employ Google products to search for publications and other information as part of their daily research routines. For obvious reasons: these services are quick, free and easy to use. Moreover, due to Google's popularity, many academics probably have integrated at least Google Web Search into their private everyday Internet routines.

So far, most studies draw a relatively coherent picture of search engine users and their practices: Usually, they only use simple queries and follow the given hierarchy in search results, mostly only considering results appearing on the first page (e.g. Fallows 2005; Machill et al. 2003; more in an overview by Lewandowski 2005, 34 ff.). The average users do not seem to regard this as a problem:

"Interestingly, search engine users are easily satisfied. When asked about the quality of the results they achieve, they usually express satisfaction with their searching strategies […]. Therefore, they don't see why they should apply sophisticated searching strategies to other search systems. If Google is able to return relevant results for a one-word query, then every other system should be able to do the same." (Lewandowski 2008, 262)

User studies among academics, however, do not show that they are more critical when it comes to search engines. For example, librarians at Cornell University reported that "there is blind trust and an increasing reliance on search results, especially on whatever appears on the first couple of screens" (Rieger 2009). The librarians are concerned "that convenience and expediency are driving the information–seeking behavior of academics" (ibid.). Many academics seem to believe that Google "represents the information space in which they are interested with excellent breadth and depth" (ibid.). Another study, observing researchers at three Swedish universities, approves Google's predominance for many different purposes:

"For many researchers, especially in the sciences, Google is the first choice for information—all kinds of information. The researchers use Google for scientific information, looking for everything from methodological information to ISSNs, and some even state having moved from subject specific databases to Google (and Google Scholar)." (Haglund and Olsson 2008, 55)

Google seems to be particularly popular among students, i.e. the next generation of academics. An American study reports "that especially the undergraduate and graduate students, consistently made remarks that reflected their trust in and loyalty to Google." (Rieger 2009). An evaluation of United Kingdom's national academic sector digital information services concluded that 45 percent of 27 students from different disciplines use Google as their first source of information, whereas the university library catalogue is second by only ten percent (Griffiths and Brophy 2005). Becker (2003) reports on Google's predominance in student's searching behavior, as well as an international representative survey by the Online Computer Library Center, that has shown that 89 percent of the students consult first a search engine and that is mostly Google (OCLC 2005).

Obviously, the company successfully established itself as a brand standing for quick, easy and helpful information gathering—also in academia. Furthermore, Google platforms other than Web Search can profit from this image, as indicated by a study comparing usage of the federated search system *MetaLib* with Google Scholar among Swedish students (Nygren et al. 2006, 43). The fact that they were already familiar with the interface from using Google regularly was viewed positively. However, the students also complained about "too many irrelevant results" (ibid.), which can be regarded as a typical Google flaw, particularly when it comes to more specific needs like in academia. As outlined above, the underlying technology is extremely sophisticated, but this complexity is hidden behind the simple-looking surfaces:

"The difficulty is that information—through Google—is seen to be both abundant and cheap. Because of this rapid ranking and return, 'anyone' can manage it. Actually, the abilities required to assess information are difficult and costly to obtain." (Brabazon 2006, 163)

Thus, Google's apparent simplicity may turn out to be a false friend:

"While the preference for very simple search engine approaches is prevalent, it is important to note that this does not mean that students are necessarily best served by this approach. Indeed, it may be that students would get better results using specialist subject gateways, but most students do not take this approach. Exclusive use of any commercial [search engine] coupled with a lack of awareness and understanding of peer-reviewed, quality resources is not in the best interest of students or academic staff." (Griffiths and Brophy 2005, 552)

This is particularly problematic in the case of Google Web Search because it largely builds on "lay indexing" (Brooks 2004): PageRank analyzes hyperlinks to estimate relevance—and linking to websites is of course not bound to expertise. But simply following Google Scholar's and Google Book's results can also be tricky because their ranking mechanisms are equally obscure and results come from a wide and largely unknown database.

The fact that obtaining academic information with Google services is undoubtedly a method with many pitfalls, does not seriously affect its popularity. Many scholars have expressed their concerns about the impact these practices have or might have on academics. Brabazon (2006) for instance, warns not only of the dangers of questionable search results, but also about a "flattening of expertise" which might be the outcome of quick superficial "googling".

One might argue obtaining academic information has always been a challenging task that requires a certain level of literacy. Thus, working with Google simply needs some understanding of its functionality, a sort of *Google literacy*, which might be established over the years. Indeed, Head (2007), for example, observed that students are more skeptical towards search engines than previous studies suggested. If applied effectively, Google's swiftness can even serve academic quality, namely when it decreases the time needed to obtain information, leaving more space for other work. From this perspective Lewandowski argues:

"Research shows that with limited time, even for scientific information needs, search engines could be a better choice for the searcher than the library's offerings." (Lewandowski 2008, 262)

Indeed, Thelwall (2002) has, for example, demonstrated Google's utility for finding journals in the web at an early stage. Today, Google's services are considered to be essential for academic work. When Google's withdrawal from China was impending, *Nature* conducted a study revealing that out of 784 responding Chinese scientists "more than three-quarters said they use Google as the primary search engine for their research" and 84 percent believe "losing Google would 'somewhat or significantly' hamper their research" (Qiu 2010).

Google products might be valuable alternatives to expensive other services (e.g. Thomson Reuter's ISI Web of Knowledge), especially for less developed countries and independent researchers with very limited funds. However, due to their flaws, it seems questionable whether they can function equally well (see also below). Anyway, it is safe to say that Google Web Search and Google Scholar have many competitors, which could replace them in principle.

The case of Google Books is different, though. Although numerous other book digitalization projects exist, none of them comes close to Google Book's pace and coverage. Especially the rich corpus of fully available historical books in the public domain makes it an attractive research tool for history, linguistics, cultural studies etc. (Brückner 2009; Gloning 2009; Bohannon 2010). Cohen highlights the advantages of Google Books by referring to his own research:

"In my book 'Equations from God' I argued that mathematics was generally considered a divine language in 1800 but was 'secularized' in the nineteenth century. Part of my evidence was that mathematical treatises, which often contained religious language in the early nineteenth century, lost such language by the end of the century. By necessity, researching in the pre-Google Books era, my textual evidence was limited—I could only read a certain number of treatises and chose to focus (I'm sure this will sound familiar) on the writings of high-profile mathematicians. The vastness of Google Books for the first time presents the opportunity to do a more comprehensive scan of Victorian mathematical writing for evidence of religious language. This holds true for many historical research projects." (Cohen 2010, 5)

Even when books are not fully accessible due to their copyright status, Google Books might be helpful for locating specific text segments. For example, it might be possible to recover quotes with missing references.

Indirect communication

Although direct communication with a view to processing knowledge is not a core functionality of search engines, two features of Google Books play a role in this context: (1) linking and (2) reviewing.

(1) Interesting communicative opportunities are given by Google Books' function of linking books and book sections. With this in mind, Kelly developed the vision of a "universal library" that is taking advantage of such functions:

"Turning inked letters into electronic dots that can be read on a screen is simply the first essential step in creating this new library. The real magic will come in the second act, as each word in each book is cross-linked, clustered, cited, extracted, indexed, analyzed, annotated, remixed, reassembled and woven deeper into the culture than ever before. In the new world of books, every bit informs another; every page reads all the other pages." (Kelly 2006)

Certainly at this early stage, all this is more of a vision than a reality (cp. also Nentwich 2003, 270ff.), not least because the limitations resulting from copyright issues and other problems hinder totally free access to the digital books (see below). Still, it is true that Google Books pulls books out of their analogue bookshelves on a large scale and makes them not only accessible (within the given limitations) but also *addressable* online. Of course, this was possible through regular citations before, but Google Books makes referencing much more instantaneous. Some journals already picked this idea up by linking references to Google Books.[110] This way it also becomes much easier to follow references and to retrace their context. Evidently, due to Google Books' limitations, visiting libraries certainly have not become obsolete yet. But it drastically speeds up and eases such processes and makes them more transparent.

The wide easy and free access of texts enables what may be called *crowdsourced peer review*. For instance, it was used to uncover plagiarism in the case of the dissertation of zu Guttenberg, a German politician (see 3.3.3). Of course, one can imagine many more ways in which linking books can be used in academic communication. Although we are not aware of any study on this subject, we can assume that it is used by many scholars on a daily basis. Kelly (2006) might be right with his assumption that with these new possibilities books will get relevant in different contexts and ways than they are now, which correspondingly will impact on scholarly communication. However, if we want to avoid technological determinism, we can hardly assess what such practices will look like and how they will shape academia. Concrete user studies would be needed to make more empirically-based statements on this issue.

(2) The same goes for Google Book's review function. It can be regarded as a new form of public ex-post peer review, potentially opening up this process to new audiences. But due to a lack of user studies, we simply do not know to what extent it is used and what impact it has on academia.

Active distribution of knowledge

We observe that the Google services discussed here significantly impact the distribution of scholarly knowledge. Two modes can be differentiated: On the one hand, knowledge is actively distributed by libraries and publishers for Google Books and Google Scholar. On the other hand, academic knowledge is indexed and ranked automatically by the search engines, leaving scholars only the passive instrument of optimizing indirectly the search results (ASEO; see below) to influence the way it is distributed. Therefore we are going to discuss Google's impact along this differentiation of *active* and *passive distribution of knowledge*.

As stated on their website, the people behind Google Books "firmly believe that this project is good news for everybody who reads, writes,

---

110 See e.g. europeangovernance.livingreviews.org.

publishes and sells books" (Google Inc. 2011e). Indeed, at first glance the book digitalization project seems to bring striking benefits to academia as well: While other digitalization projects devour immense amounts of public funds and proceed agonizingly slowly, Google scans the books not only much faster, but also free of charge. A second look reveals the pitfalls of this cooperation: Firstly, the quick progress is paid with a lack of quality, or as Cohen put it, "haste makes waste" (Cohen 2010, 3).

Google's fast OCR method soon became a matter for criticism, since it produced many errors, as shown in the example in Figure 23 below. This reduces the reliability of the service, since such pages are not only unreadable but the text can also not be indexed. Given that it comes for free to the user, one can argue an imperfect platform is better than none. Of course, academia profits from Google Books, as well as from Google Web Search and Google Scholar because these services provide many innovative possibilities that we simply did not have before, for instance access to many out-of-print books. But at the same time they deeply impact on academia (and in fact society in general)[111] in ways that are out of the control of scholarly institutions and individuals. This becomes clear when one looks at academia's passive distribution of knowledge through Google (see below), but no example illustrates this better than the case of Google Books.

When publishers and authors distribute knowledge to Google Books by voluntarily providing books or digital copies (as done in the Partner Program) this does not seem very controversial. But understandably, the corporate digitalization of millions of books from academic and public libraries without notifying their authors raises many questions and criticism—especially when it comes to books that are protected by copyright. Google dealt with this problem by referring to the *fair use* doctrine applied in United States copyright law. This allows exceptions from copyright protection for certain creative purposes, for example quoting in academia. Google believed its practice would fall within this doctrine, since it only provides excerpts of such books:

---

111 For a more general discussion on the societal impact of search engines and Google in particular, see Halavais (2009), Lehmann and Schetsche (2007), Vaidhyanathan (2011).

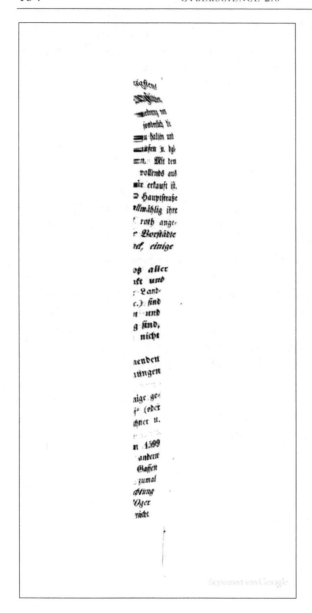

Figure 23: Wrongly scanned book in Google Books

Source: upload.wikimedia.org/wikipedia/commons/c/c1/Google_Books_scanfehler.png
(accessed May 8, 2011)

"We carefully protect copyright holders by making sure that when users find a book under copyright, they see only a card catalog-style entry providing basic information about the book and no more than two or three sentences of text surrounding the search term to help them determine whether they've found what they're looking for." (Google Inc. 2011e)

Initially, enthusiasts like Kelly (2006) celebrated this as a "clever solution", potentially helping to "unravel the Gordian knot of copydom" in the digital age. Critics however, regarded Google's interpretation as an exploitation of the fair use doctrine (Baksik 2006). As a matter of fact, the digitalization of copyrighted works for commercial purposes (one must not forget that Google is a private corporation) on this massive scale is highly debatable. Thus, some of Google Books' early proponents turned against the project. Even R. Darnton, chief of Google Books' initial partner Harvard University Libraries, denounced the project in public (he became head of the libraries after the cooperation was decided, cf. Vaidhyanathan 2011, 153). Google Books became the subject of several national and international lawsuits and until today its legal status is far from being solved. With the *Google Book Settlement* the company managed to calm down some of its opponents by financially compensating them. But since not all relevant copyright holders were part of the lawsuit, this solution was fragile from the beginning. In March 2011 the responsible American court denied a request for a final settlement approval. Therefore, we shall certainly witness further legal debates and lawsuits in the context of Google Books. Another reason for this is that due to the online accessibility of the platform, even countries without a direct Google Books presence are affected by the service. Consequently, the legal questions regarding Google Books go far beyond US copyright law and also beyond the platform itself. For example, the Google opt-out policy suggests that copyright holders can exclude their content when they actively ask for it, which has been widely criticized. However, contacting each copyright holder in advance is hardly possible. This becomes obvious, when the idea is applied to web search engines, which require caching countless websites for their indexes:

"No company, not even one as wealthy and successful as Google, could afford the time, labor, and funds it would take to secure permission to copy the billions of text passages, images and videos that Google now scours for its indexes." (Vaidhyanathan 2011, 167)

This shows how technological details are intertwined with broader legal and cultural questions. When publishers and libraries actively distribute knowledge to Google Books, a process that goes far beyond this pure act was triggered.

Passive distribution of knowledge

In fact, the active part played by publishers and libraries is more or less limited to the provision of their data to Google. Afterwards they have little or no influence on the way it is presented on the platforms. Thus we may say that academic knowledge is to a large extent *passively distributed* to Google Web Search, Google Scholar and Google Books: it is crawled, indexed and ranked automatically every day, whether scholars like it or not. At the same time, the services are widely used—by lay people as well as by scholars—so they can hardly be ignored. It is important to note this fact because it puts much of the academic criticism discussed above into perspective. Librarians may dismiss Google Scholar and Google Books for its inaccuracy and teachers may complain about the seductive, inadequate ease of Google Web Search. But as pointed out by Pomerantz: "Despite this debate, however, users are using Google Scholar" (2006, 55). In the end, these platforms gain their relevance simply by being used, thereby forcing scholars to deal with them. Mullen and Hartman spell this out in regard to the relation between Google Scholar and libraries:

"In some ways, the introduction of Google Scholar has forced academic librarians to analyze the relationships among publishers, vendors, free search engines, and research-level libraries. The relationship between libraries and Google Scholar, unprecedented in that it does not depend on sales, has implications for the library Web site. It is an example of a new type of collaboration between a commercial enterprise and academia." (Mullen and Hartman 2006, 107)

Given academia's mainly passive role in this relationship, one might wonder how collaborative it really is. As a matter of fact, the algorithms responsible for the way knowledge is distributed through the Google platforms are obscure and, more importantly, they are necessarily accepted qua their usage. Similar to Lessig's well-known notion of "code" (Lessig 1999, 2006), Schetsche (2006) coined the term "algorithmic norms" (our translation) to highlight how algorithms frame user experiences and a number of scholars have characterized search engines as "gatekeepers" to refer to the implications they trigger for information policy (see e.g. Röhle 2009).

As we pointed out earlier, Google's relevance may not necessarily be congruent with academic relevance, especially not Google Web Search.

Recalling its ranking method based on measuring hyperlinks, it is easy to argue that sheer popularity will often weigh heavier than academic scrutiny. Therefore, it is not surprising when a website questioning anthropological global warming gets better ranked than the Intergovernmental Panel on Climate Change (IPCC, König and Nentwich 2010, 21), or when websites claiming the World Trade Center was brought down by a controlled demolition receive a high Google position (König 2009b). In this way, Google thwarts the traditional way of distributing academic knowledge top-down, while producing new hierarchies at the same time. This also holds true for Google Scholar and Google Books as their even more obscure algorithms often deliver rankings that do not represent academic relevance.

The call for *academic search engine optimization*, abbreviated ASEO (Beel et al. 2010), is obviously taking this development into account by suggesting that scholarly content should be formatted search-engine-friendly. However, such attempts can hardly be seen as emancipation from the search engines. Indeed, they reinforce the logic of search engines by effectively making use of it. Fears that such practices might result in "academic search engine spam" were voiced and indeed empirically confirmed (Beel and Gipp 2010). It remains to be seen, which broader implications are triggered by this development. One of the pressing questions to be discussed is, for example, whether these new hierarchies established in search engine rankings affect offline-hierarchies as well (see chapter 3.6).

Beyond academic institutional directories and link collections

Without much exaggeration search engines may be considered a very efficient and up-to-date directory of academic institutions and personnel. Indeed, Google Web Search is used frequently by academics to find colleagues and research institutions; not least because of their high mobility and the inherent dynamics of the institutional settings of academia as a whole, the previous attempts to keep web-based lists and link collections of persons and institutions have been largely replaced by search engines. Ever more often, personal "profiles" within social network sites (2.1) are the top research results; hence search engines play an important role as intermediating actors within digital social networks.

Much of what we observed above about the passive distribution of knowledge is relevant again here. While Google provides efficient paths to individuals and institutions, they have little influence on how they appear in Google rankings. Considering that scholars are more and more using the web for all kinds of activities (as discussed in this book), we must assume that their activities are increasingly tracked (Nentwich 2009, 23) and search engines may serve to construct identities out of these traces:

"Public identities are often constructed out of what may be discovered via a search engine, and this affects how we view our colleagues, our friends, and our family members. Drawing heavily on the burgeoning exhibitionist technologies like blogs, social networking sites and photo-sharing sites, search engines help us to create portfolios of the people we interact with. In many cases, this means that they provide us with information on parts of their lives that would otherwise remain hidden, at least to most of the world." (Halavais 2009, 139)

A person's or institution's name by itself significantly frames the impact it may have because information related to unique names can of course be retrieved more easily than data connected to widely spread names. Depending on the information presented in the search engine, this can be regarded as good or bad. We might want to hide some of the information about us and our institutions that is retrievable via search engines, while we might wish other content to be more prominently ranked. As in the distribution of knowledge, scholars have little influence on how they and their institutions are presented in search engine results. Whether individuals should have more say on this, is a controversial and unsolved question even debated in courts (Rowinski 2011). It is not easy to answer because it moves along the thin and widely debated line between privacy rights and freedom of information (see 3.5).

Even if we could remove information about ourselves from search engines, other problems remain. Halavais (2009, 142) reported for example, that a student shared her name with a porn actress which made her constantly fear she might be confused with her. Of course, this principle can also be applied intentionally, for example to discredit individuals or institutions.

It goes without saying that one may also benefit from the information presented about oneself at Google. Especially for less established scholars and institutions it can be a way of getting attention independently of more restricted channels such as peer reviewed journals. The concrete consequences depend very much on individual cases. What is a person's or institution's name? Which relevant information is available online and how is it ranked? Which queries are entered and how are the results interpreted?

Correspondingly, it is an open question how these processes impact academia at a higher level. In the same vein we may address another question: Does the free infrastructure provided by Google have a democratizing effect on academia (see also 3.6)? At first sight, this might be the case because it can be used instead of other costly services. In particular, Google Scholar can be applied as a tool for citation analysis (Harzing and van der Wal 2009, 2008; Noruzi 2005), thus serving as an alternative to the traditional citation indices. Moreover, it also indexes and analyzes texts that are not considered by its competitors. However, issues related to Google Scholar's problems of retrieving metadata make it unreliable as an indicator for the impact of publications, as it was suggested (Gassmann et al. 2011). Nevertheless it is used for this purpose by external software applications[112] and of course by Google Scholar's internal ranking algorithm. This shows the two sides of Google's potential as a democratizing force. It certainly has some effects in that direction, but at the same time it has significant flaws. Moreover, scholars and institutions who decide to use Google services are forced to accept the company's policy, which leads to further issues, such as Google's privacy policy.

2.5.4 Interim conclusions

Although our case study focused on only three Google products, we can undoubtedly identify a major impact on academics caused by this company. Due to Google's stable market position based on its massive infrastructure and know-how, this is unlikely to change in the near future. However, Google's power has also increasingly become a matter of public criticism and political or juridical interventions. Especially in the case of Google Books, this impedes its impact assessment because legislation might fundamentally and rapidly change the platforms and their relation to academics.

Still, it seems safe to say Google will continue to drastically influence science, because of its dominant position on the online market. This effect is achieved due to partly overlapping goals of academia and Google. No doubt, the corporate functional logic is fundamentally different from the fact-seeking logic of academia. But the sheer omnipresent usage of Google products in academic circles intrinsically ties the two realms or, as Vaidhy-

---

112 E.g. code.google.com/p/citations-gadget, harzing.com/pop.htm.

anathan puts it: "In fact, the connections between Google and the universities of the world is more than close—it is uncomfortably familial" (2011, 186). In line with him, we believe that it is not exaggerated to speak of a "googlization" of academia.

As observed throughout this case study, this takes place in more or less all scholarly activities. Most obviously, the analyzed search products affect the production of knowledge, because they can be used to obtain all sorts of academically relevant information. Since they are popular among students as well as among faculty, one can hardly overemphasize this impact, especially because Google is actively shaping user experiences: The "googlized" way of distributing knowledge is to provide it in fragmented pieces, which are re-contextualized in hierarchically-ordered search results; the relevance of top research results created by the underlying algorithms does, however, not necessarily follow what is relevant in academia—and scholars have little means to influence it. In an analysis of search behavior of lay people in the medical field Mager (2010) has further shown that the fragmentation of information triggers new practices of evaluating information closely related to Google's way of functioning. Whether this is also the case in the academic realm needs to be further investigated.

Despite the common fears on how this will negatively impact research, one might argue that this is a particular problem of the current transition phase, which just requires a new form of literacy—a sort of *Google literacy* which helps us to understand and deal with these processes. Hence, librarians and other information professionals do not become obsolete because of Google's rise. In fact, we need these professionals more than ever to navigate us through the opaque world of search engines. However, Google challenges them with its apparently easy functionality and forces them to deal with questions such as: "Should you hide the inherent complexity to the user or let the user control it?" (Nygren et al. 2006, 56). Google's answer is obvious.

However, academia still can actively deal with such questions (for instance by teaching Google literacy). But of course, scholars cannot change the algorithms themselves, which is why they can neither control what kind of academic content is distributed here, nor how information about them or their institutions is presented. At the same time, Google's dominant position serves as an "obligatory passage point" (Mager 2010; Röhle 2010) intermediating between actors and thus shaping digital social networks within its algorithmic logic.

As yet, it is hard to say what broader effects the new emerging power structures will have on academia. Studies focusing on such questions (e.g. Mager 2010; Röhle 2010) reveal their complexity, which tells us that simplistic dichotomic assumptions (for instance, "Google helps democratizing academia", or the other way round "Google reproduces existing hierarchies" (see 3.6.2) probably do not live up to the multi-facetted impact. Further studies are needed in order to understand how exactly Google shapes digital social networks and how this influences academia.

A glimpse on the case of Google Books gives us an idea of how complex and unpredictable such connections can be. Here the digitization of books (distributed to a large extent by academic libraries), resulted in heated debates and an obscure situation with many juridical pitfalls. Such cooperations do not only raise "questions that get to the heart of copyright" (Vaidhyanathan 2011, 160), but also to academia's autonomy—with broader implications for society and culture in general. This is particularly true given the fact that we only focused on three out of many Google platforms for our case study. Of course, Google affects academia in many more ways than the ones we outlined here in regard to these platforms for text search.[113] We may reflect further on issues only incidentally touched here, for example Google's impact on user's privacy (see also 3.5), ecological effects of their infrastructure etc.

---

113 Vaidhyanathan (2011, 197) explains for example, how universities depend on Google by outsourcing crucial parts of their IT infrastructure to the company.

3 Cross-Cutting Analysis

In our case studies, we observed how digital social networks emerge in the environments of various prominent web platforms and how this affects academia. In this chapter we will further analyze the observed developments from a broader perspective. We start out by critically approaching the category of interactivity, which is crucial for Web 2.0 applications and their impact (3.1). Then we focus on the newly emerging relationship between the public sphere and academia (3.2) and, partly related, on the changes in the academic quality control system (3.3). In section 3.4 we discuss the issues of a potential information overload with regard to the multiple channels of digital social networks. Furthermore we will analyze how Web 2.0 is challenging our traditional notions of privacy and transparency (3.5). Finally, we discuss whether cyberscience 2.0 will be more "democratic" than traditional science (3.6).

3.1 Interactivity as a Crucial Category

3.1.1 Utopian and dystopian perspectives

As outlined in the introductory chapter, interactivity is a crucial attribute of Web 2.0 applications. Their open participatory architecture has been the reason for optimistic utopian visions as well as pessimistic dystopian warnings, which we will discuss throughout chapter 3. Different as these scenarios are, both sides have one assumption in common: they largely base their argumentation on the concept of active users who heavily use the given technical infrastructure. Depending on the point of view, this can be regarded as good or bad, constructive or destructive, enlightening or stultifying, an opportunity or a threat. Although one can find more differentiated contributions as well, many of the highly-cited authors who shape the contemporary discourse on Web 2.0 can be localized more or less clearly in these two parties.

On the utopian side, one finds authors stressing the positive potential of Web 2.0, starting with O'Reilly (2005) who coined the very term and referred to economic aspects, particularly the effect of "the collective power" of relatively small groups taken together, which has been described as the *long tail* by Chris Anderson in greater detail (2007). Clay Shirky (2008) claimed the new participatory architecture brings organizational benefits compared to traditional institutional structures, since, in his view supported by numerous examples, it allows easier and more effective interaction within social groups. In such optimistic perspectives, Web 2.0 contributors are conceptualized as forming a kind of collective intelligence, resulting in a "wisdom of crowds" (Surowiecki 2004). Needless to say, approaches of this kind also embrace many "Web 1.0" features, especially the possibility for wide, free and simple access to information. Enthusiasts hope this will bring societies and cultures closer together, often citing McLuhan's idea of a "global village".

Such discussions do not stay on a theoretical level, but can be found frequently in public discourses about the Internet's impact on society. Many key actors of present Internet applications share optimistic ideas of this sort—from the usually euphemistic Silicon Valley entrepreneurs such as Facebook's Mark Zuckerberg or Google's Eric Schmidt to non-profit actors such as Wikimedia's Jimmy Wales. On the user-end, one can observe a number of groups pushing utopian perspectives on the web, reaching from loosely-connected Internet-savvy bloggers to grass-rooted initiatives that might even turn into political parties, bringing their ideas to the agenda of policy-makers.[114]

Some of these views can also be identified in discourses regarding Internet usage in academia: open access advocates stress the advantages of widely-accessible publications free of charge, often favoring a reform of traditional copyright; innovative journals apply Web 2.0 elements believing they create benefits over traditional peer reviewing methods (we will come back to this issue in section 3.3); supporters of the "open science" movement promote the idea that academia should become more transparent to

---

114 Since 2006, especially in Europe, a number of *pirate parties* have emerged from the techno-enthusiastic hacker culture. Moreover, various NGOs push rather utopian visions of the Internet, e.g. the Electronic Frontier Foundation (EFF) or Germany's Chaos Computer Club.

the public (cf. sections 3.2, 3.6). For some scientists, professional blogging and other activities on the social web are even seen as an imperative for modern scholars. For obvious reasons, developers of academic Web 2.0 platforms also tend to come to rather enthusiastic assessments of their creations, overstressing positive aspects while underplaying negative ones.

On the opposite side of the spectrum, dystopians come to radically different conclusions. A common complaint is that we might suffer from a sort of "information overload"—a term that was already coined decades before the WWW was invented (Toffler 1970) but seems to be more relevant than ever today. Authors following this perspective argue that the sheer amount of information on the Internet and its fragmented and hyperlinked structure swamps our neuronal capacities and hinder deeper and coherent thoughts (Schirrmacher 2009; Carr 2010; see 3.4 below). Correspondingly, dystopian thinkers question the Web 2.0 crowd's "wisdom" and sound alarms about the decline of expertise in exchange for a "cult of the amateur" (Keen 2007). Instead of promoting the idea of collective intelligence, skeptics argue "that a hive mind is a cruel idiot when it runs on autopilot", fearing the emergence of a "digital Maoism" (Lanier 2006). Moreover, due to the digital structure of the Internet "code is law" (Lessig 1999), which means content can ultimately be regulated by algorithms that hierarchically order or even exclude its elements. As Zittrain (2008) points out, this becomes increasingly problematic as the Internet is more and more ruled by a few actors who control content through their data "clouds" and remotely controllable devices like Apple's iPhone or Amazon's Kindle. Already today, algorithms are powerfully structuring the way we perceive the Internet. According to Pariser, many of them function as "prediction engines" (2011, 9), trying to automatically assess what we want to buy, find etc. As he argues, this could lead us into a "filter bubble" with "invisible autopropaganda, indoctrinating us with our own ideas, amplifying our desire for things that are familiar" (ibid, 15). From this point of view, the Internet is not bridging societies as McLuhan's metaphor of a "global village" would suggest, but rather separates us into "cyberbalkans" (van Alstyne and Brynjolfsson 1997; Putnam 2000, 177), whose information sources lack variety and diversity. This thought becomes even weightier when we consider research on the digital divide. This strand of research points to the socially unequal availability of ICT infrastructure and literacy for its effective use. At the same time, the new possibilities for user-generated content also open doors for political and economic surveillance.

Some even conclude "web 2.0 is largely a commercial, profit-oriented machine that exploits users by commodifying their personal data and usage behaviour" (Fuchs 2009).

Again, these rather dystopian perspectives go beyond academic discussions and are also part of the broader public discourse about the Internet. They can be found among the whole political spectrum, from conservatives fearing the new participatory liberty might lead to anarchic conditions, to left-wingers, criticizing the strong influence of governments and the private sector. Understandably, such views are not popular among the major Internet companies, but are shared by some startups, who try to establish themselves as ethically better alternatives to big players (e.g. Diaspora, a social network site that gives users more control over their data, or the search engine Ecosia that donates parts of its revenue to a rainforest project).

Although the web itself is very much a product of academia, it was always accompanied by skeptical voices. Even today print journals still seem to have more authority than e-journals and peer review systems which involve Web 2.0 technology are anything but common (see 3.3). At the same time, our case studies in chapter 2 show that popular Internet platforms from Wikipedia to Google, nevertheless significantly impact academia. Many scholars do not appreciate this interference and probably every academic can tell a story about bad practices of these technologies by students or colleagues. Brabazon criticizes in her book rooted in such experiences a "fetish for information" (2007, 12) with the effect that "[c]licking replaces thinking" (ibid., 16). Such concerns about a lack of scientific quality due to an overflow of (irrelevant) information are widespread and not without foundation (for a further discussion see 3.4). Some other issues brought up by dystopian thinkers can be found in discussions on the web's impact on academia: the commercial bias is considered problematic (e.g. Vaidhyanathan 2011); the idea of open science represented in social media is discounted as a distraction; scholars would not want to share their data and thoughts at an early stage. The hope that the new participatory opportunities will help to "democratize" academia, is also questioned (see 3.6).

3.1.2 Insiders and outsiders: methodological issues

Admittedly, our picture of utopians versus dystopians is over-simplified and a little exaggerated. Of course, the reality is not that black and white, and not all of the cited authors can be clearly categorized as one or the other. Moreover, we omit more balanced perspectives in this very pointed comparison. However, we do believe that there is indeed an overweight of literature which is either optimistically or pessimistically biased. One can easily find reasons for this. First, texts with bold statements sell better and often receive many citations. It is easy to refer to them and even if one completely disagrees, such statements come in handy to build up own arguments. At the same time, they provoke counter-arguments with contradictory conclusions. Thus, although one-sided literature might be imprecise, it significantly shapes debates. This is not necessarily a bad thing, since it helps to quickly identify major issues and points of view. But of course this does not happen in a vacuum. These debates are not only situated in socio-cultural realities, they also take part in *constructing* these realities. Well-known political controversies give an idea of how this can work: differences are constructed and fortified between left and right, communistic and capitalistic, conservative and progressive, etc. A similar picture can be observed in regard to the academic usage of the Internet: we find utopians and dystopians, proponents and opponents, enthusiasts and critics. In fact, the academic usage of the Internet is to a large extent politically loaded, since institutional decisions have to be made that affect the staff's daily work: Should academics and their institutions be active on social web platforms? Which infrastructure should be used? What are the "dos" and don'ts"? Should academics get institutional credit for activities such as academic blogging? Is it desirable to open peer review and other scholarly processes to a larger audience? Which content can be trusted, what can be cited? Answering these urgent questions requires persuasion. Decision-makers have to be convinced, decisions have to be justified and strong arguments can be helpful for these purposes, no matter from which perspective they come.

It goes without saying that this tendency to exaggerate hinders a realistic assessment. This is especially problematic as there is a lack of systematic and independent empirical studies which focus on the impact of emerging Internet platforms on scholarly communication. At the same time, the sheer number of platforms and the pace of new developments in this sector hardly allow to give a truly encompassing picture of the situation. Therefore, one often depends on information and data given by the providers themselves—simply because there is nothing else available. For obvious reasons, such material will often be biased to some extent: SNS try to create an image of active and large communities; wikis want to appear like effective working environments with high quality outcome, etc. Moreover, a lot of relevant information regarding the functionality of the platforms will never be fully accessible, simply because it contains well-protected corporate secrets. For example, although research from the field of information retrieval and SEO give us a vague picture of how Google's algorithms work, the exact functionality remains unknown. Corporate Web 2.0 platforms also give only limited insights into the activities of their members because this information is a main source of their income; furthermore they are obliged to protect certain user data.

This results in a situation of *insiders and outsiders*. Even for experts, many functionalities are "black boxed" and only fully understood by the developers themselves. Needless to say, average users know even less about what is going on behind the curtain of their interface and there is an obvious gap between users and non-users. The mixture of a lack of reliable information and the specific social situation of insiders and outsiders opens the door for politically motivated arguments, misunderstandings, ignorance and arrogance. Many academics who actively involve Web 2.0 platforms in their work are frustrated because "outsider" colleagues denounce their engagement as not professionally meaningful and a waste of time. As a defensive consequence they might overestimate the benefits of their activities while underplaying related issues. At the same time, outsiders might be blind to the actual advantages of these activities.

We observed such contradictory approaches throughout all our case studies: students forced to contribute to Wikipedia, while others are forbidden to use it; academics praising their Second Life efforts which do not lead to any significant results, while others completely denounce the platform as a mere game; scientists virtually getting lost between their countless SNS representations or Twitter messages (see also 3.4), while others do not even want to try any of these services; scholars one-sidedly relying on information provided by Google, while others still consult a library for knowledge that could be retrieved more quickly and easily through a search engine.

The very divergent practices can be taken as an indicator for missing institutionalization of academic usage of the analyzed platforms. Although best practice guides and similar conventions exist for certain institutions and areas, the general handling of them is still extremely unregulated. This partly explains the formation of utopian and dystopian components. While the former try to establish their engagement as an accepted scholarly activity, the latter hold on to well-known approved practices. In case of doubt, institutions and individual scientists have to decide whether and how platforms should be used for their purposes. This can be highly controversial because such decisions touch scholars' and students' work routines and lead to larger political questions: the usage of platforms can be forbidden or enforced, staff might have to accept questionable terms of use, etc.

All this can easily cause politically heated debates between proponents and opponents, whereas it hinders a clear vision on the factual opportunities and risks of the emerging platforms for scholarly communication. The pressing question is: How can we overcome the barriers between these utopian and dystopian perspectives?

3.1.3 Overcoming the barriers between utopians and dystopians

It should be obvious by now that we neither favor utopian nor dystopian perspectives, as each of them is one-sided and biased. As we outlined above, possible reasons for their diverging judgments might be economic and political influences and a lack of systematic independent empirical studies. Since the distinct feature of Web 2.0 is the users' possibility to participate, *interactivity* has to be seen as a crucial category for assessing its impact. Looking not only at the theoretical potential of the emerging platforms but also on the actual user practices avoids techno-determinism and reveals what is factually happening—beyond hypothetical fears and hypes. Our case studies show first of all that utopian and dystopian perspectives are both right *and* wrong. Depending on what exactly is emphasized, one can reach very different conclusions. Given the strongly varying levels of interactivity, this is understandable. This can be illustrated using the example of the Wikimedia projects: The mother project, Wikipedia, is maintained and expanded by a large and active community, resulting in the world's most extensive encyclopedia and a vast bulk of related interactions between its members. Correspondingly, one can indeed find remarkable manifestations of this high interactivity. Some of them support hopes expressed by utopians, some rather remind us of dystopian concerns. There are excellent articles as well as poorly conceived so-called "stubs"; effective co-operations as well as vandalism and so-called "edit wars"; people greatly benefiting from the free and easily accessible knowledge as well as those who too trustfully rely on it or misuse it for plagiarism. Therefore, the reactions from society and academia towards the encyclopedia are equally diverse. Such a clear judgment can hardly be delivered for the sister projects Wikibooks and Wikiversity because their levels of interactivity are much lower. Although the technological architecture is almost identical, these platforms have attracted far fewer active participants, produced much less content and achieved relatively little impact. Here the crowd is neither wise nor "Maoist", simply because there is no crowd. No matter how "good" or "bad" possible consequences could be, the overall impact is just rather low. Thus, neither utopian hopes nor dystopian fears really come true, at least so far.

Although Web 2.0 platforms are crucially shaped by interactivity, we must not forget that users normally browse through them individually. Thus, experiences also differ largely from user to user. As noted above, an "outsider" with only few "followers" or "friends" will hardly recognize the full (positive as well as negative) potential of Twitter et al. But it is not only the individual social networks that frame this experience. As we stress in the subtitle of our book, these networks are *digital*, meaning they are intermediated with specific hard- and software (see 1.2.2 for a further clarification of this term). Evidently, this generally structures the user's perception as we discussed throughout our case studies. But this process can also differ largely from user to user. In recent years, we can observe a trend to track user behavior to create an indicator for relevance (Pariser 2011). This was mainly initiated by Google's web search, which capitalized on hyperlinks by interpreting them as a sort of recommendation for a web page (see 2.5). The advantage here is that it can be done automatically with the help of an algorithm weighing the different factors from case to case. In this way, Google was able to bring some order into the exponentially growing number of websites in the early web era. Today, the heavy usage of Web 2.0 produces vast amount of data which can be utilized to create additional indicators for relevance. Facebook's "like" button or Google's "+1" and rating systems from YouTube to Amazon are the most obvious examples. Beneath the surface of the user interface, all kinds of user-generated data is collected and analyzed, e.g. which websites are visited and which keywords are entered. Consequently, users shape their own web experience. However, this is performed by sophisticated algorithms, which mostly do their work unnoticed by the average user.[115]

---

115 See also the related discussion on "implicit participation" (Schäfer 2011) in 3.2.3.

This means that it is not only user-to-user interactivity we must regard as a crucial category, but also interactivity between humans and machines. In particular, we need to focus on this wherever algorithms significantly determine the user's experience. This is less prominent in the case of platforms such as Wikipedia, but search engines and social network sites increasingly apply algorithms which individually and automatized select what a user will see and how. Combined with the strong influence of personal networks and individual choices of how to use services, it is hardly possible to give an overall reply to the question of how web platforms impact scholars and other Internet users. From this point of view, it is not surprising that generalizing approaches such as the dystopian and utopian perspectives discussed above come to contradictory conclusions.

Nevertheless, our case studies reveal a number of tendencies which we will further discuss in the reminder of chapter 3. We base our assessment on our case studies which tried to avoid one-sided perspectives. Instead, we unemotionally studied the theoretical potential and the actual practices of scholars and other users of the analyzed platforms. This is probably less entertaining than utopian or dystopian approaches, but we hope it provides an assessment which is more down-to-earth.

3.2 New Windows in the Ivory Tower

Scholarly communication always had two sides: an *internal* one relating to what scholars communicate among themselves with a view to organizing collaboration and discussing scientific results; and an *external* side regarding the exchange of researchers with journalists and the wider public focusing on the presentation of scientific results. The line between these two types of communication certainly differs according to thematic fields as well as regions. While this line could be drawn quite clearly until recently—mainly by focusing on the communication partners involved and the publisher—, this is not the case any more in the digital era. Already a decade ago one of us observed that the Internet creates a new interface between the world of science and the public (Nentwich 2003, 458). Although evidently large parts of academia are still more or less strictly closed for outsiders (e.g. traditional peer review and job positions), the boundary between internal and external scholarly communication is increasingly blurred: Scholars write directly for the wider public, hence bypassing the traditional media; journalists and the interested public make use of the easier access to research results, sometimes including even primary data, and thereby bypass the interpretation by the researchers. There are various novel channels offered by the Web 2.0 that may be used by academia to reach the wider public as discussed throughout chapter 2 (cf. Nentwich 2010a): Microblogging is a qualitatively new communication channel already used frequently by many scholarly institutions and individual researchers. Science is presented in the encyclopedia Wikipedia, which is one of the most popular websites. Academic institutions may be present in virtual worlds, which can be visited by the general public (although this trend seems apparently declining). General search engines are important gatekeepers to scholarly information and they crucially shape it by their algorithmic selection and rankings. Therefore the way science and research is presented and interlinked with other websites is paramount for its perception by the general public. Science blogging is another tool to reach the wider public with research-related issues. Potentially, novel forms of open peer review may be used to include new bodies of knowledge, i.e. lay expertise, such as knowledge from practical experience—this is what Funtowicz and Ravetz (1992) call extended peer review (see 3.3). In addition, scientific content on social network sites is largely accessible for the general public—including interactive elements such as comments. Finally, also social bookmarking platforms may shed public light on inner-academic selection and rating processes among countless other emerging social media platforms.

Starting from these empirical observations we will first introduce the phenomenon from a broader perspective, and then discuss how the transformation of media formats and social roles contributes to this process of blurring. Finally, we address the concrete impact of these public windows to the formerly isolated ivory tower of academia.

3.2.1 Bringing together the academic and the public sphere

Over recent decades science has increasingly become intertwined with other social systems. This trend has resulted in mutual reactions which have been depicted as a *scientification of society* on the one hand and a *politicization of science* on the other hand (Weingart 2001, 1983). Other scholars denoted this trend by speaking of a *university-industry-government triple helix* (Etzkowitz and Leydesdorff 1997) and still others addressed the increasing convergence of so called "pure" basic science and application- or profit-driven technological innovation under the label *technoscience* (for a discussion of this term, see Forman 2007).

The thesis of a scientification of society points at an ever increasing dependence of modern societies on scientific data, insights and experts. The thereby increasing relevance of science for political decisions has led to a partial politicization of science, opening scientific research processes and scholarly discourse to political dynamics, non-scientific actors and societal interests (see Böschen et al. 2010 for an illustrative case study). At the same time, the overall pressure on science to respond to societal problem situations and economic interests has increased significantly. Scientific results are no more measured by their objectivity and truthfulness alone, they need to be applicable and powerful, a source of national competitiveness and wealth. In times of severe funding cuts and readjustments of funding schemes, researchers have to pro-actively prove the benefits their work offers to society. Widely-accepted quantitative evaluation techniques (e.g. citation indices, university rankings) seem to enable even outsiders without expertise to assess the quality of academic institutions and individuals to a certain degree. Correspondingly, Weingart concludes years before the term Web 2.0 came up:

"The 'distance' between science and the public has narrowed. The participation of the 'many' constitutes the parameters to which knowledge-production has to be orientated. The originally luxurious and relatively isolated habitat of science, the ivory tower, has become smaller, and the need to adapt has increased. This is, in large measure, exacerbated by the new role of the media." (Weingart 1997, 607)

As Weingart further points out, the mass media significantly shape public opinion, thereby affecting academia, too. As our case studies suggest, we should not only consider traditional media but add the Internet as an important arena for public opinion shaping. Unlike traditional media, its architecture allows much more and qualitatively different direct communication (as described in our case studies) between the public, academic institutions and individual researchers. Hence, the overall tendency of blurring the boundaries between academia and the public is not entirely new, but the result of a longer development that has started before the advent of Web 2.0. Internet-based technologies are not its direct cause, but their popularity may partly be explained by their fit to this overall tendency, which, in turn, they speed up to some degree. Four major technological aspects are responsible for this:

Access to individual researchers and academic institutions: While most researchers have been publicly accessible even in the pre-Internet age—everybody could have found out their contact data to approach them—the effort to do so was much higher then, and so were the obstacles for direct communication between researchers and the public. Today, a simple query in a universal search engine is often enough to retrieve contact data and other information about a researcher. E-mail has become a standard communication tool, giving fast and direct access to practically every individual in academia. Those who are active in Web 2.0 platforms provide additional channels for communication and information about themselves and their work. SNS and microblogging services even give insights into the researchers' personal networks. In addition, the informal and short communication style lowers the barrier to get in touch with an individual. Similarly, academic institutions are more and more easily accessible online not only through ordinary websites, but also via more interactive technologies such as (micro-)blogs, SNS and even virtual world representations. All this allows the public to interact much more easily and directly with researchers and their institutions.

Access to the public as research object: Researchers have new opportunities to reach the public directly for the purpose of their own research. This is particularly interesting for social scientists or psychologists, who may contact members of the public easily, for instance via online questionnaires or in experimental ways as observed in Second Life (2.4.3). Moreover, the digital traces left by individuals who interact in the web are increasingly used as raw material in the emerging fields of Internet Research and Digital Humanities.

Access to knowledge: As with access to individual researchers and academic institutions, the Internet also enables the public to retrieve scholarly knowledge. Apart from all kinds of scientific websites and databases, the trend towards open access publications is an obvious example. It lately includes a tendency to publish primary data and data processing software along with scientific papers in journals.[116] Emerging Web 2.0 platforms may even give direct insights into the process of knowledge production. (Micro-)blogging researchers, for example, write about what they read, write and think; some use this channel as an opportunity to pre-test ideas

---

116 For instance, Molecular Systems Biology, published by the Nature Publishing Group, provides structured data files, enabling further research without having direct access to lab facilities. On the idea of "open science" see Gassmann et al. (2011).

and get feedback, which is not limited to their peers, but may also include lay people. Our case studies show a number of examples of such practices of making knowledge publicly available: university libraries opening their doors for Google Books; journals and other scholarly institutions publishing content on Wikimedia projects; researchers "tweeting" live from conferences; novel ways of publicly presenting scientific knowledge in virtual worlds. Tools such as Google Scholar may provide access to free alternative versions of restricted articles; and its citation analysis gives an idea of its relevance, independently of the expensive commercial service of Thomson Reuters' ISI databases.

Participation: As usually associated with the label "Web 2.0", the public is offered completely novel ways to contribute even at the level of producing and processing academic knowledge. This may come in form of feedback to content distributed through (micro-)blogging or even by opening peer review to the public (see 3.3). Interestingly, this is not necessarily a top-down process and does not depend on initiatives from academia itself: even lay people can set up platforms that might be relevant to scholarly activities, illustrated by the case of the GuttenPlag Wiki, in which users collect potentially plagiaristic text modules (see 3.3.3). In the Wikimedia projects, the production process is formally independent from predefined roles, so one can hardly draw a line between the public sphere and academia. In this case, scholars are not able to retreat into their ivory tower, no matter whether they like it or not. Hyperlink-based search engines, such as Google, are another example, since their ranking mechanisms are not bound to scientific expertise or peer-review: the links that are at the core of Google's algorithms are not set by experts alone, and obviously, the popularity of an Internet resource does not rest solely on expertise. In such contexts, lay and expert bodies of knowledge compete directly, giving the public new possibilities to participate in the course of content production.

To sum up, the Internet, and the Web 2.0 in particular, contribute to reinforce an overall trend of blurring the previously clearer boundaries between the academic and public spheres by offering a number of additional channels or "windows" between them.

3.2.2 Blurring media formats

In addition to the "more windows" argument, the specific medial structure of the Internet apparently supports this boundary blurring process by approximating and blending formerly distinct media formats. Media theorists refer to this phenomenon as *convergence*. In a broader sense it describes how previously separated infrastructures merge, e.g. mobile and fixed-line telephony or radio and TV on the Internet. Media convergence in particular describes how different media are connected. This is an everyday practice on the modern Internet: the key technology "hyperlink" facilitates the simple and quick connection of different formats. Books may be published electronically as PDF, more or less copying its original format, but they can also be combined with audio, video or other digitally processable data. At the same time, this enables de- and re-contextualizing media content. With Google Books, for instance, specific book sections become directly linkable. Thus, they can not only be copied and pasted, but, also appear in different formats such as blogs. In addition, the application programming interfaces (APIs) render automated connections of different platforms possible, for example by integrating Twitter messages into websites. In this way, it becomes not only increasingly difficult to identify original sources, but at the same time, the contexts in which the knowledge can be presented diversify because it is distributed through multiple channels (see 3.4 for an analysis of this particular phenomenon and its impact). In the age of cyberscience 2.0, a sentence may be taken from a book excerpt at Google Books, quoted in a blog, tweeted and re-tweeted, shared and "liked" in a SNS, and retrieved as a hyperlink in search engine results.

This tendency of re-contextualization has been discussed in particular with a focus on the creative industries, where so-called *mash-ups* recombine different media sources into a more or less new product, which has caused legal controversies regarding intellectual property rights (Lessig 2006, 194 ff.). Although scientific quality standards actually exclude such creative handling of sources, this phenomenon can be found in the context of cyberscience 2.0 as well: for instance, the Wikimedia Foundation constantly fears that copyrighted content may be published on its sites and at the same time teachers complain about students copying their homework from Wikipedia articles. While there are negative examples such as plagiarism and copyright infringements, "cognitive mash-up"—creatively taking over and processing of other people's thoughts—may be considered a standard procedure in academic work. Digital social networks speed up, multiply and intensify this process, as cyberscientists 2.0 continually have to make sense of the diverse information bits and contexts they are exposed to. Arguably, this comes with the inherent risk of an information overload and researchers might easily fail to use it in a productive way (see 3.4). In any case, ideas can quickly spread and be transformed, without respecting the theoretical boundaries between "inner" (or "esoteric") and "outer" (or "exoteric") scientific communication. The new windows in the ivory tower do not only enable glimpses in and out, but they are often wide-open, consequently allowing ideas and thoughts to circulate in both directions.

For illustration, we imagine a standard work process of typical cyberscientists 2.0 embedded in digital social networks. To get a brief introduction to a new topic, they might use a search engine which will eventually lead them to a Wikipedia article written by lay people as well as academic experts. From their professional point of view, they will start to dig deeper into the topic, sort relevant and irrelevant, better and worse sources, connect ideas and eventually develop new ones. They might consult diffuse audiences of SNS, microblogs, forums and other Web 2.0 platforms in order to gain a deeper understanding of the topic. As soon as they have elaborated their own thoughts, they may post them on their blog, where they can get feedback from an even more diffuse and public audience. In a next step, a regular journal publication may follow, which involves perhaps the public in a novel peer review mechanism (see also 3.3). Finally, their insights could be used for improving the Wikipedia article which helped our model researchers in the first place.

Our empirical insights show clearly that such a highly interactive usage is far from being the norm. Many researchers do not use these services to this extent and stick to their traditional channels, which mostly exclude public participation. Large parts of the ivory tower still lack open windows, especially when it comes to competitive fields which have to protect their results to a certain degree. Still, the scenario described above is not unrealistic. When we did our empirical research for our case studies in this project, we have actually made similar experiences. Especially when processing abstract thoughts in a cyberscience 2.0 environment of diversified open media channels, it is hardly possible to draw a line between public and academic inputs. In any case, even non-cyberscientists are affected by this development because not only the media formats have become unclear but also certain social roles associated with them, which we will discuss in the next section.

3.2.3 Blurring roles

As early as a decade ago, one of us concluded that the distribution of roles in academia is changing considerably in the age of the Internet (Nentwich 2003, 235ff.); in particular, we predicted that the notion of authorship blurs in a hypertext publishing environment (ibid, 293ff.) and that the readers become empowered co-authors (ibid., 301ff.) or "wreaders". This trend is obviously reinforced in the age of digital social networks. As mentioned earlier, new terms, such as "produser" or "prodsumer", have emerged to conceptualize the transformation of formerly more or less distinct social roles. Active Wikipedians for example, are often editors, readers, reviewers and authors all at once. This also applies to SNS, where users usually write, consume and comment almost simultaneously. Moreover, users might also contribute actively, without being aware of it, which blurs formerly clear roles even further and creates new ones. Schäfer suggests differentiating between explicit and *implicit participation* to depict this phenomenon:

"Implicit participation is channeled by design, by means of easy-to-use interfaces, and the automation of user activity processes. In contrast to explicit participation, it does not necessarily require a conscious activity of cultural production, nor does it require users to choose from different methods in problem-solving, collaboration, and communication with others. Rather it is a design solution that takes advantage of certain habits users have. Users are not required to interact in social networks, nor is there a need for common objectives or shared values in order to use platforms that employ implicit participation. Such platforms provide the means for certain user activities and benefit from the user-generated content. The user activities performed on these web platforms contribute to the system-wide information management and can be exploited for different purposes, such as improving information retrieval, or gathering user information for market research." (Schäfer 2011, 51)

Especially Google has capitalized on this type of participation, since it offers a wide range of services, which allow for the collection and combination of different kinds of data. Searchers do not only passively retrieve knowledge from its services, they also take part in constructing them, since their behavior is systematically tracked and utilized for the development of the underlying technology. Here, the user automatically produces *qua* usage, no matter if intended or not. This form of implicit participation is not only hidden to average users, it also happens automatically by means of algorithms whose functional principles are largely unknown. Thus, users may become "silent producers", that is without knowing that they are producing and what exactly their product is.

This blurring of roles conflicts with academia, where they are normally clearly separated and often hierarchically organized. Usually, roles such as teacher, student, assistant, leader, author, reviewer or editor can be unambiguously identified in a given context. Correspondingly, the gateways of social inclusion are also more or less clearly defined. In pre-Internet times they could be well governed. For example, researchers who wanted to become authors are forced to get their work approved by reviewers before it gets published. With today's multiplied and diversified channels it is easy to bypass this barrier by choosing less restricted or openly available paths, directly addressing a wider audience.

No doubt, this is not entirely new as we can learn from a historic case, the World Ice Theory (Wessely 2007). At the end of the 19th century, the Austrian engineer Hanns Hörbiger came up with this theory, which basically claimed that most planets consisted of ice. After his theory had been rejected as pseudoscience by the relevant scientific experts in the field, he turned to the public as his main audience. He was remarkably successful and gained thousands of active supporters. During the Third Reich, the World Ice Theory even received the status of an officially accepted "scientific" theory because a number of influential Nazi politicians supported it.

Although the mechanism of bypassing peer review and directly addressing the public is not new, it has become much easier to use today. Consequently, there is a vast amount of pseudoscientific content on the web— which comes as no surprise. However, the label of "pseudoscience" cannot always be applied so clearly, precisely because of the blurring of formats and roles today. For instance, the *Journal for 9/11 Studies* suggests in numerous articles that New York's World Trade Center was brought down by a controlled demolition and not by the planes that hit it; the journal claims to rely on evidence-based research checked by peer review (cf. König 2009a, 2011). In our context, a pressing question arises: What constitutes a scientific journal and its peer reviewers? This "journal" might be easily discounted as a mere website with PDFs and a closed circle of reviewers, editors and authors, who support each other. But when this hypothesis is suggested with respect to an article in *The Open Chemical Physics Journal*, edited by renowned scholars at the time of its appearance, the case is less clear (Harrit et al. 2009). An observer refers to the journal as an example of fringe science, where people "publish their theories, theses, and ideas that are out of the mainstream" (Beall 2009, 30), but the editors of the *Journal of 9/11 Studies* refer to the former journal as "mainstream" and as an example of "more established journals in which scientists might more readily place their trust" (Journal of 9/11 Studies 2011). Although many colleagues will probably agree with Beall's assessment, lay people might lack the professional experience for such a judgment. Indeed, the article in case was cited and praised as scientific on countless non-academic websites. Apparently, significant parts of the public trusted the journal. Scientists may ignore such publications, but the direct channel to the public in combination with an unclear assessment of what constitutes a trusted source helps articles to gain relevance independently of scientific institutions. As prominently established by the Thomas theorem, situations do not have to be real to have real consequences. This applies in particular to the age of digital social networks, where the pace of information is much faster than the pace of quality control.

The functional logic of the big Internet players we analyzed in our case studies reinforces this point. As most Web 2.0 platforms and universal search engines are not designed specifically for academic purposes, they usually do not differentiate between the inner scientific and the public sphere. Even if this were intended, developing a mechanism for this purpose is a very challenging task. Google Scholar indicates the difficulties at hand. As discussed in 2.5, its "relevance indicators" do not always work well and despite its scholarly focus one can find a lot of non-academic literature there as well. Obviously, the criteria for being included in this database are not very demanding—with the effect that there is no definite boundary between the scientific and the public spheres. Still, it seems at least possible to separate between academic and non-academic sources, for example by including only authors who publish in defined journals. But it becomes even more complicated, when we wish to consider other factors that are used to determine relevance, especially the trend of analyzing implicit participation. Platforms such as Google Scholar are open and the developers presumably do not differentiate between academic and non-academic users when their implicit participation is tracked, so these mechanisms are simply blind to academia's criteria for exclusion and inclusion. In the traditional ivory tower, it makes a difference whether critique came from a renowned colleague or from an unknown student. By contrast, the algorithms in the age of cyberscience 2.0 do not differentiate in this respect. It does not matter whether professors or students "like", share, "tweet", cite or hyperlink items. For sure, some sources may be treated differently, e.g. when Google's PageRank weighs links from well-networked websites heavier than links from less networked ones. However, the links themselves are not in any respect bound to scholarly reputation. Even in Google Scholar, where citations are used as an indicator for relevance, the low barrier for inclusion allows items to receive citations from all kinds of sources (unlike e.g. ISI, where only established sources are counted in the citation index). In many Web 2.0 platforms, the confusion of roles has even become a sort of ideology, for example in the Wikimedia projects, where supposedly every reader should be able to become an editor, too. In a nutshell, the platforms of cyberscience 2.0 do not care about academia's differentiation of roles.

3.2.4 Bridging the boundaries?

What larger impact will the described blurring of formats and roles have? In the first place, the age of digital social networks has created numerous windows to the proverbial ivory tower. They provide new opportunities for mutual exchange, give the public novel insights into academia and allow researchers to interact with public audiences in new ways.

A decade ago one of us has put forward the hypothesis that as soon as the researchers become aware of this additional public outside academia, this "may change the way the results are presented and worded and may eventually feed back on the type of research being conducted in the first place" (Nentwich 2003, 458). There is no doubt that the majority of researchers is now aware of the "world outside academia" and some have begun to interact more or less intensively with it. The novel windows may be considered a possible "feedback-channel" from the public to science (Nentwich 2010a). Günther (2009) calls the potential long-term result the "Internet-public networked academia" (our translation): academics may perceive an informal, but growing incentive to pay attention to the new communication channels. Academia may react to the feedback from outside, for instance by addressing questions put to it. The case of the alternative interpretations of the World Trade Center collapse (see above) could be taken as an example. In the first scientific report conducted by the National Institute for Standards and Technology (NIST) on the Twin Towers, the controlled demolition hypothesis was not tested, which led to a lot of public criticism. Later, when another study on the collapse of Building 7 (a third building which collapsed on September 11, 2001) was designed, the controlled demolition hypothesis was included (cf. König 2009a; NIST 2008). One might conclude that the public significantly shaped research in this case.

A further mechanism by which the blurring of boundaries may impact on research content might be the active and systematic inclusion of public feedback in research by means of novel participatory procedures. More speculative would be what we called earlier the "shadow of the format" (Nentwich 2003, 453ff.)—the hypothesis that the communication format chosen to report the results influences the preceding research process. If research results were regularly blogged, this public format might have, perhaps unconsciously, an impact on how the research is conducted and which questions are addressed. In summary, while we would uphold this strong hypothesis, it is perhaps too early to address it empirically.

The metaphor of the windows in the ivory tower, however, falls short of helping us to fully understand the multiple consequences of the development, unless we add actors to the picture. We observe researchers who try to close the windows again, while others open them as wide as possible and enter and leave by them. Some researchers may ignore public approaches through the new channels and stick to their established routines; others go to the other extreme and bypass traditional channels in order to reach the public directly. Sometimes there is and will be a fruitful and enlightening dialogue between the two parties, at other times scientific quality might be at risk because of public interference. In other cases, scientists may be forcefully drawn out of the ivory tower, for example when fraud is exposed publicly. On the one hand, this development can be seen as liberating and democratizing (see 3.6), on the other hand, it leads to new challenges of handling the emerging channels (see 3.4). As suggested in 3.1, it is hardly possible to provide black and white answers here because the impact happens in so many different ways. For example, the new technologies could be regarded as promoting plagiarism by allowing for quick and easy "copying and pasting". But at the same time, they render the detection of plagiarism much simpler. Furthermore, on the one hand, the additional channels contribute to more transparency, but on the other, they may create new inefficiencies by merging relevant and irrelevant information.

We come to the conclusion that the last decades' process of bringing together the public and academic spheres has been accelerated by cyberscience 2.0. The latest developments have created transparent windows rather than just one-way spyholes in the ivory tower. It would be exaggerated, however, to claim that real bridges between the two spheres have been built as yet. Despite the new connections, the major scientific institutions and social mechanisms are still at work and usually they differentiate very clearly between the public and the academic realm: Researchers can still only receive a job offer if they have undergone academic education and have been successfully evaluated by submitting to the traditional academic publishing system, including book publishers and journals that have hardly changed since the advent of the Internet. While the traditional systems are still in place, the public success of the emerging platforms and their fundamentally different functional logic have initiated dynamics that cannot be ignored.

3.3 Academic Quality and Digital Social Networks

The development towards cyberscience 2.0 poses a number of challenges but also opportunities for academic quality control. In this chapter we shall reflect on the trends emerging from early cyberscience a decade ago and discuss new trends we observed in our case studies. Finally, we shall address issues regarding incentives for quality control and missing mechanisms for crediting achievements in this context.

3.3.1 Recent developments in academic quality control

When cyberscience emerged a decade ago, a number of potentially fundamental changes regarding academic quality control were identified (Nentwich 2003, 367 ff.; 2005b; Nentwich and König 2010). A main assumption was that the digital structure helps to overcome restraints resulting from the physical shape of printed publications. Indeed, not only the number of publications is increasing constantly (however only partly due to new technologies), but we can also find publishing channels that would have been unlikely to emerge in the printed era. For example, until the end of the twentieth century a lack of publication possibilities for negative results in medicine was pointed out (Varmus and others 1999). In addition to the usually presented positive results this seemed desirable, because failed experiments or studies can provide inter alia valuable methodological insights. As e-journals lower the costs considerably, this knowledge gap has been closed with the *Journal of Negative Results in Biomedicine*. Also journals on the margin of science or beyond emerged (such as the *Journal of 9/11 Studies*, see 3.2.3). Additionally, cyberscience 2.0 provides countless other channels for distributing and communicating scientific information, as we have shown in our case studies.

On the one hand, this development has been embraced as an opportunity to enhance academic quality by distributing more potentially relevant information at a faster pace. On the other hand, lowering publication hurdles raises quality concerns. Information overload is an immanent risk for researchers who are exposed to the vast amount of publications and other communication (3.4). The traditional system of academic quality control has been challenged by this development. Some journals have reacted with innovative forms of *ex ante* quality control. For instance, in *open peer review* procedures manuscripts are uploaded to preprint servers, allowing for more or less public commenting prior to the actual publication. The review process is more transparent in this model, as the identities of the reviewers are not anonymous. However, this is a double-edged sword since known reviewers may fear resentment from their colleagues. Therefore, other models that combine old and new forms have been tried out. For example, some journals apply a conventional anonymous peer review process followed by another stage of open commentary (Pöschl 2009, 2007).

The digital form and its online accessibility also allows for novel forms of *ex post* quality control. Potentially "wrong" or outdated versions can be removed or marked correspondingly and publications can be continually commented. Rating/scoring systems (similar to those applied by Amazon, but more sophisticated systems are conceivable) may be used to determine the quality of an article, as well as novel forms of citation and traffic analysis. Some journals experiment with revolutionary concepts: For example, *Philica* lets authors from all disciplines publish their ideas instantly and leaves the peer review basically open to anybody who would like to comment afterwards. It was founded by "two British psychologists who had grown dissatisfied with traditional academic journal publishing" (Philica 2011). This idea points to the problem that the circulation of information is hindered by peer review because of delaying or rejecting publication. Research on academia's quality control system has a long tradition in which such pitfalls were spelled out, often indicating biases and other issues leading to unjustified rejections (Zuckerman and Merton 1971; Fröhlich 2003;

Fischer 2004; Cole et al. 1981). Some regard novel online-driven quality control models as partial solutions to these problems (Fröhlich 2009; Pöschl 2007, 2004). However, they also pose new challenges and many open questions remain. Quality control also fulfills a crucial social function by certifying information as trustworthy (cf. Weingart 2001, 285). Many of the new experimental forms of peer review still have to earn this status and arguably radical models such as Philica will hardly be able to do so. Keeping this in mind, the openness of such formats can also be taken as a disadvantage as it does not substantially contribute to one of the core functions of academic quality control—information certification.

Apart from these journal-related institutionalized forms of peer review, academic quality, the lack of it and novel mechanisms to control it have been major issues in our case studies. The unclear status of quality control may be regarded as a major factor hindering the emergence of cyberscience 2.0. Our analysis below shows that there are indeed quality control mechanisms at work, despite difficulties to determine what constitutes a "publication" in the Web 2.0 context and whether a peer review process should be considered ex ante or ex post, as both steps often blur in digital social networks. Nonetheless, for analytical reasons we will discuss quality control along this differentiation.

3.3.2 Ex ante quality control for or through digital social networks?

A frequent argument voiced against the content communicated in digital social networks is its questionable quality. How do we know whether a (micro-)blog contribution or a Wikipedia article is trustworthy? This question has been a key issue with regard to social media as an alternative to traditional mass media, but obviously these concerns are also relevant to scholarly communication. Of course, using such content in the same way as a peer-reviewed journal article would be problematic in many cases. It might be valuable content but it is simply not certified like a traditional article and hence less trustworthy. This weakens its scholarly attractiveness, especially because it can hardly be used as a legitimate source. Nonetheless, these resources are frequently used, which leads to those controversies around quality, which we observed throughout our case studies: On the one hand, some teachers or universities ban their students from using Wikipedia or criticize them when they chose Google to retrieve scientific sources; on the other hand, others argue in favor of a reassessment of the

new platforms (see also 3.1 for a more detailed analysis of such contradictory positions).

Arguably this is mainly an issue of literacy. It is not per se problematic
to use Wikipedia articles, status updates, tweets or Google queries for academic purposes. The real question is what specific roles these practices
play in the research process. If a Wikipedia article is supposed to replace a
comprehensive literature study and if a simple Google query is meant to
list all relevant academic publications, it is indeed worrying for scholarship.
But if a Wikipedia article is merely used as a brief introduction to a new
field and if Google is consulted to find additional information outside the
narrow scope of specialized academic search engines, this seems hardly
problematic. In fact, such practices can even enhance academic quality as
they allow researchers to save time which can be invested in other stages of
their work. Whether researchers manage to use digital social networks
effectively largely depends on their digital literacy. This is not really a new
problem since research methodology has always been crucial for scholarship. Results of traditional inquiries can be as easily misinterpreted as
Google results, status updates or Wikipedia articles.

A crucial problem seems to be that literacy for the new platforms has
yet to be developed. This is particularly difficult for three reasons:

- *Dynamics:* The market for web platforms is extremely dynamic. New
  ones emerge continually and others disappear. Many platforms grow
  epidemically before a deeper understanding of their functionality could
  have been gained. Often they are released as unready "beta" versions
  and even the developers need to learn about their functionality "in the
  field". In such cases users act as involuntary testers. This also goes for
  many "older" established platforms such as Google Web Search,
  which is also continually modified. In addition, the platforms are also
  subject to social dynamics, which are often even harder to understand
  and cope with.

- *Opacity:* Since even the developers need to learn about their products,
  they usually remain "black boxes" to lay users. Mostly technical details
  are protected and therefore even advanced users and experts from
  outside the developer team can hardly obtain a clear picture of the inner workings. Similarly, many social processes within the platforms
  cannot be studied because access is restricted. There are exceptions,
  such as the fairly transparent Wikimedia projects. However, many
  questions regarding the impact of such platforms remain unanswered

because of their novelty. Moreover, the functional logic is often fundamentally different and requires completely new forms of literacy.

- *Role reversal:* Without overstressing the picture of "digital natives", we may assume that in many cases younger tech-savvy researchers at the beginning of their careers have gained a more sophisticated literacy for the new platforms than their older and established colleagues. Academia's hierarchical structure will often hinder a role reversal in which the younger teach the older. Instead, reactions such as a rigorous ban of Wikipedia could be read as a defense mechanism to maintain status hierarchies.

Since we are obviously still at an early stage of a long transformation process, ways of dealing with the new development are emerging but slowly. A specific literacy for the academic usage of digital social networks is part of this. It seems reasonable to assume that many of the widely-perceived quality issues will be resolved as academics learn how to apply the new platforms effectively. A possible way of doing this is to regard digital social networks not as publication contexts with a lack of quality control but instead to consider them as tools *for* quality control *prior* to publication. Used carefully, they can play a valuable role during the different stages of academic activities—from knowledge production, to communication and distribution. Vague ideas might be posted and discussed with colleagues and useful information might be gathered through the multiple new channels.

However, this requires a deeper understanding of the new technologies. Without such understanding researchers are likely to suffer from an information overload of irrelevant sources, which hinders their work (3.4). We need to give differentiated answers regarding who actually can profit from the new platforms and which social changes they may trigger inside academia (3.6). It also largely depends on the individual interactive possibilities, namely which digital social networks a researcher can build on (3.1). They can work as a social filter and in that sense as a form of quality control. We may, for example, only pay attention to certain actors whom we trust.

Another increasingly important form of quality control in digital social networks is executed automatically: software determines the structure in which information can be distributed and communicated. It regulates user behavior and forces them to accept certain limitations. Word limits are a common example that is not only applied by microblogging platforms,

SNS and the like, but also in many academic submission processes. Many journals already use web-based forms which make it impossible to exceed a predefined number of words in an abstract. Such practices will probably become more sophisticated with new technological developments. In the future, our article submissions might be even prescreened to identify plagiarism and linguistic mistakes.

3.3.3 Ex post quality control in digital social networks

As mentioned above, it is difficult to draw a clear line between *ex ante* and *ex post* quality control in digital social networks. Wikipedia and its related projects are good examples to examine this blurred boundary: In most cases users can create and edit articles freely and the outcome is visible to others immediately. In that sense, they are "published" in that very moment—but in heavily disputed issue areas these contributions might only last for a couple of minutes until they are undone by other users. Additionally, templates can be added to mark the questionable quality status of an article. In 2008 the German Wikipedia established the system of *sighting* in which trusted and experienced users check edits before they become public. Still, the unsighted version can be accessed but only through the page history and not directly in form of the actual current article. It is thus a matter of opinion whether such an article is considered as "published" or not. Again it is a matter of literacy how adequately the quality status of an article is assessed. Templates indicating the status might be helpful to a certain degree but in fact it takes profound knowledge about Wikipedia's system of quality control to get a realistic picture of an article's status. To use the example from above, sighting should not be mistaken as a form of thorough editorial quality control as it mainly aims at preventing vandalism. At the same time, content which was not checked by the Wikipedia community may have undergone serious peer review at an earlier stage. The journal RNA Biology, which publishes sections of its articles in Wikipedia, can be taken as an example (2.3.3).

This also shows that in digital social networks "ex post" is an ongoing process rather than a closed status. This is obvious in the case of wikis since the permanent opportunity to edit is a core idea of these platforms. But also status updates, tweets, blog posts etc. can be revised continuously, either by editing the content itself and creating new versions or by commenting it. In contrast to traditional ex post quality control this can be done in the direct context of the reviewed content. With hyperlinks it is even possible to refer to longer statements and related articles published elsewhere.

Given this procedural character, we could also describe the peer review in digital social networks as *continuous or accompanying quality control*. Together with the ex-ante mechanisms described above, the whole writing process can be accompanied by reviewers. For example, G. Andrews wrote her doctoral thesis in an open wiki environment, making the entire writing process transparent to a public audience.[117] In fact, outsiders could have even taken part in writing the thesis themselves. But as she stated, only one single "spammer" did that and also the other interactive possibilities were barely used. Instead readers rather used e-mails to get in touch with her.[118] Once more this warns us to not overestimate the potential of the new platforms based on their mere technological opportunities. Many examples for low user participation could be added from our case studies here, from Wikiversity, Wikibooks and Second Life to much of what we observed on SNS. Whether one welcomes or neglects such new possibilities for peer reviewing, the often low participation relativates much of the potential impact.

Nevertheless, especially when public interest is involved, the emerging technologies can be used efficiently for novel forms of quality control. This can be illustrated by a look at the case of the dissertation of Germany's former defense minister Karl-Theodor zu Guttenberg. When law professor Andreas Fischer-Lescano read it, he entered text fragments in Google and discovered they were taken from another text and not quoted correctly (Preuß 2011). Soon after this became public, the *GuttenPlag Wiki* was setup to collaboratively search further hints for plagiarism. Google Books was one of the sources used to identify and prove it quickly.[119] Since no special skills are required to do so and it can be done comfortably without extraordinary equipment, this process could effectively be "crowd-sourced": Only two weeks after the initial suspicion of plagiarism went public, zu Guttenberg resigned from his position as defense minister—the political pressure became too high and due to its detailed documentation the accusation of plagiarism could hardly be denied. Thus we can regard

---

117 See here: studyplace.org/wiki/User:Gusandrews/SearchProject/Outline1208.

118 Personal e-mail correspondence, December 4, 2011.

119 See de.guttenplag.wikia.com/wiki/Seite_283 for an example of how Google Books is used to link to text fragments.

this incident as a case of *crowdsourced peer review*, in which Google (Books) played an important role in combination with a wiki platform. Numerous comparable projects followed in the meantime,[120] so this case may mark the beginning of a new kind of public scrutiny.

Spectacular as this case may be, it can hardly serve as a role model for academic quality control. There is no doubt that the large public interest resulting from political sensitivity was a major driving force in this case. This is of course anything but typical for academic publications. Moreover, screening for plagiarism does not require the disciplinary expertise that is normally required for reviewing. This reminds us of the idea of differentiated peer review as proposed by Kircz (Kircz 2001; Kircz and Roosendaal 1996), where the peers are not responsible for the whole paper, but for specific functional fragments of it, e.g. for the module on "methods". Wikipedia partly applies this idea, when certain users specialize on grammatical mistakes, or when disciplinary projects focus on particular sections of an article related to their field of expertise, while not looking at other aspects of the same article. In any case, an effective review process needs motivated contributors and, so far, academics do not have much incentive to contribute to these novel forms of quality control. We are going to discuss this issue in more detail below (3.3.4).

Just as there are automated forms of ex ante quality control (3.3.2), we can also identify such automated mechanisms that work ex post. Obvious examples are "bots" in Wikipedia, which are small programs that perform automatically simple editing tasks. Search engines are further examples: their algorithms determine what is relevant and how it is ranked. Also many SNS apply algorithms to order news feeds. Especially in multipurpose platforms they do not necessarily represent academic relevance, and even the specialized algorithms of Google Scholar appear questionable in this regard. Thus we may conclude that this type of automated quality control is not very efficient and can hardly replace human reviewing processes. Nonetheless, these mechanisms already do that to a certain degree because they powerfully pre-structure what content appears on our screens. This is not so much a form of reviewing, but certainly a form of controlling. It is highly questionable if this contributes to academic quality.

---

120 For example, VroniPlag Wiki focuses on the dissertation of Veronica Sass, daughter of former Bavarian Ministerpräsident (prime minister) Edmund Stoiber, and suggests contributing by using Google Books, Google Scholar etc. (de.vroniplag.wikia.com/wiki/WieKannIchHelfen).

The blurred boundaries to the non-scientific world with their different "impact factors" challenge the common academic routines, to say the least (3.2). Whether this is to be seen as a wishful form of "democratization" has to be assessed carefully in a differentiated way as we point out below. With regard to quality, we should be particularly concerned about potential effects of *populism*, as popularity appears to be an important factor in digital social networks (3.6). The technical infrastructure might be misused in a manipulative way, for example when rating systems are not secured properly and content is massively over- or underrated by unfair means. A similar concern has already been voiced with regard to possible "spam" in the context of academic search engine optimization (Beel and Gipp 2010; cf. 2.5.3). Equally, we must carefully assess how far the challenge of information overload runs counter to the benefits of the new forms of quality control (3.4).

3.3.4 Crediting and incentives

At the current stage, scholarly activity in digital social networks is mostly based on voluntary engagement. Since academic evaluations usually do not consider such activity, academics have little direct incentive to get involved here. Collaborative platforms such as the Wikimedia projects additionally complicate the crediting of single contributors. Activities on non-academic platforms such as Facebook or Second Life might even be seen as negative in the record of a researcher. From this perspective, it is not surprising that many researchers are not very keen on participating here and that engagement is often limited to self-marketing. Of course, this is problematic for the quality control in digital social networks as it largely depends on the interactivity of its users (3.1).

Enthusiasts often embrace the openness of the new platforms and stress its democratizing effects. But not only are these democratizing effects questionable (3.6), openness may also be a major obstacle for less idealistic colleagues since it causes the challenge of information overload (3.4) and privacy concerns (3.5). Additionally, openness is the exact opposite of the widely-desired prestige given by the exclusiveness of elite journals, grants and boards. There are already calls for "opening up science" (Gassmann et al. 2011) and taking into account the new channels, e.g. by applying "scientometrics 2.0" which consider impact achieved on the Web 2.0 (Priem and Hemminger 2010). However, such novel forms of measuring impact and creating new incentives meet a number of challenges. On the one hand, they are political: new scientometrics 2.0 should be designed carefully, ideally avoiding, for example, the risks of populism and manipulation mentioned above. On the other hand they are methodological: if the technical issues around the proposed evaluation tools are solved, they could be more encompassing, covering impact more completely. But as long as exclusiveness is a driving-force in academia, more inclusive measurements are unlikely to become powerful alternatives. Of course, decisions in the realm of research policy play a major role in this context. If significant sponsoring institutions choose to give credit to such new evaluation factors, this could change drastically. As the established ways of doing scientometrics are already controversial, we should watch closely how potential new methods might impact academia.

Thinking further, scholarly engagement in digital social networks could be enforced top-down when institutions give incentives for it. This may also help to reduce effects of populism: In such a model, researchers would contribute more for professional reasons and not so much simply because they like to. This could help academia to draw a better picture of itself on influential platforms such as Wikipedia. However, especially when it comes to commercial actors such engagements have to be assessed carefully because of the different interests and values involved.[121]

3.4 Information Overload or Information Paradise?

The developments of the last decade reinforces one of our observations made with respect to the changing academic working patterns (Nentwich 2003, 212ff.): on the one hand, the productivity of researchers is improved in many ways, not least by the increased access to ever more information from the desk—an "information paradise"; on the other hand, the enormously increasing amount of information available in the Internet may lead to information overload. Web 2.0 adds to the wealth of information available as many more individual information providers contribute today by sharing through the various networks and beyond. This may be particularly fruitful for some research fields: for instance, historical or political science

---

121 The problems caused by academia's cooperation with Google Books may be taken as a warning example (2.5).

research may be enriched by unofficial reports, assessments and opinions; another example may be the collection of data in the geosciences regarding earthquakes, weather phenomena or climate data. In addition, the big search engines such as Google give us instantaneous access to an increasing amount of data, books, images, and so on. At the same time, this becomes problematic as the sheer amount of information easily brings researchers into a situation of information overload. The multitude of communication channels which emerged over the last decade increase the severity of this problem. In this section, we shall mainly focus on this communicative dimension.

3.4.1 The evolution and diversification of communication channels in academia

The early academics of the modern age sent letters bilaterally to each other, called on each other to discuss in person, and wrote books with mostly low circulation. The culture of writing letters eventually led to the publication of the first scientific journals in the seventeenth century ("Letters of...") as an organized multilateral communication form; speeches to colleagues, in particular in the academies, were put into writing ("Annals of...", see Nentwich 2003, 408f.). In the early days of the twentieth century bilateral telephone calls in the fixed line network and later the fax machine have been added to the set of academic communication channels. While print publication in books and journals was and still is the norm, pre-publication became a new habit in the 1970s and 80s: so-called grey literature, such as pre-prints and working papers, shortened the time from authoring to reading and added the opportunity to receive comments before final print publication. Document delivery services (DDS) further increased the turnover of publication exchange. Decreasing travel cost and increasing internationalization of research let academic conferences proliferate over the course of the twentieth century and became an important forum of scientific exchange, including the new format of the "conference paper". With the establishment of the Internet towards the end of the last century, communication channels multiplied and pre-publication turned electronic and instantaneous. At the same time, bilateral surface mail letters have become rare today, the fax machine, frequently used only ten years ago, is almost off duty. Traditional phone calls among academics seem decreasing—despite an increasing level of (international) cooperation, and against the trend of more telephoning in the private sphere. Academic journals—much increasing in numbers—are still printed, but they reach most scientists in an electronic format and are eventually printed locally. When it comes to books, however, everything seems mostly as it was a hundred years ago and e-books and e-readers have not widely taken over yet. However, appearances are deceiving: While the genuine electronic-only book enters the market only very slowly, the academic book's "back-end" is electronic indeed: the complete production process is electronic; books are printed only on-demand in increasing numbers; more and more books are searchable in full text mode, not least through Google Books (cp. 2.5).

The beginning of the twenty-first century brought about two further changes: First, communication becomes increasingly mobile, also among academics, as the terminal equipment (phone, computer) is now wireless and there is a trend towards being online virtually everywhere at any time. Indeed, many scientists are increasingly online while traveling to conferences and even at night or during their holidays. Second, Web 2.0 added qualitatively new communication channels, as discussed in this volume. For example, microblogging in various forms quickly distributes short pieces of information, questions or statements to medium-sized groups of peers (2.2). Although by far not all scientists communicate with these latest channels, we observe that a growing fraction of them actually does, in particular the younger generation.

Summing up this ongoing development throughout the history of (internal) science communication, we see that the academic communication channels became increasingly diversified, more and more based on electronic means, and ubiquitous. The number of ways to reach a typical researcher is greater than ever in the past. Most of these channels rely on electronic means, so the computer infrastructure has become a basic requirement for a scientist's daily routines—with the side effect that a growing part of the day is devoted to interacting with electronic devices and their interfaces. The spatial layout of doing science—of which communication is an important element—undergoes further change as compared to traditional science (see already Nentwich 2003, 185ff., for the era of early cyberscience). Cyberscience 2.0 potentially completes this process of relativization of time and space for academia (Nentwich 2003, 185ff.).

Analyzing the evolution of the communication media in science sheds light on yet another important issue. The various channels are not mutually neutral. With regard to the relationship between an older and a newer communication tool we may distinguish between substitution, superposition, amendment, expansion and insignificant effect (Nentwich 2003, 481ff.). To give a few examples: the fax seems to have been substituted by e-mail with scanned attachments; the advent of the E-book has had no significant effect on the printed book, as yet[122]; Internet-based (video-) phoning via software on one's working computer seems to superpose the traditional telephone; e-mail has largely substituted paper letters, and so have, for many researchers Google, online full text literature databases and Wikipedia practically replaced the traditional library services. For the latest new communicative tools, we are in a stage of experimentation: overall, they do not superpose or substitute the traditional channels and are rather utilized as amending pre- and co-existing practices.

This is particularly true for microblogging, either via a dedicated platform such as Twitter or as part of the standard communication in SNS. For most academic users, microblogging is an add-on, but no replacement for other means of communication. Nonetheless, while for most academics the inbox of the e-mail account has become the central platform of one's daily communication, at least some members of the younger generation even in academia put equal or even more focus on the new online social communication tools. It may well be in the not-so-distant future, that e-mail—which has just largely substituted traditional letter writing and, to some extent, phone calls—may lose their central position. It would be conceivable not to start one's e-mail program in the morning as the standard way of communicating professionally, but to log on to one's preferred social network and check messages and microblogs there.

Expanding on this projection, a possible future development may be what one might call a "one-stop-service 2.0", integrating all communicative needs in one unambiguous academic communication space. As we have argued in relation to SNS (2.1.3) there are three possible paths to this: (1) monopolization, (2) multi-functionality or (3) interface harmonization. One the one hand, tools such as Tweetdeck rely on the third option, interface harmonization, by integrating services offered by multiple other platforms (in this case microblogging). On the other hand, the big players try to attract as many people as possible to their services, obviously striving for a central or monopolistic position in the communication space, mainly by combining the first two options: Google integrates ever more services

---

122 It may, however, have one in the not-so-distant future, but this is not the topic of this book.

under one roof. While the market of academic SNS is still highly competitive, Facebook, though challenged by some competitors, in particular Google, is obviously the most successful so far in achieving a monopoly. This trend towards monopolization does not go unnoticed and uncriticized. Some already argue that this trend will eventually lead to the recognition that these core Internet services are part of our future basic services—with the possible consequence that they will be heavily regulated (Callas 2011). We are, however, not there as yet.

3.4.2 Quantitative impacts of multi-channel communication

As we have seen, the current status quo is characterized by the simultaneous existence of a huge number of communication channels that are partly equivalent and partly redundant to each other, despite the differences in details. This state of affairs generates what we call the *multi-channel phenomenon*: communication is scattered, it may start in one medium, e.g. Twitter, and switch to another, e.g. e-mail, and return to a web-based forum or SNS. As the characteristics of these different platforms vary, the communication styles have to be adapted. In particular, some of the channels are public, others are only semi-private, some allow for longer texts, others for very short messages only. This change of channels may also mean that varying communication partners participate along the way. Note further that most of this communication is in written form; this form requires special care and concentration and is inherently at risk to produce misunderstandings, probably even more than verbal communication (Nentwich 2003, 196ff.). We assume that this is reinforced by both the swiftness of social media and the typical switching from one platform to the next.

Furthermore, not all of the partners are available on all platforms or, even when they have an account, they may not observe them regularly, with the effect that communication is severely hampered and may reach deadlocks. Although this may be an interim state only, as we have discussed above, it will most probably take a long time to be established. In the meantime, academic users of these digital social networks have to invest considerable time and effort to keep track of their widespread partners and preferred communication patterns. We may conclude that this is one of the main reasons not to join these networks for most scientists.

Next to these rather practical aspects—communication styles and partners—we observe that these channels also fulfill different functions, some of which could not be addressed before or at least not as easily and quickly. Among them we discussed in chapter 2 in particular the following: fast, multilateral information exchange by pointing at further resources, spreading news, answering questions, commenting current events, including ongoing offline conferences, presenting one's research or expertise, rating and tagging of online resources. If a cyberscientist wants to profit from this flow of information, they have to participate in these digital social networks by, first, actively contributing, in order to build up reputation so that others will later be willing to help in turn. Second, they have to follow the multilateral communication in the networks, in order to pick up those pieces of new information that relate to one's own research. In other words, whatever the activity level, our ideal typical cyberscientist needs to allow various streams of information to reach his or her attention. At first sight, this could be considered a nightmare and may easily lead to information overload (a term coined already decades ago by Toffler 1970).

Obviously, this user-generated stream of information has to be filtered in order to be valuable and "digestible". The in-built, Web 2.0 typical filter is a social filter: the very idea of the social web is that only those pieces of information reach the researcher which have been found useful, interesting, exciting, worth looking at by those people who you are "following", that is whose messages you have subscribed to. One could say, it resembles a "personalized newspaper featuring (and created by) your friends", as Pariser (2011, 37) puts it. In a professional context, such as the academic world, the cyberscientist relies, as usual, on peers, i.e. mainly other academics from his or her field, plus further experts or informants. Therefore, the information is somehow rated by others who one trusts or at least grants some leap of faith. Choosing and continually updating your network then becomes crucial. It should neither be too small, because then it would not generate enough return, nor too big, because it would then not reduce the potentially infinite flow of information to a workable size. Furthermore, the filtering is not only done indirectly by the other users and their assessment of the flow of information, but increasingly also by the in-built platforms' algorithms, which make some elements more relevant than others. This is most obvious with Google and the opaque ways of structuring and presenting information (cf. 2.3.1). While the ranking of the search results is an easy-to-use filtering mechanism, it is highly debatable whether it is adequate for academic research. Similar hidden mechanisms are also at work with Facebook and other Web 2.0 services (Pariser 2011). As the underlying algorithms are hidden to the user, professional information workers, such as academics, should not rely on them unconsciously.

While already discussed before the number of individual information providers skyrocketed on the basis of Web 2.0 services (Nentwich 2003, 212f.), the later aggravate a further problem: the inherent tendency of electronic communication in the Internet to multiply and vary pieces of information, resulting in fluidity over time and in virtual space. The original source often gets blurred and the variations between seemingly identical documents are not transparent (see also 3.2 for a discussion of blurred boundaries). While it certainly is an advantage that information spreads widely, it is problematic for the scientist and researcher who needs to keep track of his sources and to quote them properly.

To sum up: the filtering or selection problem is not new (Fröhlich 1996, 10; Harasim and Winkelmans 1990, 398; Nentwich 2003, 212f.; Gresham 1994; Harnad 1990, 3), but it gets intensified by the sheer increase of information and additional challenges such as opaque filter mechanisms. In other words, whether or not Web 2.0 platforms and the mechanisms devised to overcome the selection problem lead to information overload cannot be answered in general, but is mainly an individual issue, depending on one's specific digital social networks. It is moreover a question of individual literacy with regard to this new environment (see section 4).

3.4.3 Qualitative impacts?

In the previous sub-section we addressed the quantitative aspect of the issue of information overload. There is also a qualitative side to it, namely the potential *impacts of Web 2.0 communication on research results*. May the typically quick and short communication contribute to in-depth insights—the main purpose of science and research—or possibly even lead to the contrary as some have claimed (e.g. Carr 2010; Schirrmacher 2009)?

As argued throughout this volume, science can obviously only be supported by bits of 140 characters as in Twitter messages, never exclusively done in such a medium. This supportive function may, however, be quite substantial. Depending on the field, the swiftness of the information gathering process may be very advantageous. In particular in research fields in which the object of research develops very fast, for instance in political science, media studies or Internet research, keeping up-to-date regarding one's object of study is crucial and facilitated by the matching speed of Web 2.0 communication. For many, if not the majority of fields, however, this is not the core activity. In the laboratory sciences, for instance, the main sources of information to feed into the research process stem from the experiments, not from outside information. Although keeping track of the research literature may be assisted by digital social networks, we assume that the comprehensive traditional, now electronic, alerting services may do the job equally well.

The argument put forward by adversaries of Web 2.0 goes even further and in two directions. Similar to our earlier observations in the context of cyberscience 1.0 (Nentwich 2003, 213), the first apprehension is that continual use of Web 2.0, in particular of various platforms in parallel, has the effect that one's mind is distracted from the researcher's main tasks as the constant inflow of information attracts attention. We have to distinguish between *intentional active usage*, on the one hand, and *non-targeted passive usage*, on the other hand. In the first case, it is not necessarily distracting, but helping to focus on one's main task, as Internet-based information retrieval is easier and may be more efficient than, for instance, a visit in the library (note however, that irrelevant results may also be distracting; cf. 2.5). The second case is different, as the researcher is not actively seeking information, but "following" a stream of information that is only indirectly related to his research focus. Consequently, it may turn out that the main task would be fulfilled less efficiently as it takes more time, or it would even be poorly performed as errors may be overlooked. Practically, both types can of course easily be mixed as we know from e-mail clients: most of them check for new mail in regular intervals and they alert the user when new mail has arrived. It largely depends on the user's experience and "e-mail literacy" how he or she copes with the challenge of incoming information. While there may be some professions where one has to be constantly reachable and responsive, this is not usually the case in research contexts. Cyberscientists are normally allowed to check mails at longer intervals in order not to be distracted from their main tasks. The situation is somewhat different with Web 2.0 services. In many cases, the communication here is neither clearly synchronous nor asynchronous, but something in between: While it is only of limited importance in a typical asynchronous medium, such as e-mail, when one reacts to it, the situation is different for most Web 2.0 communication: status messages, questions raised, pointers at events and news age rather quickly. For example, to read a question put to

the community half a day after it has been posted may be of no use anymore as it has likely already been answered or is otherwise obsolete. So in
some respect, if one does not continually participate in the flow of information, one may be less distracted, but may miss the essence of the medium. In any case, it would need a special kind of Web 2.0 literacy to cope
with this dilemma.

The second hypothesis put forward in this context goes much further.
The multi-tasking that comes along with intensive Web 2.0 use, the abbreviated style, speed, informality and spontaneity of Web 2.0 communication
may slowly change the way the minds of intensive users work altogether. A
growing number of observers argues that an overall superficiality may
result; this would mean that we would not only have to expect less efficiently produced results or overlooked errors, but even no in-depth insights altogether (e.g. Carr 2010; Davidow 2011; Turkle 2011).

For instance, Nicholas Carr's book "The Shallows. What the Internet Is
Doing to Our Brains" (2010) draws on up-to-date research of the neuro-
sciences. Carr starts out with anecdotal evidence and the self-observation
that, on the one hand, reading habits change—the ability to stay focused
on longer pieces of writing diminishes. On the other hand, he points out
that heavy Web 2.0 users would consider themselves more creative and
smarter because they would profit from more external influences and a
"networked thinking process", as opposed to the "old linear thought process"; Carr, referring to McLuhan, speaks of a possible "moment of transition between two very different modes of thinking" (ibid., 10). His main
argument focuses on the concept of neuroplasticity: our brains physiology
(anatomy and biochemistry) adapt to repeated experiences—and working
intensively with the current Internet, its multiple signals and heavy multi-
tasking is indeed a different experience. In particular, what he calls "deep
reading" (ibid., 63)—concentrated and focused engagement with a longer
text over a long period of time—can hardly be practiced while reading
from the Internet. Furthermore, the technologies of hyperlinking and multimedia, as well as digital searching favor distraction as the content is fragmented and de-contextualized. Finally, there is evidence that because of
information overload—so much parallel input and too little time to digest
each piece of information before the next one arrives—the transfer from
the working to the long-term memory is hampered. The latter, however, is
crucial for learning and understanding. Although this is certainly not irre-

versible because of neuroplasticity,[123] Web 2.0-trained brains will work partly differently in the end. Carr's argument is not specifically about science and research, but it is obvious that if this neurological evidence would be reconfirmed, it would entail remarkable consequences for an activity that heavily relies on the brain and its deep reasoning capacities. Indeed, superficiality and shallowness would be serious threats to science and research.

It is certainly premature to decide whether Carr's and others' forecasts are right in the long term. It may, however, be advisable to carry out further research in this field and, in the meantime, to add cautious and perhaps retentive use of the Web 2.0 to the list of issues to address when it comes to Web 2.0 literacy (see chapter 4).

3.5 Between Transparency and Privacy

In the age of traditional science the private sphere of individual researchers was well protected and only partly opened inside one's own institution and at conferences. We may even say that academia was not particularly transparent so that only insiders knew who was working at which institute and on which topics. The age of cyberscience 1.0 turned academia into a much more transparent place as researchers started to upload professional information to freely accessible institutional websites and their personal homepages. This included short curricula vitae, publication lists, and contact details. Some explored the new possibilities of the Internet even further and revealed not only professional information, but also private photographs, hobbies etc. However, this was still the exception from the rule. In this section, we shall focus first on the dodgy relationship between privacy and transparency, then contribute to a privacy impact assessment of social media use in academia, and finally discuss the perspectives of a transparent and privacy-friendly academic Web 2.0.

---

123 Carr argues, however, that it will be much harder to reverse the trend as it seems particularly difficult to abstain from using all the mobile "gadgets" and interactive multimedia services. Our brains seem to be greedy for news and connections, so they become easily addicted to this mode of communicating and thinking. Furthermore, it may be even more difficult for the next generation to acquire deep reading capabilities after not having made this experience in their adolescence.

3.5.1 Privacy versus transparency in the Web 2.0

Potentially, Web 2.0, by its very nature, turns this upside down as social media heavily rely on the users being prepared to share as much information about themselves as possible. Many of the praised features, such as user-specific attention-directing services and, in particular, the automated support for building up one's network, only function satisfactorily if the users become somewhat transparent. We may distinguish between (1) the data, which the users upload onto the platforms, such as the profile information or photographs, and (2) the seemingly ephemeral traces they leave in the course of actively using the platforms. The individual user activity is stored and analyzed in order to enhance the service: What kind of information a user is visiting, rating or linking to, what information, questions or statements he or she shares with others as a status message, what queries are entered in search boxes—all this is processed by sophisticated algorithms to predict interests and future behavior. Indeed, it is very convenient if "the machine" offers appropriate suggestions to new publications, potential collaborators or upcoming conferences that fit the user's personal interests and preferences. But it comes at the price of becoming more and more transparent.

Data-protection and privacy issues are high on the agenda of the worldwide public debate around social media (e.g. Barnes 2006; Lewis et al. 2008; Zheleva and Getoor 2009; Bonneau and Preibusch 2010; Preibusch et al. 2007; Leenes 2010; Fuchs 2009, 2010), but still "severely underresearched", as Preibusch et al. (2007, 11) put it. It is important to note that while SNS "share many privacy problems (and therefore solution possibilities) with other Web applications, there are also important new challenges" (ibid., 1), because they concern not only the individual, but also the relations in the social network, For example, if a "user reveals data about himself, as well as a list of his friends, this 'network' information could lead to revelations that had not been intended by his friends" (ibid., 11). The usefulness of a SNS, e.g. its contribution to one's reputation, increases with the size of one's network—and so does the threat to privacy. Practically all of the big commercial Web 2.0 players, such as Facebook and Google, are under constant observation and critique with regard to their privacy policies (Bonneau and Preibusch 2010). These policies are obviously a unilaterally set and dynamic compromise between the perceived wishes of the users, the requirements of novel functions on these platforms and the commercial needs. This is not the place to discuss privacy issues related to the commercial Web 2.0 in general, sometimes labeled as "economic surveillance"(Fuchs 2010). Instead, our purpose is to assess the situation with respect to the academic use of social media.

3.5.2 Privacy impact assessment of academic use of social media

While the general user of Web 2.0 services tends to share private information, such as hobbies, relationship status, photographs, political or religious convictions, this is not usually the case in the professional contexts. There are two kinds of data to be considered in this context, namely those actively uploaded and the data traces left while using the services:

(1) *Uploaded data:* Even if a platform asks for more private information, we observed that researchers rarely provide it, but rather only upload the elements of typical professional curricula vitae, office contact details and classification of their expertise; some also add wallet-size photographs, and the more active users among the researchers upload publication lists, including occasionally even full texts. At first sight, this first type of data is per se relatively harmless as it corresponds to the information already available via institutional homepages and other databases. However, what is new in the Web 2.0 environment is that cross-linking of the various profiles is often promoted, for instance between Facebook and ResearchGate. Furthermore, users, in particular for professional purposes, tend to use the same screen names on various platforms; therefore, data-mining activities in the Web 2.0 will succeed in relating the various profiles of one person and generate a highly sensitive meta-profile that encompasses data from across all platforms.[124] Such a meta-profile will most likely also include private profiles, even if the person uses pseudonyms in private contexts. In any case, the boundaries between professional and private use of Web 2.0 are blurred or fluid.

2) *Data traces:* The data of the second type, the traces left by actively using the platforms, are novel and highly sensitive information. Whether or not someone likes or has read a particular publication was not known outside small circles, but can now be revealed to potentially all peers with a mouse click. Similarly, a researcher's network was only known to her or

---

124 These "meta profiles" are increasingly also generated indirectly by the users themselves. For instance, when using a series of services of Google, from Google+ and Mail to Groups and Docs etc., this leads to a very encompassing profile. In addition, there are services with the sole purpose to integrate data from very platforms (see also 3.4.1).

him alone, others could only speculate about it. In a SNS or a microblogging service, the lists of followers and people followed, the friends or contacts are openly accessible to everyone interested, including data-mining software. Access to contributions to web forums and group discussions are often not restricted and—quite different from the offline world—stored and accessible even for people who have not been involved in a discussion at the time.

In the early days of ResearchGate, users were regularly informed who has visited one's profile and who has rated or commented on which contributions of one's network members. Although this particular feature is not available anymore[125], it hints at the hidden layer of information: Even if not, or not currently, made available to its users, the platforms store and analyze a lot more than what is visible on the surface. These data are used to improve the above mentioned attention-directing services and are potentially very useful for targeted advertising, even in science-specific SNS. In other words, this user-generated data is commercially valuable, not only for the providers of the original platform where the data has been generated, but also for others, whether they are in a business relationship with the provider or not. From a privacy protection perspective the potential reuse of data generated in one context in another is particularly opaque and dangerous, because the contextual information may be lost so that information is likely to be misinterpreted.[126]

In a scenario in which most researchers would continually and actively use Web 2.0 services for all kinds of communicative purposes, there is no doubt that the "fully transparent researcher" may become reality, unless the users actively control their privacy settings, inasmuch as they are available. While access to basic information as quickly and easily as possible is certainly an overall positive development because it facilitates cooperation and exchange, we may seriously ask whether it is desirable and acceptable to go beyond that: transparent research is not necessarily equal to transparent researchers. In a fully-fledged cyberscience 2.0 scenario, an increasing part of a researcher's daily activities—from Internet browsing to multilat-

---

125 The list of "notification settings" in ResearchGate, however, includes, by the time of writing (October 2011), approximately 50 different types of activities on the platform about which you can chose whether to be notified or not and in which form.

126 Many SNS providers, including ResearchGate, cooperate, for instance, with the marketing enterprise ScorecardResearch (scorecardresearch.com), which collects Internet web browsing data across platforms.

eral communication—would be watched, kept track of and observed by peers, machines and providers of targeted information. In some cases, this may be a deliberate and understandable choice by the individual. For instance, one may deliberately share behavioral data in order to be offered useful hints to latest developments in one's field of expertise, such as new publications or blogs. However, the amount of data generated and stored for this purpose, but also made available to other persons, even beyond the network, may be a big threat to overall privacy. While it may be desirable for the user to have only one platform instead of many (cf. 3.4), monopolization or centralization is particularly dangerous from a privacy point of view, because it renders abusive behavior, such as spamming or identity theft[127], even more attractive. Note that as yet no international regulatory framework has been implemented that sets effective limits to the disclosure or allowed time of storage of users' traces. Thus it is conceivable that some of a researcher's traces, such as microblogs or ratings of a publication, may play a role in his or her later career if easily available to, for instance, a tenure committee.

3.5.3 Paths towards transparent and privacy-friendly academic Web 2.0?

In the face of the tension between the wish to protect one's private sphere, the trend towards more transparent academia and the needs of a state-of-the-art social media infrastructure for science and research, there seem to be three paths forward: non-usage, educated usage, and privacy-friendly design; we shall address them in turn.

Non-usage: The first path would be individual or collective decisions not to use the platforms at all. Although this is not a deliberate choice for many so far, because some non-users simply do not know yet of Web 2.0 at all, the majority of researchers are non-users. Privacy concerns may prolong the list of arguments against becoming cyberscientists 2.0. The downside of this option is that one could not enjoy the advantages of those digital social networks. Moreover, there may be even traces and data of non-members of such networks because others may refer to them in their contributions (cf. 3.6.2).

---

127 With regard to identity theft, see in general OECD (2008) and the literature and cases collected at combat-identity-theft.com.

Educated usage: The second path would be to enhance user awareness of the privacy threats and to spread the knowledge how to cope with them in practice. As most Web 2.0 platforms today pose some risks to privacy, this strategy would probably lead to rather careful and restricted use of them. This path, less radical than the first, would be an imperfect solution because, again, the users could not realize in practice many of the potential advantages and, in addition, could not overcome some of the current restrictions to effective privacy protection. To illustrate this, Zheleva and Getoor (2009) come to the conclusion that, from a privacy point of view, it would be advisable to join only groups with diverse membership and not homogenous groups—advice that is difficult to follow in professional environments without risking to remain an outsider of the inner circles of expertise.

Privacy-friendly design: The third possible solution would be to address the challenge by designing the platforms in a privacy-friendly or privacy-enhancing way.[128] There is, for instance, the well-known initiative to create such a SNS by the name "Diaspora"[129]; and Holtz (2010) describes a prototype, called "Clique", a product of an EU project[130] implementing vigorously data protection principles. Apart from data-security measures, such as cryptography and scrambling, privacy-friendly SNS would put much more emphasis on user control over disclosure and non-disclosure of his or her data and restrict the secondary use (for instance for the purpose of advertisement) to a minimum or exclude it altogether; they would support audience segregation (Leenes 2010) so that it would become easier to distinguish who would be a recipient of which information[131]; data, such as those generated by usage traces, would not be stored for ever, not be made available for data-mining, and could be deleted partly or completely by the user at any time. There is a chance that within the realm of academia this scenario might be realized as soon as the Web 2.0 becomes recognized as useful. We see three options: commercially-driven activity, regulation, and public initiatives.

---

128 There is a growing body of research regarding "privacy enhancing technologies" (PETs) and "privacy by design", see for instance privacybydesign.ca/publications.

129 See joindiaspora.com.

130 EU project PrimeLife at www.primelife.eu.

131 Still, it would be difficult to implement this segregation in everyday practice, even it is technically feasible.

(a) *Commercially-driven activity:* The providers of already existing Web 2.0 services for academia respond to the calls for privacy-enhancing design. As most of those providers have their own roots in academia it is not unlikely that this path may be at least partly successful, and some of the providers already do so. Bonneau and Preibusch (2010), however, argue that despite the "evidence that social network providers are making efforts to implement privacy enhancing technologies with substantial diversity in the amount of privacy control offered [...] privacy is rarely used as a selling point". Obviously, privacy concerns are not too important for the general user. It remains to be seen whether the academic user behaves differently.

(b) *Regulation:* At some point privacy regulation could be implemented to induce providers to respond to these needs (similar Callas 2011). This could come in three forms, either through hard law, i.e. binding statutes, or through jurisdiction (court law), or soft law, such as international codes of conduct (Hoeren and Vossen 2010). No doubt, this option faces considerable problems given the international dimension of the Internet.

(c) *Public initiatives:* Like the rest of the research infrastructure, including the communication infrastructure[132], it could be publicly financed and designed according to the needs of the research community, not of the commercial actors. These needs would certainly include privacy issues. Some initiatives in this direction are already on the way, for example Vivo as a broader solution or Les Carnets2 at Paris Descartes University as a local one.

We conclude that, on the one hand, more open access and more transparency is certainly a desirable perspective for academia as a whole—"Science, after all, is ultimately an Open Source enterprise." (DiBona et al. 1999, 1). On the other hand, the digital social networks pose a serious threat to the private sphere of the researchers when they make the individual researchers transparent. While we are convinced that it would be possible to conceive a privacy-friendly *and* transparent solution, we are not sure whether it will be chosen unless it receives support by the academic institutions and, ultimately, politics. Therefore, we advocate starting an open and broad discourse about how the future digital academic network should be designed—inside and outside academic circles.

---

132 Such as telephone lines, Internet access, the pan-European research data network GÉANT, see geant.net, and so on.

3.6 Towards Democratization of Science?

The decentralized networked structure of the Internet has triggered hopes that it will potentially democratize society in general and academia in particular. Apparently, the new communication channels created an independency of knowledge authorities, which is historically novel. Never before was it so easy to obtain knowledge regardless of the social status of a group or an individual and the emergence of Web 2.0 has also given broad access to means of knowledge distribution. This has potentially drastic effects on academia, which has established extraordinarily high hurdles for publication with its peer review systems.

Indeed, we were able to observe windows in the ivory tower, which have blurred the boundaries between academia and the public (3.2). However, many open questions remain, starting with the unclear concept labeled as "democratization". Therefore, our discussion of this term will lead us to distinguish between democratization in an internal and in an external sense. Finally, we will address key issues for assessing the "democratization of science".

3.6.1 What does democratization mean?

Clearly, the term describes a process of moving towards democracy. But what exactly constitutes a democracy is less obvious and has led to many different understandings. Etymologically, it comes from the Greek words *"demos"* which basically means "people" and *"kratos"* which can be translated as "power". From this basic understanding, democracy is an organizational power structure which is governed by the people. But who belongs to "the people" and how should its powers be designed can be answered very differently. For example, in the Greek Polis, the "mother" of all democracies, slaves and women were excluded from the *demos*. Although the modern understanding of democracy is much more inclusive and liberal, most forms are organized as representative democracies, in which the *demo* has only indirect power by voting for its governors.

From this perspective, we may wonder what the popular catchphrase of a "democratization of science" actually describes. Who is the *demos* in this concept and which powers does it have over whom to do what? In the related discussions two understandings are common, which first of all have different ideas of who is the *demos*.

(1) The public in the broad sense of civil society is seen as the *demos*. Here, democratization may describe a power shift that strengthens extra-academic elements—which is why we may call it *external democratization*.

(2) In a narrower sense, democratization refers to science in particular—to all members of the academic communities—and to a possible weakening of the inner-academic hierarchies; therefore, we may call it *internal democratization*.

In modern societies democratization usually has a positive connotation and is regarded as desirable. Nevertheless, applying a concept originally formed to organizing power relations in the realm of the state to the social system of science is much more troublesome than it appears on the pleasing first sight. In fact, a non-democratic organization could be seen as a core-principle of science. Academia is entirely built on the idea that not every-one, but only individuals with certain (more or less clearly defined) exper-tise and skills are allowed to participate. This organizational model of sci-entific knowledge production has evolved in a long process, in which other models have slowly lost influence. In contrast to the theocentric model which dominated for a long time and bound knowledge production and distribution to the membership in clerical circles, the scientific model ide-ally reduces selection mechanisms to methodological principles and reputa-tion based on the ability to apply them. In this sense, it could be seen as democratic since it bounds participation primarily to *skills* and not to social status per se. Although status plays an important role in academia (e.g. in form of titles, impact factors etc.) it is supposed to reflect skills and is not given qua inheritance and the like.

Needless to say, this ideal form is often not achieved and many studies from the field of science and technology studies have shown how other (social) factors impact on scientific knowledge production and distribution. Therefore, the call for a "democratization of science" could be heard al-ready decades ago, when science was regarded increasingly not only as a solver, but also as a *cause* of problems (cf. 3.2). The underlying hope is that softening hierarchies could help to diminish such unwanted effects in favor of a mode of knowledge production and distribution which is closer to the ideal of science. We will discuss this argument with regard to the emerging platforms of our case studies along the differentiation between internal and external democratization.

3.6.2 Internal democratization?

Potentially democratizing effects on academia triggered by ICT have already been discussed in relation to the early shift to cyberscience (Nentwich 2003, 250 ff.). The core arguments were similar to what we described in regard to the windows in the ivory tower created by the emerging technologies (3.2): ICT apparently provides easier access to invisible colleges and (scarce) information, diminishes status cues, brings new publication opportunities and due to the higher ICT literacy of younger people it might partly even turn dependencies around. Fröhlich describes what we would call internal democratization as follows:

"the moderation of the Matthew effect[133], the encouragement of transitive scientific critique beyond closed 'invisible communities' with their exclusive information distribution, 'citation cartels' and courtesy reviews, the reduction of inequalities in the access to academic resources, and the dissemination of academic works according to quality criteria and not according to the recognition of the name of the author" (Fröhlich 1993, 7, our translation).

It is remarkable that he expressed these hopes already in the early 1990s, based on the observation of emerging disciplinary information systems and computer networks. At first sight, Web 2.0 seems to support such a "democratization of science" even more, since it facilitates the handling of ICT. The more people are able to use it, the less it is limited to early adopters. Indeed, there is no doubt that it was never easier to distribute and access knowledge and to get insights into (informal) communication and social networks of scientists. The functional principles of the new platforms apparently support this development because they are mostly "blind" to academic status and hierarchies, as we pointed out above (3.2).

However, this does not apply to their users who might consider reputation as an important factor for deciding who to interact with. A good example to illustrate this is Twitter. Technically, all users have the same possibilities to communicate and publish their thoughts. But of course, high-impact researchers have much higher chances to get noticed. Popular authors such as Clay Shirky and Lawrence Lessig have far over 100.000 followers who they can contact with their tweets. Needless to say, a random student who has just set up a Twitter account will hardly be able to address such an audience. Additionally, Twitter strengthens such hierarchies by explicitly showing the ratio between "followers" and "following", indicat-

---

133 "Those who have, will be given." See below.

ing the popularity and success of a user. So, renowned academics will often have a head start compared to less known colleagues and therefore we must stress that conventional reputation and hierarchies also play a significant role in gaining visibility and impact in digital social networks.

Already in the early age of cyberscience, skepticism towards the democratizing potential of the Internet was expressed (Nentwich 2003, 253 ff.). A main argument goes back to Merton who prominently identified a "Matthew effect" in science, meaning a favoring of already established scientists and concurrently a withholding of recognition from those who have not achieved this status yet. Interestingly, he already pointed out in 1968 that more publication possibilities might even enforce status hierarchies:

"There is reason to assume that the communication function of the Matthew effect is increasing in frequency and intensity with the exponential increase in the volume of scientific publications, which makes it increasingly difficult for scientists to keep up with work in their field. [... S]cientists search for cues to what they should attend to. One such cue is the professional reputation of the authors." (1968, 449)

As information overload becomes a permanent challenge in the age of digital social networks (3.4), selection of information becomes a crucial task for users and platforms. Reducing content and communication to the most important actors and publications appears to be a logical strategy in this context. The digital structure may even support this because it partly allows for effectively excluding content and individuals. For example, users can often ban others from their news streams and algorithms may regard contributions as irrelevant, resulting in a low ranking or even complete exclusion. The latter automated selection is mostly executed implicitly without transparent indicators. As we pointed out above (3.2), these mechanisms do not necessarily represent academic relevance. Instead, a main functional logic here is *popularity*, which is of course not tantamount to scientific relevance (see also our related discussion of academic quality in digital social networks, 3.3). The digital structure requires quantifiable indicators, for instance, the number of back-links pointing to a website or article, how many comments, "shares" and "likes" an item has received or the amount of "followers" an individual or institution has gathered. As the Matthew effect suggests, this may very well reproduce and escalate status hierarchies.

But since these indicators are not directly bound to academic factors, they can also work in favor of individuals and positions on the margin of the scientific community. As we are still in an early and ongoing transformation process—from cyberscience to cyberscience 2.0—many practices in this context are not institutionalized yet. Early adopters (who are typically rather young users at the beginning of their career) can profit from this. They have already gained the necessary technical skills to navigate through the emerging digital social networks before their more established colleagues start with it. More importantly, they had a head start in constructing them. As we argued above (3.1), interactivity plays a crucial role for shaping the individual experience, but also the platforms themselves. The users create groups, content, comments, networks etc. and they also develop certain structures and cultures of communication. Simply because the most active users are usually not also the most reputable academics (if they are academics at all, see 3.2) these structures do not mirror academia's offline status hierarchies.

Students may be founders and moderators of groups that represent certain fields or institutions, users with various backgrounds establish rules for wiki projects and communication cultures on the different platforms, bloggers and webmasters set up powerful link-networks which have a major impact on the visibility of content. Whoever wants to take part here has to walk on this path paved by the previous users. In many cases this turns academia's common top-down hierarchies upside-down: Often young tech-savvy scholars can draw on an extensive network and their content is well-positioned—optimized for search engines, linked, shared and commented by their friends and colleagues. In contrast, their less tech-savvy but established colleagues may have difficulties to gain a position online that reflects their offline status. Even very popular scholars with a celebrity-like status do not automatically benefit from their offline reputation. It may help them to gain quick and wide impact also online, but they still need to manage the new channels effectively to take advantage of them. Prominent visibility also means to be exposed to criticism from various sides, often with little opportunities to intervene. It is practically impossible to control or even react to the countless channels through which criticism can be expressed. To a large extent, the multiple channels relativize themselves because potential audiences face the same problem as the criticized researcher: they cannot process everything. Nevertheless, central points may evolve that can hardly be ignored: The first hits of a Google name search, related Wikipedia articles, "viral tweets", i.e. Twitter messages that have been forwarded ("re-tweeted") by many, widely-perceived pertinent blogs, mailing lists or groups. While some researchers lack attention, others get too much—or to be more precise—too much *unwanted* attention. This way, researchers are often part of digital social networks even if they do not actively contribute. For example, during many conferences presentations are commented publicly via Twitter and other platforms even before they are over.

From this perspective, the scenario of an (internal) democratization of science is already partly accomplished. Thoughts can be distributed quickly and widely regardless of a researcher's status. Due to the accountability within cyberscience 2.0 it becomes increasingly difficult to maintain controversial results based on reputation and hierarchies only. But at the same time, powerful conventional status hierarchies remain and the main factors to evaluate academics are still located outside of cyberscience 2.0: Reputation is measured in journal publications, citations and grants, not in tweets, wiki edits or activity in social network sites. At the current state, engagement might even turn against the researchers as "irrelevant" activity. Hence, some already identified "a need to develop a system of 'scientific impact 2.0'" (Gassmann et al. 2011, 24) that takes account of the new platforms. However, so far academia has been rather reluctantly adapted to this trend (cf. 3.3.4).

Even if cyberscience 2.0 gained more significance for evaluation processes, it would be premature to equate this with a "democratization of science". We can already observe various mechanisms to create and maintain hierarchies. In some respect, these mechanisms have a partly democratizing effect because they usually do not represent existing offline hierarchies one-to-one. This may however change in the longer run as cyberscience 2.0 becomes increasingly institutionalized and professionalized. This trend can already be observed for the business world: After the first "wild years" of the Internet, many companies have adapted by actively incorporating online platforms into their business strategies. They contact potential clients with targeted advertisements, monitor what is said about their companies in social media, use crowd-sourcing to their benefit, optimize content for search engines and sometimes "brighten" widely accessible information sources (such as Wikipedia articles) in a rather unethical manner. Well-situated actors are better equipped to execute such activities as compared to weaker competitors. This also applies to academia. In fact, such processes can be identified: some propose "academic search engine optimization" (Beel et al. 2010), libraries and scientific institutions start to focus on social media for public relations, and some develop their own platforms.

Finally, we must also carefully examine whether the widely-discussed *digital divide* hinders the envisioned democratization of science. This tends to be a blind spot of scholars in the developed world who often take the necessary ICT infrastructure for granted. For instance, whether developing countries actually benefit from open access (OA) is not as clear as one might assume. In a study comparing citation rates from different countries, Norris et al. (2008) noticed that OA articles received far fewer citations in low income regions and conclude:

"It may be that the lack of reliable telecommunications networks in these low income countries could hinder access to OA articles. In this case, scholars in these countries may rely on a limited number of printed journals for which they have subscriptions." (ibid., 342)

Given that OA articles apparently have a citation advantage[134] and many OA publishers charge expensive author fees, we may furthermore critically ask whether authors with good resources profit from this emerging practice, whereas scholars with less financial support could be alienated by these costs.

All things considered, we conclude that cyberscience 2.0 has some remarkable effects on academic status hierarchies, but it would go too far to diagnose a general internal democratization of science. Especially the expected increasing professionalization of cyberscience 2.0 may work counter the potential of democratization in the long run.

3.6.3 External democratization?

The elitist model of scientific expertise challenges democratically-organized societies (for a detailed study of this relationship see: Fischer 2009). While the first half of the twentieth century was rather techno-optimistic with a generally positive view on science, technology and expertise, this began to crumble when the public became increasingly aware of problems associated with this development. Starting in the 1960s a wide debate emerged about ecological damage, in particular, damage caused by science and technology themselves (Beck 1992; Giddens 1990). Correspondingly, the image

---

134 In his annotated bibliography of studies regarding this topic, Wagner (2010) concludes that 39 of the 46 studies at hand see an open access citation advantage.

of experts as problem solvers as it was outlined in technocratic visions, came under pressure. At the same time, complex knowledge societies heavily depend on expertise, which leaves them in a kind of dilemma, a "risk society" as Beck (1992) has labeled it. One suggestion to deal with this situation is a call for the democratization of expertise and science (e.g. Nowotny 2003), e.g. by involving laypeople in decision-making as it is done in many participatory procedures nowadays (Durant 1999; Joss and Bellucci 2002). The architecture of the Internet apparently supports this development and various experiments with "e-participation" are trying to take advantage of it.

Indeed, the Internet has created new windows in the academic ivory tower, intertwining it more and more with the public, as we have discussed in detail above (3.2). It has raised quality and privacy concerns (3.3/3.5), but in view of the problematic relationship between democracy and expertise, many have also embraced this development. Similar to internal democratization processes some believe that this opening will rather enhance the quality of academic work and the new transparency is weighed heavier than privacy issues. Especially, active cyberscientists have impelled a "democratization of science" with the help of the Internet. Using quotation marks here seems necessary because often descriptive elements are mixed with normative assumptions and wishful thinking, so that it is unclear if the desired "democratization" actually is or can be achieved.

For example, Marc Scheloske, former senior editor for the German scientific blog platform *ScienceBlogs.de*, has argued that blogging would help to partly overcome the "asymmetric monologue" (2008, our translation) of regular science communication, leading to a society in which citizens could responsibly deal with academic knowledge. In line with the common argument for OA, Scheloske furthermore stresses that most research is publicly-funded and should therefore be publicly available, too. Günther (2009) makes a similar point with her proposed "Internet-public networked academia" (our translation, cf. 3.2). Cyberscience 2.0 could go beyond the mere publication of results by giving insights into the production and communication process. Klaus Graf, a historian who runs the academic blog platform *Archivalia*, takes this argument to the extreme. When he was asked at a conference whether he believes that scientists who do not blog are bad scientists, he answered with only one word: "Yes".[135]

---

135 The case has been further discussed here: schmalenstroer.net/blog/2011/09/wissen-schaft-bloggen-und-die-ffentlichkeit.

From this perspective, cyberscience 2.0 is regarded as an *imperative* for researchers. In such a scenario, the question is not how scholars could be motivated to take part in digital social networks, but they simply have to. This may be regarded as utopian (or—depending on the point of view— as dystopian), but in some domains we have already come close to this scenario. To give a few examples: the Journal *RNA Biology* publishes abstracts in Wikipedia; some faculty or students are obliged to join a certain SNS; or public pressure is caused by the sheer impact of a platform. Google Books transferred academia's analogue work into the realm of digital social networks—to a large extent without the authors' permission. The harsh controversies which arose from this case may be taken as an example for how problematic a "cyberscience 2.0 imperative" is.

Moreover, our observations of the functionality and practices of digital social networks do not allow the assumption that they are inherently democratic. In many regards they do not support democratization processes but rather the emergence of (partly new) powerful hierarchies, as we have discussed above (3.6.2). Ironically, Scheloske and his platform Science-Blogs.de (which he praised as democratic) were accused of "cyber-mobbing" by users with a rather esoteric point of view (Fritzsche 2010). Apparently, harsh measures were taken against the opponents who constantly "disturbed" the consensual thinking on the website. Similar exclusion politics could have been observed for Wikipedia (König 2009a, 2011).

Of course, one might question these practices themselves, but the more interesting point is that this indicates the need for mechanisms for exclusion. In many cases, digital social networks have to deal with the issue of information overload (3.4) and it is an illusion to believe that every point of view can be represented equally. Exclusion of information is inevitable. Thus, we should discuss the criteria and the design for such measurements rather than holding on to the illusion of total inclusion.

Again, the digital divide has to be addressed as an obstacle for democratization. By the time of writing, we are not aware of any study which focuses on the specific issue of a digital divide in regard to external science communication. However, numerous studies have critically assessed the general democratizing potential of the Internet (Schrape 2010; Grunwald et al. 2006) and in line with the above thoughts we can conclude that it would be naïve to assume that the emergence of cyberscience 2.0 itself would help an external democratization of science.

3.6.4 Obstacles for assessing democratization processes

Our analysis reveals a number of key issues which hinder the assessment of potential democratization processes triggered by cyberscience 2.0. First of all, the term itself is often not clearly defined. We hope that our understanding of democratization in an internal and in an external sense may be a first step towards a sharper conceptualization of the term. This should avoid misunderstandings and help to identify what it actually describes. Secondly, it seems necessary to draw a clearer line between the descriptive analysis of democratization and normative approaches. Many discussions reflect the political implications of the issue and the problems we have outlined in regard to utopian and dystopian perspectives on cyberscience 2.0 (3.1). Only when it is clear what "democratization" actually means, can we conceptualize how it can be measured. Normative elements (e.g. how democratization should be designed and how it can be achieved) could be addressed at the next level. Of course, it depends on the actual concept whether democratization is seen as desirable at all. The positive image of the word should not distract us from assessing potential risks and other problems. For example, when new ways for measuring impact in cyberscience 2.0 are proposed, it should not be assumed that they will be per se more democratic. Instead, the often undemocratic or populist structure has to be considered and realistically assessed.

4 Overall Conclusions and Outlook

This book started by asking what role the digital social culture triggered by Web 2.0 plays in the academic world at present and what the potentials are of the related platforms. Our main concern is what impact they and the socio-technical practices around them may have. As we stated from the outset, the Internet in general and Web 2.0 in particular are moving targets, and so are the potential roles and impacts they may play in academia. Despite this uncertainty we tried to give an encompassing overview of the present state of affairs in our case studies (section 2), and discussed some of the key impacts of the development in our analysis section (section 3). In this final chapter, we summarize our findings and go one step further by looking ahead. We proceed in two steps: In 4.1 we look at the status quo, asking whether we reached the age of cyberscience 2.0; after negating this, we consider in 4.2 what the future may possibly be like by assessing the influence of key intervening factors playing a role in this development. With section 4.3 we conclude this book with an outlook on and assessment of the likely further development.

4.1 Maturing Cyberscience

In 2011, the vast majority of the members of the scientific communities are indeed cyberscientists: their working lives are heavily influenced by the Internet, and it is hardly conceivable to do without Internet-based communication, such as e-mail, online databases and other resources, which are so easily accessible without even leaving one's desk. Many work flows are completely organized online: for instance, papers are submitted, reviewed and published electronically and they are usually retrieved through online search engines and databases. No doubt, cyberscience is reality. Our study revealed that those new tools that are generally associated with the term Web 2.0 have already started to play a significant role in science and research: academics blog about their research, communicate via microblogging services, contribute to collaborative wiki resources, activate profiles in social network sites, and some even populate virtual worlds.

Web 2.0 is obviously a forceful trend outside academia with hundreds of millions participating more or less actively. There is no indication that the Internet in general would return to a non-participatory, not interactive, top-down kind of communication space. Could the academic world be different? On the one hand, there is evidence that an increasing number of academics, though still the minority, actively explore how Web 2.0 may help them in performing their tasks. Many academics report favorable experiences. On the other hand, we analyzed throughout this book whether the new tools are functional, whether they satisfy genuine needs of the highly differentiated and professionalized academic world. Our results show that not all of them do and many hindering factors remain. At the present state of development, the problem of multiple channels and information overload, or of lacking participation in evolving processes of bottom-up quality control, for instance, show that there is still need for further development and adaptation, both technically and regarding the social embedding of these technologies. It would be premature to say that the activity of science bloggers today heralds an age in which all researchers are virtually obliged to blog, just like they have to write academic articles in books and journals. Similarly, there is no intrinsic necessity of e-mail being gradually replaced by web-based communication within social network sites. However, we found a number of hints that those proficient in the Web 2.0 actually enjoy some advantages, for instance, when it comes to information gathering, networking, collaborating, self-marketing, and publishing.

Based on our analysis, fully-fledged cyberscience 2.0 would be a very different place from the present:

- It could be characterized by a new quality of transparency and exchange between the inner spheres of academia and its environment.
- Internally, it could be much more communicative with a constant exchange of small pieces of information, queries and statements.
- It could have a much more diversified system of communication and publication channels, from traditional ex-ante peer-reviewed journal articles, written by identifiable authors, to highly cooperative and dy-

namically evolving knowledge resources and new types of transdisciplinary publications.

– In this new environment, the researcher's identity and status might be defined to a lesser degree by traditional offline achievements, such as printed articles and papers given at conferences in person, but more by the totality of one's activities in the world-wide academic social networks, in particular the digital ones.

– The individual researcher would partially lose control over his or her incoming flow of information as the complex Web 2.0 mechanisms order and pre-structure the information and knowledge space in which one navigates. Attention-directing services, triggered by other users or by sophisticated computation on the basis of a user's previous activities, or sorting by search engines according to non-scientific relevance criteria, will have a considerable influence on research activities and even content. On a macro level, popular platforms put pressure on academia as their wide societal impact can hardly be ignored.

All of the above characteristics can, in part, be observed even today—and are indeed, for some actors, reasons for concern and even non-participation. Our conclusion at this point is that some researchers may already rightfully be called cyberscientists 2.0, but, on the whole, we do not live in the age of cyberscience 2.0, but are observers of mature cyberscience 1.0 with elements of "cyberscience 2.0 in the making" in an environment that is increasingly influenced by Web 2.0. So even if researchers do not actively decide to use them, social media and in particular the most popular platforms do affect academia.

4.2 The Cyberscience 2.0 Prospects

In such a dynamic and complex environment, it is certainly highly speculative to predict whether fully-fledged cyberscience 2.0 will ever become reality. Nonetheless, we shall try do find a tentative answer, applying our well-tried conceptual framework (as outlined in 1.3). The framework's core is a model of change in which three types of intervening factors play a crucial role: institutional (general, cultural, economic), actor-related, and functional/technical factors. In principle, all types of factors may serve both as drivers and impediments. We shall briefly discuss them in turn.

Cultural factors: From an institutional perspective, the overall trend towards Web 2.0 in modern societies is an important cultural factor. Even without direct links, such a forceful societal trend may certainly indirectly influence the developments in the academic world, as all of its members are also part of wider society; in addition academia is increasingly connected to its environment (cf. 3.2). It seems safe to say that the popularity of these interactive platforms is likely to trickle down. Already today we can observe parts of academia moving towards such popular platforms. Since they also provide a prominent space for communicating science, academia has a vital interest in being properly represented on these platforms.

Economic factors: Most of the general social media platforms are run by enterprises with strong commercial interests that are not necessarily compatible with those of the academics using them. While some of the science-specific Web 2.0 tools are of a non-commercial character so far, this may change in the long run. The big players may have the resources to enter the academic market—just as they did with regard to citation analysis or scientific journals, which are to a large extent under the control of a few profitable enterprises. An early example in this respect is Google Scholar. Furthermore, many of the now not-for-profit platforms may see the necessity to switch to income-generating activities at some point. Both developments may have a considerable influence on how these platforms are further developed, either taking or not taking account of academic concerns. Another economic factor that will play a role is the research field's closeness to economic application and its competitiveness (Nentwich 2003, 160ff.)—both characteristics act against the Web 2.0-typical transparent and open communication modes in the early stages of research. A more general conclusion in this respect would be that the concrete shape of cyberscience 2.0 will be specific for each discipline, perhaps for each specialty—as we have seen in the case of cyberscience 1.0.

Actor-related factors: As previously noted in the original cyberscience study, actors are crucial in any diffusion process. So far, most researchers are mainly passive observers. While there are only very few outspoken adversaries of the development, we observed some "cyber-entrepreneurs" who actively experiment with the tools, shape them, and involve others. Whether they will be successful in generating enough activity to attract a sufficient number of fellow researchers to reach the tipping point, is an open question, but a demographic development may work in their favor:

the younger generation of researchers grew up with the Internet and they are more likely than the older generation to take the Web 2.0 way of doing things for granted, including research-related communication. Other important actors are the academic institutions, such as universities, but also the learned societies. Their appraisal and whether they give incentives or disincentives for certain academic activities in the Web 2.0 may be crucial. While so far only a few have actually been active in this respect (such as supporting university-based SNS or issuing microblogging guidelines), this may change as the general impact of social media on society becomes ever more obvious.

Technical factors: Looking at the development from a technical perspective, we observe that many of the platforms are obviously sufficiently developed enough for very widespread use. However, we found some shortcomings of the general purpose platforms for academic purposes (such as archiving of messages; technical reliability and limitations of some tools; non-transparent functionalities). Also with regard to the academically oriented platforms we can find technical flaws (e.g. lacking integration of a writing environment in multi-purpose SNS; citation analysis in Google Scholar). In some cases the providers try to solve these technical difficulties. For example, Google Scholar will be increasingly adapted to academia's needs because its (economic) success depends on this main target group. But since academics play only a minor role in more generally oriented platforms, there is little incentive to accommodate this rather specific target group.

Functional factors: As we have seen, many of the tools seem indeed functional for academic purposes, e.g. for world-wide networking, long-distance collaboration, swift information gathering and so on, while others seem to be inimical to academic work, e.g. the proliferation of resources of unknown quality or the distraction from a researcher's core tasks. Probably, the concern of information overload may be the single most important issue when it comes to individual decisions whether to adopt the new bundle of tools. From a broader perspective, that is for academia or a discipline as a whole, the issue of quality seems paramount. The current system of hierarchical and organized quality control is, despite all shortcomings, well-established and widely accepted. So any competing systems, such as open peer review, still have to prove their worth. The inherent transparency-enhancing character of most tools seems to be useful for science as a whole—not least because it serves the interest of the funders of research in society to obtain information and to be involved. By contrast, data and privacy protection is an important concern in some circumstances. We assume that this "mixed bag" will lead to differentiated usage practices, with some functions being adopted and others discarded in the long run.

So where do we go from here? What will the future development look like, considering those factors? What has been said of the "mixed bag" in the previous paragraph may be the core of our overall answer: It is most likely that today's cyberscientists will pick and choose specific platforms for specific purposes. The ideal "fully-fledged" version of cyberscience 2.0 will probably never become reality. Instead, the likely "real" version of it will consist of a combination of novel Web 2.0 elements alongside the well-known Internet tools cyberscientists use today on a daily basis. Since Web 2.0 applications mainly depend on the interactivity of their users, the usefulness of cyberscience 2.0 and its success will vary drastically from person to person, platform to platform and somewhat from discipline to discipline. The multiple communicative possibilities from SNS could potentially replace many channels from cyberscience 1.0. But due to the remaining problems and fragmented usage, this is unlikely to happen in the near future. Some researchers will keep using these channels for specific purposes, mostly public relations and self-marketing—the most common form of usage we observed. Microblogging fulfills similar functions and might increasingly be combined with SNS, as it is done already in a number of cases.

Whether cyberscience 2.0 will prevail also depends on political decisions within academic institutions. So far, most engagement in cyberscience 2.0 occurs bottom-up. As mentioned above, providing incentives may drastically increase interactivity on the platforms and hence directly influence their success. In addition, academic institutions may not only act as passive technology users, but also as active contractors and initiators promoting the design of "tailor made" platforms for specific needs, thereby possibly addressing a number of the current problems. Either way, there is still a lot to learn in this early transformation process. Therefore we shall see many promising experiments fail. Second Life appears to be one of them, despite the early enthusiasm it received. In contrast, not even its founders believed in the later success of Wikipedia, which exceeded all expectations. Therefore, the future developments have to be studied very carefully, avoiding unfounded optimism as well as fear mongering.

4.3 An Ambivalent Overall Assessment

In summary, our analysis of potential impacts of Web 2.0 on science and research is ambivalent. On the one hand, some of the platforms and services have become an integral part of the academic workaday life. This is especially true for the search engines of Google, but Wikipedia is also intimately connected with academia. Even scientists who do not use these services cannot deny their relevance for students and the wider public. These platforms operate, however, on the basis of a functional logic that is usually distinct from scientific logic, for instance regarding indicators for relevance or reputation—whereas academia has no direct influence on these mechanisms. Consequently, impact on the science system is beginning to show, for instance when novel publication forms, such as blogs, are cited in academic papers, or when academic journals ask their authors to contribute to Wikipedia. On the other hand, many of these platforms still fall short of their potentials, whether welcome or not: for instance, social network sites or virtual worlds are today apparently used rather experimentally within academia. All things considered, we may be only at the beginning of a broad and lengthy transformation process, which may result in a novel institutionalized form at some point.

We do not doubt that the current evolution of cyberscience 2.0 will lead to increasing professionalization in dealing with the new media. This will mean two things: first, academic institutions, including universities, will discover these platforms for their own purposes, for public relations as well as for internal communication with staff and students. There are already examples: universities started blogging to reach a wider public, institutional SNS emerged, etc. In the long run, this will drive us away from the present experimental and exploratory environment towards standardization and suitability for daily use.

Second, some kind of Web 2.0 literacy is likely to emerge. The authors of this volume do neither believe in the dystopian scenario of shallow minds caused by intensive consumption and use of Web 2.0 tools, nor in the optimistic scenario that all will turn out for the best. We rather reach the conclusion that scientists will be confronted with a new environment, which challenges some of our traditional ways of doing research. In order to cope with these challenges and to profit most from the digital social networks, a novel kind of literacy is mandatory and has to be built up individually. To give a few examples of topics to be included in this learning process: how to update and select one's peer group (whom to follow); how to avoid becoming distracted by the steady flow of Web 2.0 messages; how to use search engines most efficiently without getting trapped in unwanted artifacts; how to interact with the public the "Web 2.0 way"; etc. While most of these activities have to be performed on an individual level, it rests with the academic institutions to provide an auxiliary framework. This may mean offering advanced training courses as well as elaborating guidelines.

Whether or not one comes to the conclusion that cyberscience 2.0 is a desirable or even likely future, each researcher and each academic institution has to deal with this ongoing development towards increased use of ICT and Web 2.0 in particular. While passively ignoring it is a theoretical option, it seems advisable to address the issue actively as we are confronted with it every day. So far, only a number of individual "cyberentrepreneurs" and trail-blazing institutions actively shape the emerging cyberscience 2.0 landscape, while the majority is only observing or even ignoring. We assume that taking part in the design phase, both in technical and organizational terms, is worthwhile given the potential advantages of interactive and networked digital formats for external and internal scientific communication and collaboration. Following this line of thinking, some academic organizations may come to the conclusion that actively promoting certain forms of doing research in a Web 2.0 mode would help to avoid inconsistencies with the present system and induce desirable impacts. And on the individual level, we see no reason to fear the emerging cyberscience 2.0 environment.

Abbreviations

2D	two-dimensional
3D	three-dimensional
API	application programming interface
apps	application(s)
ASEO	Academic Search Engine Optimization
CERN	Centre Européen de Recherche Nucléaire (Geneva)
DDS	document delivery service
DSN	digital social networks
EFF	Electronic Frontier Foundation
ICT	information and communication technology (-ies)
INSA	Institut National des Sciences Appliquées (Toulouse)
IQOQI	Institute for Quantum Optics
ISSN	International Standard Serial Number
IT	information technology
ITA	Institute of Technology Assessment
NASA	National Aviation and Space Agency (US)
NCRR	National Center for Research Resources
NIH	National Institutes of Health
NOOA	National Oceanic and Atmospheric Administration (US)
NPL	National Physical Laboratory (UK)
NPOV	neutral point of view (a Wikipedia principle)
OAW	Österreichische Akademie der Wissenschaften (Austrian Academy of Sciences)
OCR	optical character recognition
OPAC	online public access catalogue
PDA	personal digital assistant

PDF	Portable Document Format
PET	privacy enhancing technologies
PLoS	Public Library of Science
SEO	Search Engine Optimization
SL	Second Life
SMS	short message service
SNS	social network site(s)
SRF	Social Research Foundation (US)
STS	science and technology studies
SURL	Second Life-specific address
TA	technology assessment
UK	United Kingdom
URL	unified resource locator (web address)
US	United States (of America)

List of Tables

List of Figures

Bibliography

Alexander, Andrew (2009). *Post Editor Ends Tweets as New Guidelines Are Issued* (Blogpost) 25.9. http://voices.washingtonpost.com/ombudsman-blog/2009/09/post_editor_ends_tweets_as_new.html.

Anderson, Chris (2007). *The Long Tail : How Endless Choice is Creating Unlimited Demand.* London: Random House Business Books.

Anderson, Richard J., Tamy Vandegrift, Steven Wolfman, and Ken Yasuhara (2003). Promoting interaction in large classes with computer-mediated feedback. In *Designing for change in networked learning environments*, 119–123. Bergen: CSCL.

APS (2011). *APS Wikipedia Initiative.* http://www.psychologicalscience.org/index.php/members/aps-wikipedia-initiative.

Aspden, Elizabeth J., and Louise P. Thorpe (2009). "Where Do You Learn?": Tweeting to Inform Learning Space Development. *EDUCAUSE Quarterly Magazine 32*/1 http://www.educause.edu/EDUCAUSE+Quarterly/EDU CAU-SEQuarterlyMagazineVolum/WhereDoYouLearnTweetingtoInfor/163852.

Baksik, Corinna (2006). Fair use or exploitation? The google book search controversy. *Portal-Libraries and the Academy,* 6, 4, 399–415.

Bampo, Mauro, Michael T. Ewing, Dineli R. Mather, David Stewart, and Mark Wallace (2008). The Effects of the Social Structure of Digital Networks on Viral Marketing Performance. *Information Systems Research,* 19, 3, 273–290 http://www.marketingsa.co.za/content/ISR.pdf.

Barnes, Susan B. (2006). A privacy paradox: Social networking in the United States. *First Monday,* 11, 6 http://firstmonday.org/issues/issue11_9/barnes/index.html.

Beall, Jeffrey (2009). Bentham Open. *The Charleston Advisor,* 11, 1, 29–32.

Becher, Tony (1989). *Academic Tribes and Territories.* Milton Keynes: Open University Press.

Beck, Ulrich (1992). *The Risk Society: Towards a New Modernity.* Sage: London.

Becker, Nancy J. (2003). Google in perspective: understanding and enhancing student search skills. *New Review of Academic Librarianship,* 9, 1, 84–100.

Beel, Joeran, and Bela Gipp (2010). Academic Search Engine Spam and Google Scholar's Resilience Against it. *Journal of Electronic Publishing,* 13, 3 http://quod.lib.umich.edu/j/jep/3336451.0013.305?rgn=main;view=fulltext.

Beel, Jöran, and Bela Gipp (2009). Google Scholar's Ranking Algorithm: An Introductory Overview. In Larsen, Birger, and Jacqueline Leta (eds.). *Proceedings of the*

12th International Conference on Scientometrics and Informetrics (ISSI'09), 230–241. Rio de Janeiro: International Society for Scientometrics and Informetrics http://www.sciplore.org/publications/2009-Google_Scholar's_Ranking_Algorithm_--_An_Introductory_Overview_--_preprint.pdf.

Beel, Jöran, Bela Gipp, and Erik Wilde (2010). Academic Search Engine Optimization (ASEO): Optimizing Scholarly Literature for Google Scholar and Co. *Journal of Scholarly Publishing*, 42, 2, 176–190.

Beer, David (2008). Social network(ing) sites ... revisiting the story so far: A response to Danah Boyd & Nicole Ellison. *Journal of Computer-Mediated Communication*, 13, 2, 516–529 http://onlinelibrary.wiley.com/doi/10.1111/j.1083-6101. 2008.-00408.x/full.

Bergman, Michael K. (2001). The Deep Web: Surfacing Hidden Value. *Journal of Electronic Publishing*, 7, 1 (August) http://quod.lib.umich.edu/j/jep/3336451. 0007.104?rgn=main;view=fulltext;q1=Bergman.

Berners-Lee, Tim (2006). *developerWorks Interviews, 28 July 2006, transcript*, http:// www.ibm.com/developerworks/podcast/dwi/cm-int082206.txt.

Beus, Johannes (2009a). *Twitter: Nutzung* (Blogpost) 6.11. http://www.sistrix.de/ news/910-twitter-nutzung.html.

Beus, Johannes (2009b). *Twitter: Wachstum* (Blogpost) 5.11. http://www.sistrix.de/ news/909-twitter-wachstum.html.

Biermann, Kai (2010). Facebook, bing und Skype vernetzen sich. *Die Zeit online* (15.10.) http://www.zeit.de/digital/internet/2010-10/facebook-bing-skype.

Bignell, Simon, and Vanessa Parson (2010). *Best Practices in Virtual Worlds Teaching. A guide to using problem-based learning in Second Life. Version 2.1, January* http:// previewpsych.org/BPD1.2.pdf.

Bittarello, Maria Beatrice (2008). Another Time, Another Space: Virtual Worlds, Myths and Imagination. *Journal of Virtual Worlds Research*, 1, 1, 1-18 http:// journals. tdl.org/jvwr/article/view/282/213.

Björk, Bo-Christer, Annikki Roos, and Mari Lauri (2009). Scientific journal publishing: yearly volume and open access availability. *Information Research*, 14, 1 http://informationr.net/ir/14-1/paper391.html.

Björk, Bo-Christer, Patrik Welling, Mikael Laakso, Peter Majlender, Turid Hedlund, and Guðni Guðnason (2010). Open Access to the Scientific Journal Literature: Situation 2009. *PLoS ONE*, 5, 6, e11273 http://www.plosone.org/ article/info:doi/10.1371/journal.pone.0011273.

Boellstorff, Tom (2008). *Coming of Age in Second Life: An Anthropologist Explores the Virtually Human*. Princeton: Princeton University Press.

Bohannon, John (2010). Google Opens Books to New Cultural Studies. *Science*, 330, 17, 1600 http://dericbownds.net/uploaded_images/Science-2010-Bohannon.pdf.

Bonetta, Laura (2009). Should You Be Tweeting? *Cell*, 139, 3, 452–453 http:// www.cell.com/fulltext/S0092-8674%2809%2901305-1.

Bonneau, Joseph, and Sören Preibusch (2010). The privacy jungle: On the market for data protection in social networks. In Moore, Tyler, David Pym, and Christos Ioannidis (eds.). *Economics of Information Security and Privacy*, 121–167. New York et al.: Springer http://citeseerx.ist.psu.edu/viewdoc/download?doi=10. 1.1.153.7796&rep=rep1&type=pdf.

Borgmann, Christine L. (2007). *Scholarship in the Digital Age: Information, Infrastructure, and the Internet.* Cambridge (MA)/London: MIT Press.

Böschen, Stefan, Karen Kastenhofer, Ina Rust, Jens Soentgen, and Peter Wehling (2010). Scientific Nonknowledge and Its Political Dynamics: The Cases of Agri-Biotechnology and Mobile Phoning. *Science, Technology, and Human Values*, 35, 6, 783–811.

Bourke, Paul (2008a). *Evaluating Second Life as a tool for collaborative scientific visualisation.* Paper presented at the Computer Games and Allied Technology, 29.4., Singapur http://local.wasp.uwa.edu.au/~pbourke/papers/cgat08.

Bourke, Paul (2008b). Evaluating Second Life for the Collaborative Exploration of 3D Fractals. *Computers & Graphics*, February, 113-117 http://local.wasp. uwa.edu.au/~pbourke/papers/cg2008/

Boyd, Danah, Scott Golder, and Gilad Lotan (2010). *Tweet Tweet Retweet: Conversational Aspects of Retweeting on Twitter.* Paper presented at the HICSS-42, Persistent Conversation Track, 5.–8.1., Kauai http://www.danah.org/papers/Tweet TweetRetweet.pdf.

Boyd, Danah M., and Nicole B. Ellison (2007). Social Network Sites: Definition, History, and Scholarship. *Journal of Computer-Mediated Communication*, 13, 1, 11 http://jcmc.indiana.edu/vol13/issue1/boyd.ellison.html.

Brabazon, Tara (2006). The Google Effect: Googling, blogging, wikis and the flattening of expertise. *Libri*, 56, 3, 157–167.

Brabazon, Tara (2007). *The University of Google: Education in a (post) information age.* Aldershot: Ashgate.

Bradley, David (2009). *scientwist* (Blogpost) 1.8. http://www.sciencebase.com/ science-blog/scientwists.html.

Brand-Finance (2011). *Google tops the BrandFinance Global 500* (News). http://brand finance.com/news/in_the_news/google-tops-the-brandfinance-global-500.

Brin, Sergey, and Lawrence Page (1998). *The Anatomy of a Large-Scale Hypertextual Web Search Engine.* Paper presented at the Seventh International World-Wide Web Conference (WWW 1998), 14.–18.4., Brisbane http://ilpubs.stanford. edu: 8090/361/1/1998-8.pdf.

Brooks, Terrence A. (2004). The nature of meaning in the age of Google. *Information Research*, 9, 3 http://informationr.net/ir/9-3/paper180.html.

Brückner, Dominik (2009). Die Google Buchsuche als Hilfsmittel für die Lexikographie. *Sprachreport. Institut für Deutsche Sprache (IDS)*, 3, 26–31.

Bruns, Axel (2008). *Blogs, Wikipedia, Second Life, and Beyond: From Production to Produsage.* New York: Peter Lang.

Bry, François, and Jana Herwig (2009). Kreidetafel und Lounge 2.0 – Der Einzug sozialer Medien in Technik und Wissenschaft. *IM-Fachzeitschrift für Information Management und Consulting*, 24, 1, 26–33.

Büffel, Steffen, Thomas Pleil, and Jan Sebastian Schmalz (2007). Net-Wiki, PR-Wiki, KoWiki – Erfahrungen mit kollaborativer Wissensproduktion in Forschung und Lehre. In Stegbauer, Christian, Klaus Schönberger, and Jan Schmidt (eds.). *Wikis – Diskurse, Theorien und Anwendungen, Sonderausgabe von kommunikation@gesellschaft*, 8 http://www.soz.uni-frankfurt.de/K.G/F2_2007_Bueffel_Pleil_Schmalz.pdf.

Butler, Brian, Elisabeth Joyce, and Jacqueline Pike (2008). *Don't Look Now, But We've Created a Bureaucracy: The Nature and Roles of Policies and Rules in Wikipedia.* Paper presented at the CHI 2008, Florence.

Butler, Declan (2008). *Publish in Wikipedia or perish* (Webnews) http://www.nature.com/news/2008/081216/full/news.2008.1312.html.

Cain, Jeff, Doneka R. Scott, and Paige Akers (2009). Pharmacy Students' Facebook Activity and Opinions Regarding Accountability and E-Professionalism. *American Journal of Pharmaceutical Education*, 73, 6, 104 http://www.ajpe.org/aj7306/aj7306104/aj7306104.pdf.

Callas, Jon (2011a). Google, Facebook und der Staat. *Die Zeit online* (1.10.) http://www.zeit.de/2011/40/Jon-Callas-ueber-Facebook.

Callas, Jon (2011b). Über Facebook. *Die Zeit online* (1.10.) http://www.zeit.de/2011/40/Jon-Callas-ueber-Facebook.

Carr, Nicholas G. (2010). *The Shallows: What the Internet Is Doing to Our Brains.* London/New York: Norton & Company.

Casey, Michael E., and Laura C. Savastinuk (2006). Library 2.0 – Service for the next-generation library. *Library Journal* 1, 9 http://www.libraryjournal.com/article/CA6365200.html.

Chapman, Paige (2010). Second Life To Drop Educational Discount. *The Chronicle of Higher Education* (5.10.) http://chronicle.com/blogs/wiredcampus/second-life-to-drop-educational-discount/27458.

Cohen, Dan (2010). *Is Google Good for History?* (Blogpost) 7.1. http://hdl.handle.net/1920/6101.

Cole, Stephen, Jonathan R. Cole, and Gary A. Simon (1981). Chance and Consensus in Peer Review. *Science*, 214, 4523, 881–886.

Connell, Ruth Sara (2009). Academic Libraries, Facebook and MySpace, and Student Outreach: A Survey of Student Opinion. *Libraries and the Academy*, 9, 1, 25–36.

Crane, Diana (1972). *Invisible Colleges – Diffusion of Knowledge in Scientific Communities.* Chicago/London: The University of Chicago Press.

Dambeck, Holger (2009). Bebenforscher rüsten sich mit Twitter und Volks-Seismografen. *Spiegel online* (17.12.) http://www.spiegel.de/wissenschaft/natur/0,1518,667260,00.html.

Danowski, Patrick, and Lambert Heller (2006). Bibliothek 2.0: Die Bibliothek der Zukunft? *Bibliotheksdienst*, 40, 11, 1259–1271 http://www.zlb.de/aktivitaeten/bd_neu/heftinhalte2006/DigitaleBib011106.pdf.

Davidow, William H. (2011). *Overconnected: The Promise and Threat of the Internet*. New York: Delphinium.

DiBona, Chris, Sam Ockman, and Mark Stone (1999). Introduction. In DiBona, Chris, Sam Ockman, and Mark Stone (eds.). *Open Sources: Voices from the Open Source Revolution*. Cambridge et al.: O'Reilly http://www.oreilly.com/catalog/open sources/book/intro.html.

Dröge, Evelyn, Parinaz Maghferat, Cornelius Puschmann, Julia Verbina, and Katrin Weller (2011). Konferenz-Tweets. Ein Ansatz zur Analyse der Twitter-Kommunikation bei wissenschaftlichen Konferenzen. In *Proceedings of the 12th International Symposium for Information Science*, in print. Boizenburg: Verlag Werner Hülsbusch http://ynada.com/pubs/isi2010.pdf.

Duguid, Paul (2007). Inheritance and loss? A brief survey of Google Books. *First Monday*, 12, 8 http://firstmonday.org/htbin/cgiwrap/bin/ojs/index.php/fm/article/viewArticle/1972/1847.

Durant, John (1999). Participatory technology assessment and the democratic model of the public understanding of science. *Science and Public Policy*, 26, 5, 313–319.

Dutton, William H., and Paul W. Jeffreys (eds.) (2010). *World Wide Research: Reshaping the Sciences and Humanities*. Cambridge (MA): MIT Press.

Dvorak, John C. (2009). *Nine Ways to Use Twitter* (Blogpost) 23.9. http://www.pcmag.com/article2/0,2817,2343672,00.asp.

Ebner, Martin, and Hermann Maurer (2009). Can Weblogs and Microblogs Change Traditional Scientific Writing? *Future Internet*, 1, 1, 47–58 http://www.mdpi.com/1999-5903/1/1/47.

Elmer, Greg (2004). *Profiling Machines*. Cambridge (MA): MIT Press.

Emrich, Eike, and Jens Flatau (2004). Kaffeetrinken in Organisationen. *sozialersinn*, 3, 507–522.

Etzkowitz, Henry, and Loet Leydesdorff (eds.) (1997). *Universities and the Global Knowledge Economy. A Triple Helix of University-Industry-Government Relations*. London/Washington: Pinter.

Evans, Mark (2010). *An Update on the State of the TwitterSphere* (Blogpost) 17.12. http://blog.sysomos.com/2010/12/17/an-update-on-the-state-of-the-twittersphere.

Everts, Sarah (2007). Second Life Science. Take a scientific Field Trip to a digital world. *Chemical & Engineering News*, 85, 26, 49 http://pubs3.acs.org/cen/science/85/8526sci3.html.

Fallows, Deborah (2005). *Search Engine Users. Internet searchers are confident, satisfied and trusting – but they are also unaware and naïve*. Washington: Pew Internet & American Life Project http://www.pewinternet.org/~/media//Files/Reports/2005/PIP_Searchengine_users.pdf.pdf.

Ferdig, Richard E., Kara Dawson, Erik W. Black, Nicole M. Paradise Black, and Lindsay A. Thompson (2008). Medical students' and residents' use of online social networking tools: Implications for teaching professionalism in medical education. *First Monday*, 13, 9 http://firstmonday.org/htbin/cgiwrap/bin/ojs/index.php/fm/article/viewArticle/2161/2026.

Fischer, Frank (2009). *Democracy and Expertise: Reorienting Policy Inquiry*. New York: Oxford University Press.

Fischer, Klaus (2004). Soziale und kognitive Aspekte des Peer Review-Verfahrens. In Fischer, Klaus, and Heinrich Parthey (eds.). *Evaluation wissenschaftlicher Institutionen. Wissenschaftsforschung Jahrbuch 2003*, 23-62. Berlin: Gesellschaft für Wissenschaftsforschung http://www.wissenschaftsforschung.de/JB03_23-62.pdf.

Forman, Paul (2007). The Primacy of Science in Modernity, of Technology in Postmodernity, and of Ideology in the History of Technology. *History and Technology* 23, 1/2, 1–152.

Fritzsche, Claus (2010). *Marc Scheloske und die Schlangengrube ScienceBlogs: Cyber-Mobbing, Agitation, Fanatiker und militante "Skeptiker"* (Blogpost) 25.11. http://www.psychophysik.com/h-blog/?p=12464.

Fröhlich, Gerhard (1993). 'Demokratisierung' der Wissenschaftskommunikation durch Fachinformationssysteme und Computernetze? In Institut für Höhere Studien (ed.) *Information und Macht*, 63–73. Wien.

Fröhlich, Gerhard (1996). The (Surplus) Value of Scientific Communication. *Review of Information Science*, 1, 2 http://www.inf-wiss.uni-konstanz.de/RIS/1996iss02_01/articles01/02.html.

Fröhlich, Gerhard (2003). Anonyme Kritik: Peer Review auf dem Prüfstand der Wissenschaftsforschung. *medizin – bibliothek – information*, 3, 2, 33-39.

Fröhlich, Gerhard (2009). Die Wissenschaftstheorie fordert Open Access. *Information Wissenschaft & Praxis*, 60, 5, 253-258

Fuchs, Christian (2009). *Social Networking Sites and the Surveillance Society. A Critical Case Study of the Usage of studiVZ, Facebook, and MySpace by Students in Salzburg in the Context of Electronic Surveillance*. Salzburg/Wien: ICT&S Center (University of Salzburg), Forschungsgruppe Unified Theory of Information http://twinic.com/duploads/0000/0509/ICT_Use_-_MySpace_Facebook_2008.pdf

Fuchs, Christian (2010). Facebook, Web 2.0 und ökonomische Überwachung. *Datenschutz und Datensicherheit (DuD)*, 7, 453–458.

Funtowicz, Silvio O., and Jerome R. Ravetz (1992). Three types of risk assessment and the emergence of post-normal science. In Krimsky, S., and D. Golding (eds.). *Social Theories of Risk*, 251–273. London: Praeger.

Gargouri, Yassine, Chawki Hajjem, Vincent Lariviere, Tim Brody, Yves Gingras, Les Carr, et al. (2010). Self-Selected or Mandated, Open Access Increases Citation Impact for Higher Quality Research. *PLoS ONE* 10, 5, e11273 http://www.plosone.org/article/info:doi/10.1371/journal.pone.0013636.

Gassmann, Oliver, Bastian Widenmayer, Sascha Friesike, and Thomas Schildhauer (2011). *Opening up Science: Towards an Agenda of Open Science in Industry and Academia*. Paper presented at the 1st Berlin Symposium on Internet and Society, 25.–

28.10., Berlin http://berlinsymposium.org/sites/berlinsymp osium.org/files/ open_science.pdf.

Geiger, R. Stuart (2011). The Lives of Bots. In Lovink, Geert, and Nathaniel Tkacz (eds.). *Critical Point of View: A Wikipedia Reader* 78–93. Amsterdam: Institute of Network Cultures http://networkcultures.org/wpmu/portal/publications/ inc-readers/critical-point-of-view-a-wikipedia-reader/.

Gewin, Virginia (2010). Collaboration: Social networking seeks critical mass. *Nature*, 468, 993–994.

Gibbons, Michael, Camille Limoges, Helga Nowotny, Simon Schwartzman, Peter Scott, and Martin Trow (1994). *The new production of knowledge – The dynamics of science and research in contemporary societies.* London et al..: Sage.

Giddens, Anthony (1990). *Consequences of Modernity.* Cambridge: Polity Press.

Giles, Jim (2005). Internet encyclopaedias go head to head. *Nature,* 438, 7070, 900–901.

Gloning, Thomas (2009). Digitale Textcorpora und Sprachforschung. Ältere Koch- und Kräuterbücher. In Hofmeister, Wernfried, and Andrea Hofmeister-Winter (eds.). *Wege zum Text. Überlegungen zur Verfügbarkeit mediävistischer Editionen im 21. Jahrhundert. Grazer Kolloquium 17. –19. September 2008,* 53-71. Tübingen: Max Niemeyer Verlag.

Google Inc. (2006). *Official Google Blog: Testimony: The Internet in China* (Blogpost) 15.2. Retrieved 12.5.2011 http://googleblog.blogspot.com/2006/02/testimony -internet-in-china.html.

Google Inc. (2008). *Official Google Blog: The future of search* (Blogpost) 10.9. http://googleblog.blogspot.com/2008/09/future-of-search.html.

Google Inc. (2011a). *About Google Books.* http://books.google. com/intl/en/ googlebooks/history.html.

Google Inc. (2011b). *About Google Scholar* http://scholar.google.com/intl/en/ scholar/about.html.

Google Inc. (2011c). *Company.* http://www.google.com/intl/en/corporate/.

Google Inc. (2011d). *Google Books Library Project.* http://books.google.com/intl/ en/googlebooks/library.html.

Google Inc. (2011e). *Google Books Perspectives.* http://books.google.com/intl/en/ googlebooks/issue.html.

Google Inc. (2011f). *Library Partners.* http://books.google.com/intl/en/google-books/ partners.html.

Google Inc. (2011g). *Technology overview* (Webpage). http://www.google.com/intl/ en/corporate/tech.html.

Google Inc. (2011h). *What you'll see when you search on Google Books* http://books. google. com/intl/en/googlebooks/screenshots.html.

Grange, Camille, and Izak Benbasat (2009). *Information Technology Capabilities for Digital Social Networks.* Paper presented at the International Conference on Computational Science and Engineering, 29.–31.8., Vancouver http://thesocial-mobileweb.org/smw09/papers/smw09_information_tech_cap_social_ net.pdf.

Gresham, John L. (1994). From invisible college to cyberspace college: computer conferencing and the transformation of informal scholarly communication networks. *Interpersonal Computing and Technology*, 2, 4, 37–52 http://jan.ucc.nau.edu/~ipct-j/1994/n4/gresham.txt.

Griffiths, Jillian R., and Peter Brophy (2005). Student Searching Behavior and the Web: Use of Academic Resources and Google. *Library Trends*, 53, 4, 539–554.

Grosseck, Gabriela, and Carmen Holotescu (2008). *Can we use Twitter for educational purposes?* Paper presented at the 4th International Scientific Conference eLSE "eLearning and Software for Education", 17–18.4., Bucharest http://www.scribd.com/doc/2286799/Can-we-use-Twitter-for-educational-activities.

Grunwald, Armin, Gerhard Banse, Christopher Coenen, and Leonhard Hennen (2006). *Netzöffentlichkeit und digitale Demokratie: Tendenzen politischer Kommunikation im Internet*. Berlin: Edition Sigma.

Günther, Tina (2009). *Was bedeutet "Internetöffentliche Netzwerkwissenschaft"? Ein Brainstorming* (Blogpost) 3.5. http://sozlog.wordpress.com/2009/05/03/ internetoeffentliche-netzwerkwissenschaft/.

Haber, Peter, and Jan Hodel (2007). Das kollaborative Schreiben von Geschichte als Lernprozess. Eigenheiten und Potenzial von Wiki und Wikipedia. In Merkt, Marianne, Kerstin Mayrberger, Rolf Schulmeister, Angela Sommer, and Ivo van den Berk (eds.). *Studieren neu erfinden – Hochschule neu denken*, 43–53. Münster: Waxmann http://www.hist.net/fileadmin/user_upload/redaktion/107932.pdf.

Haber, Peter, and Jan Hodel (2009). Wikipedia und die Geschichtswissenschaft. Eine Forschungsskizze. *Schweizerische Zeitschrift für Geschichte*, 59, 4, 455–461 http://www.histnet.ch/dox/109803.pdf.

Haglund, Lotta, and Per Olsson (2008). The Impact on University Libraries of Changes in Information Behavior Among Academic Researchers: A Multiple Case Study. *The Journal of Academic Librarianship*, 34, 1, 52–59.

Halavais, Alexander (2009). *Search Engine Society*. Cambridge: Polity Press.

Halavais, Alexander, and Derek Lackaff (2008). An Analysis of Topical Coverage of Wikipedia. *Journal of Computer-Mediated Communication*, 13, 2, 429–440.

Hammwöhner, Rainer (2007). Qualitätsaspekte der Wikipedia In Stegbauer, Christian, Jan Schmidt, and Klaus Schönberger (eds.). *Wikis – Diskurse, Theorien und Anwendungen, Sonderausgabe von kommunikation@gesellschaft*, 8 http://www.soz.uni-frankfurt.de/K.G/B3_2007_Hammwoehner.pdf

Harasim, Linda M., and Tim Winkelmans (1990). Computer-Mediated Scholarly Collaboration – A Case Study of an International Online Educational Research Workshop. *Knowledge: Creation, Diffusion, Utilization*, 11, 4, 382–409.

Harley, Diane, Sophia Krzys Acord, Sarah Earl-Novell, Shannon Lawrence, and C. Judson King (2010). *Assessing the Future Landscape of Scholarly Communication: An Exploration of Faculty Values and Needs in Seven Disciplines*. Berkeley: The Center for Studies in Higher Education http://escholarship.org/uc/item/ 15x7385g.

Harnad, Steven (1990). Scholarly Skywriting and the Prepublication Continuum of Scientific Inquiry. *Psychological Science*, 1, 342–343 http://users.ecs.soton.ac.uk/harnad/Papers/Harnad/harnad90.skywriting.html.

Harrit, Niels H., Jeffrey Farrer, Steven E. Jones, Kevin R. Ryan, Frank M. Legge, Daniel Farnsworth, et al. (2009). Active Thermitic Material Discovered in Dust from the 9/11 World Trade Center Catastrophe. *The Open Chemical Physics Journal*, 2, 7–31.

Harzing, Anne-Wil K., and Ron van der Wal (2008). Google Scholar as a new source for citation analysis. *Ethics in Science and Environmental Politics*, 8, 1, 61–73.

Harzing, Anne-Wil K., and Ron van der Wal (2009). A Google Scholar h-Index for Journals: An Alternative Metric to Measure Journal Impact in Economics and Business. *Journal of the American Society for Information Science and Technology*, 60, 1, 41–46.

Head, Alison J. (2007). Beyond Google: How do students conduct academic research? *First Monday*, 12, 8 http://firstmonday.org/issues/issue12_8/head/index.html.

Heidemann, Julia (2010). Online Social Networks – Ein sozialer und technischer Überblick. *Informatik-Spektrum*, 33, 3, 262–271 http://www.uni-augsburg.de/exzellenz/kompetenz/kernkompetenzzentrum_fim/Forschung/paper/paper/wi-272.pdf.

Herring, Susan C. (2007). A Faceted Classification Scheme for Computer-Mediated Discourse. *language@internet*, 4, 1 http://www.languageatinternet.org/articles/2007/761.

Herwig, Jana (2009). *Liminality and Communitas in Social Media: The case of Twitter.* Paper presented at the Internet Research 10.0: Critical, annual conference of the Association of Internet Researchers, 8.–10.10., Milwaukee http://digiom.files.wordpress.com/2009/10/herwig_ir10_liminalitycommunitastwitter_v5 oct09.pdf.

Herwig, Jana, Axel Kittenberger, Michael Nentwich, and Jan Schmirmund (2009). *Microblogging und die Wissenschaft. Das Beispiel Twitter. Steckbrief IV im Rahmen des Projekts Interactive Science.* Wien: Institut für Technikfolgen-Abschätzung http://epub.oeaw.ac.at/ita/ita-projektberichte/d2-2a52-4.pdf.

Hey, Tony, and Anne Trefethen (2008). E-Science, Cyberinfrastructure, and Scholarly Communication. In Olson, Gary M., Ann Zimmermann, and Nathan Bos (eds.). *Scientific Collaboration on the Internet*, 15–31. Cambridge (MA)/London: MIT Press.

Hindman, Matthew, Kostas Tsioutsiouliklis, and Judy A. Johnson (2003). *Googlearchy: How a few heavily-linked sites dominate politics on the web.* Paper presented at the Annual Meeting of the Midwest Political Science Association, 31.3., Chicago.

Hoeren, Thomas, and Gottfried Vossen (2010). Die Rolle des Rechts in einer durch das Web 2.0 dominierten Welt. *Datenschutz und Datensicherheit (DuD)*, 7, 463–466.

Holotescu, Carmen, and Gabriela Grosseck (2008). *Can we use Twitter for educational activities?* Paper presented at the 4th International Scientific Conference eLSE 'eLearning and Software for Education', 17.–18.4., Bucharest http://www.scribd.com/doc/2286799/Can-we-use-Twitter-for-educational-activities.

Holtz, Leif-Erik (2010). Datenschutzkonformes Social Networking: Clique und Scramble! *Datenschutz und Datensicherheit (DuD)*, 7, 439–443.

Honeycutt, Courtenay, and Susan C. Herring (2009). Beyond Microblogging: Conversation and Collaboration via Twitter. In *Proceedings of the 42nd Hawaii International Conference on System Sciences*. Los Alamitos: IEEE Computer Society Press http://ella.slis.indiana.edu/~herring/honeycutt.herring.2009.pdf.

Huss, Jon W., Camilo Orozco, James Goodale, Chunlei Wu, Serge Batalov, Tim J. Vickers, et al. (2008). A Gene Wiki for Community Annotation of Gene Function. *PLoS Biology*, 6, 7, 1398–1402 http://www.plosbiology.org/article/info: doi/10.1371/journal.pbio.0060175.

Initiative D21, and TNS Infratest (2010). *Digitale Gesellschaft. Die digitale Gesellschaft in Deutschland – Sechs Nutzertypen im Vergleich. Sonderstudie im Rahmen des (N)ONLINER Atlas* http://www.initiatived21.de/category/digitale-gesellschaft.

Jacsó, Péter (2005). Google Scholar: the pros and the cons. *Online Information Review*, 29, 2, 208–214.

Jacsó, Péter (2008). Google Scholar revisited. *Online Information Review*, 32, 1, 102–114 http://comminfo.rutgers.edu/~tefko/Courses/e530/Readings/Jaszo%20 Google%20scholar%202008.pdf.

Jacsó, Péter (2009). Google Scholar's Ghost Authors, Lost Authors, and Other Problems. Why the popular tool can't be used to analyze the publishing performance and impact of researchers. *Library Journal* (24.9.) http://www.library-journal. com/article/CA6698580.html?q=jacso.

Jaschik, Scott (2007). A Stand Against Wikipedia. *Inside Higher Ed.* (26.1.) http:// www.insidehighered.com/news/2007/01/26/wiki.

Java, Akshay, Xiaodan Song, Tim Finin, and Belle Tseng (2007). Why We Twitter: Understanding Microblogging Usage and Communities. In *Proceedings of the Joint 9th WEBKDD and 1st SNA-KDD Workshop* http://ebiquity.umbc.edu/_file _directory_/papers/369.pdf.

Johnson, Kirsten A. (2011). The effect of Twitter posts on students' perceptions of instructor credibility. *Learning, Media and Technology*, 36, 1, 21–38.

Joss, Simon, and Sergio Bellucci (eds.) (2002). *Participatory Technology Assessment. European Perspectives.* London: Center for the Study of Democracy.

Journal of 9/11 Studies (2011) http://www.journalof911studies.com.

Kaplan, Andreas M., and Michael Haenlein (2010). Users of the world, unite! The challenges and opportunities of Social Media. *Business Horizons*, 53, 1, 59–68.

Keen, Andrew (2007). *The Cult of the Amateur: How blogs, MySpace, YouTube, and the rest of today's user-generated media are destroying our economy, our culture, and our values.* New York: Doubleday.

Keim, Brandon (2007). News feature: WikiMedia. *Nat Med*, 13, 3, 231–233.

Kelly, Kevin (2006). Scan This Book! *The New York Times online* (14.5.) http:// www.nytimes.com/2006/05/14/magazine/14publishing.html?_r=2&oref=slo gin&pagewanted=all.

Kemp, Jeremy W., Daniel Livingstone, and Peter R. Bloomfield (2009). SLOODLE: Connecting VLE tools with emergent teaching practice in Second Life. *British Journal of Educational Technology*, 40, 3, 551–555.

Kerres, Michael, and Annabell Preussler (2009). Soziale Netzwerkbildung unterstützen mit Microblogs (Twitter). In Hohenstein, Andreas, and Karl Wilbers (eds.). *Handbuch E-Learning*, 4.3.4. Köln: Fachverlang Deutscher Wirtschaftsdienst.

Kircz, Joost G. (2001). *New practices for electronic publishing: how to maintain quality and guarantee integrity*. Paper presented at the UNESCO-ICSU Conference Electronic Publishing in Science, 20.–23.2., Paris http://users.ox.ac.uk/~icsuinfo/kirczppr.htm.

Kircz, Joost G., and Hans E. Roosendaal (1996). Understanding and shaping scientific information transfer. In *Electronic publishing in science – Proceedings of the joint ICSU Press – UNESCO Expert Conference*, 106–116. Paris http://www.science.uva.nl/ projects/commphys/papers/unescom.htm.

Kirkpatrick, Marshall (2008). *How We Use Twitter for Journalism* (Blogpost) 25.8. http://www.readwriteweb.com/archives/twitter_for_journalists.php.

Kleimann, Bernd, Murat Özkilic, and Marc Göcks (2008). *Studieren im Web 2.0. Studienbezogene Web- und E-Learning-Dienste* (HISBUS-Kurzinformation). Hannover: HIS Hochschul-Informations-System GmbH https://hisbus. his.de/hisbus/docs/hisbus21.pdf.

Knorr, Eric (2003). The Year of Web Services. *CIO* (15.12.) http://www.cio.com.

Koch, Daniel, and Johannes Moskaliuk (2009). Onlinestudie: Wissenschaftliches Arbeiten im Web 2.0. *e-learning and education*, 5.7. http://eleed.campussource.de/archive/5/1842/.

König, René (2009). *Eine Bewegung für die Wahrheit? Gesellschaftliche Wirklichkeitskonstruktion in Wikipedia am Beispiel alternativer Deutungen des 11. September 2001*. Unpublished Diplomarbeit, Universität Bielefeld http://nbn-resolving.de/urn/resolver.pl?urn=urn:nbn:de:hbz:361-17633.

König, René (2011). *Wikipedia: Participatory Knowledge Production or Elite Knowledge Representation?* Paper presented at the Participatory Knowledge Production 2.0: Critical Views and Experiences, 23.3., Virtual Knowledge Studio, Maastricht http://renekoenig.eu/Publikationen/RK_Extended%20Abstract.pdf.

König, René, and Michael Nentwich (2008). *Wissenschaft in "Second Life". Steckbrief I im Rahmen des Projekts Interactive Science*. Wien: Institut für Technikfolgen-Abschätzung http://epub.oeaw.ac.at/ita/ita-projektberichte/d2-2a52-1.pdf.

König, René, and Michael Nentwich (2009). *Wissenschaft in Wikipedia und anderen Wikimedia-Projekten. Steckbrief II im Rahmen des Projekts Interactive Science*. Wien: Institut für Technikfolgen-Abschätzung http://epub.oeaw.ac.at/ita/ita-projekt berichte/d2-2a52-2.pdf.

König, René, and Michael Nentwich (2010). *Google, Google Scholar und Google Books in der Wissenschaft. Steckbrief III im Rahmen des Projekts Interactive Science*. Wien: Institut für Technikfolgen-Abschätzung http://epub.oeaw.ac.at/ita/ita-projekt berichte/d2-2a52-4.pdf.

Kramer, Staci D. (2009). *WaPo's Social Media Guidelines Paint Staff Into Virtual Corner; Full Text of Guidelines* (Blogpost) 27.9. http://paidcontent.org/article/419-wapos-social-media-guidelines-paint-staff-into-virtual-corner.

Krotoski, Aleksandra K. (2009). *Social Influence in Second Life: Social Network and Social Psychological Processes in the Diffusion of Belief and Behaviour on the Web*. Unpublished Doctoral thesis, University of Surrey, Guildford http://epubs.surrey.ac. uk/2252.

Kuhlen, Rainer (2005). *Wikipedia – Offene Inhalte im kollaborativen Paradigma – eine Herausforderung auch für Fachinformation* http://www.kuhlen.name/MATERI-ALIEN/Publikationen2005/wikipedia_141005.pdf.

Kumar, Sanjeev, Jatin Chhugani, Changkyu Kim, Daehyun Kim, Anthony Nguyen, Pradeep Dubey, et al. (2008). Second Life and the New Generation of Virtual Worlds. *Computer* 41, 9, 46–53.

L'Amoreaux, Claudia, Claudia Linden, John Lester, and Pathfinder Linden (2007). *Proceedings of Second Life Education Workshop 2007. Part of the Second Life Community Convention Chicago 24.-26.8.* http://www.simteach.com/slccedu07proceedings.pdf.

Lack, Caleb, Lisa Beck, and Danielle Hoover (2009). Use of social networking by undergraduate psychology majors. *First Monday*, 14, 12 http://firstmonday. org/htbin/cgiwrap/bin/ojs/index.php/fm/article/view/2540/2407.

Lang, Andrew SID, and Jean-Claude Bradley (2009). Chemistry in Second Life. *Chemistry Central Journal*, 3, 14 http://journal.chemistrycentral.com/content/3 /1/14.

Lanier, Jaron (2006). Digital Maoism: The Hazards of the New Online Collectivism. *Edge* (30.5.) http://www.edge.org/3rd_culture/lanier06/lanier06_index. html.

Leenes, Ronald (2010). Context is everything: sociality and privacy in Online Social Network Sites. In Bezzi, M., P. Duquenoy, S. Fischer-Hübner, M. Hansen, and G. Zhang (eds.). *Privacy and Identity, IFIP AICT 320*, 48–65. Heidelberg/Berlin/New York: Springer http://works.bepress.com/ronald_ leenes/3.

Lehavot, Keren (2009). MySpace or Yours? The Ethical Dilemma of Graduate Students' Personal Lives on the Internet. *Ethics & Behavior*, 19, 2, 129–141.

Lehdonvirta, Vili (2008). *Virtual worlds don't exist*. Paper presented at the Breaking the Magic Circle, 10.–11.4., Tampere http://virtual-economy.org/files/Lehdonvirta-VWDE.pdf.

Lehmann, Kai, and Michael Schetsche (eds.) (2007). *Die Google-Gesellschaft. Vom digitalen Wandel des Wissens*. Bielefeld: Transcript.

Lessig, Lawrence (1999). *Code and Other Laws of Cyberspace*. New York: Basic Books.

Lessig, Lawrence (2006). *Code. Version 2.0*. New York: Basic Books http://codev2. cc/download+remix/Lessig-Codev2.pdf.

Lewandowski, Dirk (2005). *Web Information Retrieval. Technologien zur Informationssuche im Internet*. Frankfurt (a.M.): Deutsche Gesellschaft für Informationswissenschaft und Informationspraxis e.V. http://www.durchdenken.de/lewandowski/web-ir.

Lewandowski, Dirk (2007). Nachweis deutschsprachiger bibliotheks- und informations-wissenschaftlicher Aufsätze in Google Scholar. *Information Wissenschaft und Praxis*, 58, 3, 165–168.

Lewandowski, Dirk (2008). Search engine user behaviour: How can users be guided to quality content? *Information Services & Use*, 28, 261–268.

Lewandowski, Dirk, and Philipp Mayr (2006). Exploring the academic invisible web. *Library Hi Tech*, 24, 4, 529–539 http://eprints.rclis.org/9156/.

Lewis, Kevin, Jason Kaufman, and Nicholas Christakis (2008). The Taste for Privacy: An Analysis of College Student Privacy Settings in an Online Social Network. *Journal of Computer-Mediated Communication*, 14, 1.

Lifton, Joshua, and Joseph A. Paradiso (2009). Dual Reality: Merging the Real and Virtual. In Lehmann-Grube, Fritz, and Jan Sablatnig (eds.). *Facets of Virtual Environments (FaVE)*, 12–28. Berlin: Springer.

Lisa (2007). *Twitter: A New Conference Tool* (Blogpost) 21.9. http://www.thebalcom group.com/node/124.

Lovink, Geert, and Nathaniel Tkacz (eds.) (2011). *Critical Point of View: A Wikipedia Reader*. Amsterdam: Institute of Network Cultures http://networkcultures.org /wpmu/portal/publications/inc-readers/critical-point-of-view-a-wikipedia-reader.

Machill, Marcel, Christoph Neuberger, Wolfgang Schweiger, and Werner Wirth (2003). Wegweiser im Netz: Qualität und Nutzung von Suchmaschinen. In Machill, Marcel, and Carsten Welp (eds.). *Wegweiser im Netz. Qualität und Nutzung von Suchmaschinen*, 13–490. Gütersloh: Verlag Bertelsmann Stiftung.

Mack, Daniel, Anne Behler, Beth Roberts, and Emily Rimland (2007). Reaching Students with Facebook: Data and Best Practices. *Electronic Journal of Academic and Special Librarianship*, 8, 2 http://southernlibrarianship.icaap.org/content/ v08n02/mack_d01.html.

MacKenzie, Donald, and Judy Wajcman (1988). *The Social Shaping of Technology – How the Refrigerator got its Hum*. Milton Keynes: Open University Press.

Madrigal, Alexis (2010). Inside the Google Books Algorithm. *The Atlantic* (1.11.) http://www.theatlantic.com/technology/archive/10/11/inside-the-google-books-algorithm/65422.

Mager, Astrid (2009). Mediated health: sociotechnical practices of providing and using online health information. *New Media & Society*, 11, 7, 1123–1142.

Mager, Astrid (2010). *Mediated Knowledge: Sociotechnical practices of communicating medical knowledge via the web and their epistemic implications*. Unpublished Dissertation, Universität Wien http://sciencestudies.univie.ac.at/publikationen#c147112.

Mathews, Brian S. (2006). Do you Facebook? Networking with students online. *College and Research Libraries News*, 67, 5 http://www.ala.org/ala/mgrps/divs/ acrl/publications/crlnews/2006/may/facebook.cfm.

Matzat, Uwe (2004). Academic Communication and Internet Discussion Groups: Transfer of Information or Creation of Social Contacts? *Social Networks*, 26, 3, 221–255 http://www.tue-tm-soc.nl/~matzat/matzat-social-networks-2004.pdf.

Mayr, Philipp, and Anne-Kathrin Walter (2007). An exploratory study of Google Scholar. *Online Information Review*, 31, 6, 814–830.

McConaghy, T. Troy (2007). *Using Second Life for Knowledge Transfer and Collaboration*. Paper presented at the International Workshop on Managing Knowledge for Space Missions, 19.7., Pasadena http://km.nasa.gov/pdf/182785main_Mc Conaghy_Second_Life.pdf

Mendez, Jesse P., John Curry, Mwarumba Mwavita, Kathleen Kennedy, Kathryn Weinland, and Katie Bainbridge (2009). To Friend or Not to Friend: Academic

Interaction on Facebook. *International Journal of Instructional Technology and Distance Learning* 6, 9, 33–47.

Merton, Robert K. (1968). The Matthew Effect in Science. *Science*, 159, 3810, 56–63.

Merz, Marina (1998). Nobody Can Force You When You Are Across the Ocean – Face to Face and E-Mail Exchanges Between Theoretical Physicists. In Smith, Crosbie, and Jon Agar (eds.). *Making Space for Science*, 313-329. London: Macmillan.

Miller, Christopher (2007). Strange Facts in the History Classroom: Or How I learned to Stop Worrying and Love the Wiki(pedia). *Perspectives Online*, 45, 5 http://www.historians.org/perspectives/issues/2007/0705/0705vie1.cfm.

Miller, Vincent (2008). New Media, Networking and Phatic Culture. *The International Journal of Research into New Media Technologies* 14, 4, 387–400 http://con. sagepub.com/cgi/content/abstract/14/4/387.

Mischaud, Edward (2007). *Twitter: Expressions of the whole self. An investigation into user appropriation of a web-based communications platform.* Unpublished MSc Dissertation, London School of Economics and Political Science http://www2.lse.ac.uk/media@lse/research/mediaWorkingPapers/MScDissertationSeries/Mishaud_Final.pdf.

Möller, Erik (2005). *Die heimliche Medienrevolution – Wie Weblogs, Wikis und freie Software die Welt verändern.* Hannover: Heise http://medienrevolution.dpunkt.de/files/Medienrevolution-1.pdf.

Möller, Erik (2009). *Scholarly community gives feedback regarding Wikipedia* (Blogpost) 27.4. http://blog.wikimedia.org/2009/04/27/scholarly-community-gives-feedback-regarding-wikipedia/.

Moskaliuk, Johannes, Joachim Kimmerle, Ulrike Cress, and Friedrich W. Hesse (2011). Knowledge Building in User-Generated Online Virtual Realities. *Journal of Emerging Technologies in Web Intelligence,* 3, 1, 38–46.

Mullen, Laura Bowering, and Karen A. Hartman (2006). Google scholar and the library web site: The early response by ARL libraries. *College & Research Libraries,* 67, 2, 106–122.

Nature (2011). Editorial: Copy and paste. *Nature,* 473, 7348, 419–420 http://www.nature.com/nature/journal/v473/n7348/full/473419b.html.

Nentwich, Michael (1999). *Cyberscience: Die Zukunft der Wissenschaft im Zeitalter der Informations- und Kommunikationstechnologien,* Working papers no. 99/6 http://www.mpi-fg-koeln.mpg.de/pu/workpap/wp99-6/wp99-6.html.

Nentwich, Michael (2003). *Cyberscience: Research in the Age of the Internet.* Vienna: Austrian Academy of Sciences Press http://hw.oeaw.ac.at/3188-7.

Nentwich, Michael (2005a). Cyberscience. Modelling ICT-induced changes of the scholarly communication system. *Information, Communication & Society (iCS),* 8, 4, 542–560.

Nentwich, Michael (2005b). Quality control in academic publishing: challenges in the age of cyberscience. *Poiesis & Praxis. International Journal of Ethics of Science and Technology Assessment,* 3, 3, 181–198.

Nentwich, Michael (2009). *Cyberscience 2.0 oder 1.2? Das Web 2.0 und die Wissenschaft, ITA manu:script* no. ITA-09-02 http://epub.oeaw.ac.at/ita/ita-manuscript/ita_09_ 02.pdf.

Nentwich, Michael (2010a). Neue Fenster im Elfenbeinturm? Wissenschaftskommunikation und Web 2.0. In Bieber, Christoph, Benjamin Drechsel, and Anne Lang (eds.). *Kulturen im Konflikt. Claus Leggewie revisited*, 421–428. Bielefeld: Transcript.

Nentwich, Michael (2010b). Technikfolgenabschätzung 2.0. *Technikfolgenabschätzung – Theorie und Praxis*, 19, 2, 74–79 http://www.itas.fzk.de/tatup/102/nent 10a.pdf.

Nentwich, Michael, and René König (2010). Peer Review 2.0: Herausforderungen und Chancen der wissenschaftlichen Qualitätskontrolle im Zeitalter der Cyber-Wissenschaft. In Gasteiner, Martin, and Peter Haber (eds.). *Digitale Arbeitstechniken für die Geistes- und Kulturwissenschaften*, 143–163. Wien et al.: Böhlau.

Neuhaus, Chris, Ellen Neuhaus, Alan Asher, and Clint Wrede (2006). The depth and breadth of Google Scholar: An empirical study. *Portal – Libraries and the Academy*, 6, 2, 127–141.

NIST (2008). *NIST NCSTAR 1A: Federal Building and Fire Safety Investigation of the World Trade Center Disaster: Final Report on the Collapse of World Trade Center Building 7*. Washington: US Department of Commerce http://wtc.nist.gov/NCSTAR1/PDF/NCSTAR%201A.pdf.

Nordan, Nurul Aini M., Ahmad I. Z. Abidin, Ahmad K. Mahmood, and Noreen I. Arshad (2009). Digital Social Networks: Examining the Knowledge Characteristics. *International Journal of Human and Social Sciences*, 4, 8, 574–580 http://www.waset.org/journals/ijhss/v4/v4-8-73.pdf.

Norris, Michael, Charles Oppenheim, and Fytton Rowland (2008). *Open access citation rates and developing countries*. Paper presented at the ELPUB2008. Open Scholarship: Authority, Community, and Sustainability in the Age of Web 2.0 – 12th International Conference on Electronic Publishing, Toronto http://elpub.scix.net/cgi-bin/works/Show?335_elpub2008.

Noruzi, Alireza (2005). Google Scholar: The new generation of citation indexes. *Libri*, 55, 4, 170-180.

Novak, Tom (2007). *Concept Plan for eLab City: Live, Work, Play in the Virtual World* http://api.ning.com/files/pDJhpOrp-t5goR6lfwzqhEkyz7BgJYckKYHjZis 0mWs_/eLabCityConceptPlanNov52007.pdf.

Nowotny, Helga (2003). Democratising expertise and socially robust knowledge. *Science and Public Policy*, 30, 3, 151–156.

Noyes, Katherine (2008). Virtual Space Travel, Part 2: Surfing to Mars. *TechNewsWorld* (10.10.) http://www.technewsworld.com/story/63387.html.

NPG (2005). Wiki's wild world. *Nature*, 438, 7070, 890–890.

Nunberg, Geoffrey (2009). Google's Book Search: A Disaster for Scholars. *The Chronicle of Higher Education* (31.3.) http://chronicle.com/article/Googles-Book-Search -A/48245/.

Nygren, Else, Glenn Haya, and Wilhelm Widmark (2006). *Students experience of Metalib and Google Scholar*.

O'Reilly, Tim (2005). *What is Web 2.0? Design Patterns and Business Models for the Next Generation of Software*, http://www.oreilly.de/artikel/web20.html.

OCLC (2005). *Perceptions of Libraries and Information Resources. A Report to the OCLC Membership*. Dublin (Ohio): OCLC Online Computer Library Center http://www.oclc.org/reports/pdfs/Percept_all.pdf.

Oder, Norman (2009). Google, "The Last Library," and Millions of Metadata Mistakes. *Library Journal* (3.9.) http://www.libraryjournal.com/article/CA66 87562. html?nid=2673&source=title&rid=1407498533.

OECD (2008). *Scoping Paper on Online Identity Theft*. Seoul: Organisation for Economic Co-operation and Development, http://www.oecd.org/dataoecd/35 /24/40644196.pdf.

Okerson, Ann Shumela (1997). *Introduction to the 6th Edition (1996) of the Directory of Electronic Journals, Newsletters and Academic Discussion Lists* http://www.people.virginia.edu/~pm9k/libsci/96/intro.html.

Olson, Gary M., Ann Zimmermann, and Nathan Bos (eds.) (2008). *Scientific Collaboration on the Internet*. Cambridge (MA)/London: MIT Press.

Page, Lawrence, Sergey Brin, Rajeev Motwani, and Terry Winograd (1998). *The PageRank Citation Ranking: Bringing Order to the Web*: Stanford InfoLab http://ilpubs.stanford.edu:8090/422/.

Pariser, Eli (2011). *The Filter Bubble. What the Internet is Hiding from You*. New York: Penguin.

Parsons, Cherilyn (2008). Second Life offers healing, therapeutic options for users. *San Francisco Chronicle* (13.7.), F-1 http://www.sfgate.com/cgi-bin/article.cgi?f=/c/a/2008/07/11/LVL211GP5C.DTL.

Penfold, Paul, and Gigi Au Yeung (2008). *Hospitality & Tourism Management Students' Experience of Learning in the Virtual World of Second Life* http://www.scribd.com/doc/4612817/SL-Hotel-and-Tourism-Student-Feedback.

Petrides, Lisa, and Cynthia Jimes (2008). Building Open Educational Resources from the Ground Up: South Africa's Free High School Science Texts. *Journal of Interactive Media in Education*, 2008, 07 http://jime.open.ac.uk/2008/07/ jime-2008-07.pdf

Philica (2011). *A short history of Philica* (Webpage) http://philica.com/about.php.

Pomerantz, Jeffrey (2006). Google Scholar and 100 percent availability of information. *Information Technology and Libraries*, 25, 2, 52–56.

Pöschl, Ulrich (2004). Open Access: Interactive peer review enhances journal quality. *Research Information* September/October http://www.researchinformation.info/features/feature.php?feature_id=99.

Pöschl, Ulrich (2007). Mehr Transparenz und Effizienz. Interaktives Open Access Publizieren und gemeinschaftliche Fachbegutachtung. *Forschung & Lehre*, 6, 334–335.

Pöschl, Ulrich (2009). *Interactive Open Access Publishing & Collaborative Peer Review for Improved Scientific Communication & Quality Assurance*. Paper presented at Kommunikationsformate und ihre Dynamik in der digitalen Wissenschaftskommunikation. Erste Meilensteintagung des Forschungsverbundes Interactive Science 9.–11.9., Rauischholzhausen http://www.atmospheric-chemistry-and-physics.net/pr_acp_interactive_open_access_publishing_icsti. pdf.

Prattichizzo, Domenico (2009). Robotics in Second Life. *IEEE Robotics & Automation Magazine*, 16, 1, 99–102.

Preibusch, Sören, Bettina Hoser, Seda Gürses, and Bettina Berendt (2007). *Ubiquitous social networks – opportunities and challenges for privacy-aware user modelling*. Paper presented at the Data Mining for User ModellingWorkshop (DM.UM'07), June, Corfu http://citeseerx.ist.psu.edu/viewdoc/download?doi=10.1.1.139. 5376&rep=rep1&type=pdf.

Preuß, Roland (2011). Summa cum laude? "Mehr als schmeichelhaft". *Süddeutsche Zeitung online* (16.2.) http://www.sueddeutsche.de/politik/guttenbergs-doktor-arbeit-summa-cum-laude-mehr-als-schmeichelhaft-1.1060779.

Priem, Jason, and Bradely H. Hemminger (2010). Scientometrics 2.0: New metrics of scholarly impact on the social Web. *First Monday*, 15, 7 http://firstmonday. org/htbin/cgiwrap/bin/ojs/index.php/fm/article/viewArticle/2874/257.

Procter, Rob, Robin Williams, and James Stewart (2010). *If you build it, will they come? How researchers perceive and use web 2.0*: Research Information Network http:// www.rin.ac.uk/our-work/communicating-and-disseminating-research/use-and -relevance-web-20-researchers.

Putnam, Robert D. (2000). *Bowling Alone. The Collapse and Revival of American Community*. New York: Simon & Schuster.

Qiu, Jane (2010). A land without Google? *Nature*, 463, 1012–1013.

Rankin, Monica (2009). *Some general comments on the "Twitter Experiment"* (Webpage) http://www.utdallas.edu/~mar046000/usweb/twitterconclusions.htm.

Ravid, Gilad, Yoram M. Kalman, and Sheizaf Rafaeli (2008). Wikibooks in higher education: Empowerment through online distributed collaboration *Computers in Human Behavior*, 24, 5, 1913–1928.

Reagle, Joseph Michael Jr. (2010). *Good Faith Collaboration: The Culture of Wikipedia*. Cambridge (MA)/London: MIT Press.

Rector, Lucy Holman (2008). Comparison of Wikipedia and other encyclopedias for accuracy, breadth, and depth in historical articles. *Reference Services Review*, 36, 1, 7–22.

Reinhardt, Wolfgang, Martin Ebner, Günter Beham, and Christina Costa (2009). How People are using Twitter during Conferences. In Hornung-Prähauser, Veronika, and Michaela Luckmann (eds.). *Creativity and Innovation Competencies on the Web. Proceeding of the 5th EduMedia conference*, 145–156. Salzburg: Salzburg Research http://citeseerx.ist.psu.edu/viewdoc/download?doi=10.1.1.148.12 38& rep=rep1&type=pdf.

Richter, Alexander, and Michael Koch (2007). *Social Software – Status quo und Zukunft* (Technischer Bericht). München: Fakultät für Informatik, Universität der Bundeswehr München http://www.unibw.de/wow5_3/forschung/social_ software.

Richter, Alexander, and Michael Koch (2008). Funktionen von Social-Networking-Diensten. In Bichler, Martin, Thomas Hess, Helmut Krcmar, Ulrike Lechner, Florian Matthes, Arnold Picot, Benjamin Speitkamp, and Petra Wolf (eds.). *Multikonferenz Wirtschaftsinformatik 2008*, 1239–1250. Berlin: GITO-Verlag http://ibis.in.tum.de/mkwi08/18_Kooperationssysteme/04_Richter.pdf.

Rieger, Oya Y. (2009). Search engine use behavior of students and faculty: User perceptions and implications for future research. *First Monday*, 14, 12 http://firstmonday.org/htbin/cgiwrap/bin/ojs/index.php/fm/article/view/2716/2385.

Rogers, Everett M. (1995). *Diffusion of Innovations* (4 ed.). New York/London: The Free Press.

Rogers, Richard (2009). The Googlization Question, and the Inculpable Engine. In Becker, Konrad, and Felix Stalder (eds.). *Deep Search: The Politics of Search Engines beyond Google*, 173–184. Innsbruck: Studienverlag.

Röhle, Theo (2009). Dissecting the Gatekeepers. Relational Perspectives on the Power of Search Engines. In Becker, Konrad, and Felix Stalder (eds.). *Deep Search: The Politics of Search Engines beyond Google*, 117–132. Innsbruck: Studienverlag.

Röhle, Theo (2010). *Der Google Komplex. Über Macht im Zeitalter des Internets*. Bielefeld: Transcript.

Rosenman, Michael A., Gregory Smith, Mary-Lou Maher, Lan Ding, and David Marchant (2007). Multidisciplinary collaborative design in virtual environments. *Automation in Construction*, 16, 1, 37–44.

Rowinski, Dan (2011). Spain Asks Google for the Right To Be Forgotten. *Read Write Web* (21.4.) http://www.readwriteweb.com/archives/spain_asks_ google _ for_the_right_to_be_forgotten.php.

Sajjapanroj, Suthiporn, Curtis J. Bonk, Mimi Miyoung Lee, and Meng-Fen Grace Lin (2008). A Window on Wikibookians: Surveying their Statuses, Successes, Satisfactions, and Sociocultural Experiences. *Journal of Interactive Online Learning*, 7, 1, 36-58 http://www.ncolr.org/jiol/issues/PDF/7.1.3.pdf.

Saunders, Neil, Pedro Beltrão, Lars Jensen, Daniel Jurczak, Roland Krause, Michael Kuhn, et al. (2009). Microblogging the ISMB: A New Approach to Conference Reporting. *PLoS Computational Biology*, 5, 1.

Schäfer, Mirko Tobias (2011). *Bastard Culture! How User Participation Transforms Cultural Production*. Amsterdam: Amsterdam University Press http://www.mtschaefer.net/media/uploads/docs/Schaefer_Bastard-Culture_ 2011.pdf.

Scheloske, Marc (2008). *Demokratisierung der Wissenschaftskommunikation durch wissenschaft-liche Blogs. Wege in eine "wissenschaftsmündige" Gesellschaft* (Blogpost) 14.3. http://www.wissenswerkstatt.net/2008/03/14/demokratisierung-der-wissenschaftskommunikation-durch-wissenschaftliche-blogs-wege-in-eine-wissenschaftsmuendige-gesellschaft/.

Schetsche, Michael (2006). Die digitale Wissensrevolution – Netzwerkmedien, kultureller Wandel und die neue soziale Wirklichkeit. *zeitenblicke*, 5, 3 http://www.zeitenblicke.de/2006/3/Schetsche.

Schetsche, Michael, Kai Lehmann, and Thomas Krug (2007). Die Google-Gesellschaft. Zehn Prinzipien der neuen Wissensordnung. In Lehmann, Kai, and Michael Schetsche (eds.). *Die Google-Gesellschaft. Vom digitalen Wandel des Wissens.* Bielefeld: Transcript.

Schiff, Stacy (2006). Know It All. Can Wikipedia conquer expertise? *The New Yorker* (31.7.) http://www.newyorker.com/archive/2006/07/31/060731fa_fact.

Schirrmacher, Frank (2009). *Payback: Warum wir im Informationszeitalter gezwungen sind zu tun, was wir nicht tun wollen, und wie wir die Kontrolle über unser Denken zurückgewinnen.* Munich: Karl Blessing Verlag.

Schmidt, Jan (2009). *Das neue Netz. Merkmale, Praktiken und Folgen des Web 2.0.* Konstanz: UVK.

Schrape, Jan-Felix (2010). *Neue Demokratie im Netz? Eine Kritik an den Visionen der Informationsgesellschaft.* Bielefeld: Transcript.

Sherman, Chris, and Gary Price (2003). The Invisible Web: Uncovering Sources Search Engines Can't See. *Library Trends,* 52, 2, 282–298.

Shirky, Clay (2008). *Here Comes Everybody: The Power of Organizing Without Organizations.* London: Penguin Press.

Smith, Aaron, and Lee Rainie (2010). *8% of online Americans use Twitter* (Report). Washington D.C.: Pew Research Center's Internet & American Life Project, http://pewinternet.org/Reports/2010/Twitter-update-2010.aspx.

Smith, Stephanie (2008). Second Life Mixed Reality Broadcasts: A Timeline of Practical Experiments at the NASA CoLab Island. *Journal of Virtual Worlds Research,* 1, 1 http://journals.tdl.org/jvwr/article/view/295/226.

Soto, José Felipe Ortega (2009). *Wikipedia: A quantitative analysis.* Unpublished Doctoral thesis, Universidad Rey Juan Carlos, Madrid http://de.wikipedia.org/wiki/Datei:Thesis-wkp-quantanalysis-1.pdf.

Speakman, David (2008). *Introduction to Paleoanthropology: As Appears on Wikibooks, a Project of Wikipedia.* Santiago: Seven Treasures Publications.

Steuer, Jonathan (1992). Defining Virtual Reality: Dimensions Determining Telepresence. *Journal of Communication,* 42, 4, 73–93.

Stieger, Stefan, and Christoph Burger (2009). Let's Go Formative: Continuous Student Ratings with Web 2.0 Application Twitter. *CyberPsychology & Behavior,* 13, 2, 163–167.

Surowiecki, James (2004). *The Wisdom of Crowds: Why the Many Are Smarter Than the Few and How Collective Wisdom Shapes Business, Economies, Societies and Nations.* Anchor: Doubleday.

Sysomos Inc. (2010). *Twitter Statistics for 2010. An in-depth report at Twitter's Growth 2010, compared with 2009* (Report) http://www.sysomos.com/insidetwitter/twitter-stats-2010/.

Thagard, Paul (1997). *Internet Epistemology: Contributions of New Information Technologies to Scientific Research.* http://cogprints.org/674.

Thelwall, Mike (2002). Research note: In praise of Google: Finding law journal Web sites. *Online Information Review,* 26, 4, 271–272.

Timmer, John (2007). Prof replaces term papers with Wikipedia contributions, suffering ensues. *ars technica* 30.10. http://arstechnica.com/old/content/2007/10/prof-replaces-term-papers-with-wikipedia-contributions.ars.

Toffler, Alvin (1970). *Future Shock*. New York: Random House.

Turkle, Sherry (2011). *Alone Together: Why We Expect More from Technology and Less from Each Other*. New York: Basic Books.

Vaidhyanathan, Siva (2011). *The Googlization of Everything. And Why We Should Worry*. Berkeley/Los Angeles: University of California Press.

van Alstyne, Marshall, and Erik Brynjolfsson (1997). Widening Access and Narrowing Focus: Could the Internet Balkanize Science. *Science*, 274, 5292, 1479–1480.

Varmus, Harold, and others (1999). *PubMed Central: An NIH-Operated Site for Electronic Distribution of Life Sciences Research Reports*. http://www.nih.gov/about/director/pubmedcentral/pmcprint.htm.

Wagner, A. Ben (2010). *Open Access Citation Advantage: An Annotated Bibliography* (Webpage). http://www.istl.org/10-winter/article2.html.

Waldrop, M. Mitchell (2008). Science 2.0: Great New Tool, or Great Risk? *Scientific American* (9.1.) http://www.scientificamerican.com/article.cfm?id=science-2-point-0-great-new-tool-or-great-risk.

Walsh, John P., and Todd Bayma (1996). The Virtual College: Computer-mediated Communication and Scientific Work. *The Information Society*, 12, 4, 343–363.

Wannemacher, Klaus (2008). Wikipedia – Störfaktor oder Impulsgeberin für die Lehre? In Zauchner, Sabine, Peter Baumgartner, Edith Blaschitz, and Andreas Weissenbäck (eds.). *Offener Bildungsraum Hochschule. Freiheiten und Notwendig-keiten*, 147–155. Münster: Waxmann http://waxmann.com/kat/inhalt/2058Volltext .pdf.

Weingart, Peter (1983). Verwissenschaftlichung der Gesellschaft – Politisierung der Wissenschaft. *Zeitschrift für Soziologie* 12, 3, 225–241.

Weingart, Peter (1997). From 'Finalization' to 'Mode 2': old wine in new bottles? *Social Science Information*, 36, 4, 591–613.

Weingart, Peter (2001). *Die Stunde der Wahrheit? Zum Verhältnis der Wissenschaft zu Politik, Wirtschaft und Medien in der Wissensgesellschaft*. Weilerswist: Velbrück.

Weller, Katrin, Evelyn Dröge, and Cornelius Puschmann (2011). *Citation Analysis in Twitter: Approaches for Defining and Measuring Information Flows within Tweets during Scientific Conferences*. Paper presented at the #MSM2011,1st Workshop on Making Sense of Microposts, 30.5., Heraklion/Crete http://files.ynada.com/papers/msm2011.pdf.

Wessely, Christina (2007). Koalitionen des Nichtwissens? Welteislehre, akademische Naturwissenschaften und der Kampf um die öffentliche Meinung, 1895–1945. In Nikolow, Sybilla, and Arne Schirrmacher (eds.). *Wissenschaft und Öffentlichkeit als Ressourcen füreinander. Studien zur Wissenschaftsgeschichte des 20. Jahrhundert*, 225–243. Frankfurt (a.M.): Campus Verlag.

Wikimedia (2011a). *Category: Wikipedia protected pages without expiry*. Retrieved 4.6.2011 http://en.wikipedia.org/w/index.php?title=Category:Wikipedia_protected_pages_without_expiry&oldid=397157023.

Wikimedia (2011b). *Meta-Wiki: Founding principles.* Retrieved 1.6.2011 http://meta.wikimedia. org/wiki/Founding_principles.
Wikimedia (2011c). *Mission statement.* Retrieved 25.5.2011 http://wikimediafoundation.org/w/index.php?title=Mission_statement&oldid=21859.
Wikimedia (2011d). *Wikibooks: Dewikify.* Retrieved 7.6.2011 http://en.wikibooks.org/w/index.php?title=Wikibooks:Dewikify&oldid=1917514.
Wikimedia (2011e). *Wikibooks: Welcome.* Retrieved 6.6.2011 http://en.wikibooks.org/w/index.php?title=Wikibooks:Welcome&oldid=2010673.
Wikimedia (2011f). *Wikibooks: What is Wikibooks?* Retrieved 7.6.2011 http://en.wikibooks.org/w/index.php?title=Wikibooks:What_is_Wikibooks&oldid=2061673.
Wikimedia (2011g). *Wikipedia power structure.* Retrieved 5.5.2011 http://meta.wikimedia.org/wiki/Power_structure.
Wikimedia (2011h). *Wikipedia: Academy.* Retrieved 30.5.2011 http://en.wikipedia.org/w/index.php?title=Wikipedia:Academy&oldid=418151624.
Wikimedia (2011i). *Wikipedia: Core content policies.* Retrieved 5.6. http://en.wikipedia.org/w/index.php?title=Wikipedia:Core_content_policies&oldid=432216609.
Wikimedia (2011j). *Wikipedia: Five pillars.* Retrieved 1.6. http://en.wikipedia.org/w/index.php?title=Wikipedia:Five_pillars&oldid=431871252.
Wikimedia (2011k). *Wikipedia: Policies and guidelines.* Retrieved 26.5.2011 http://en.wikipedia.org/w/index.php?title=Wikipedia:Policies_and_guidelines&oldid=430502418.
Wikimedia (2011l). *Wikipedia: School and university projects.* Retrieved 3.6.2011 http://en.wikipedia.org/w/index.php?title=Wikipedia:School_and_university_projects&oldid=433288899.
Wikimedia (2011m). *Wikipedia: User access levels.* Retrieved 5.5.2011 http://en.wikipedia.org/w/index.php?title=Wikipedia:User_access_levels&oldid=43102254 2.
Wikimedia (2011n). *Wikiversity: Main Page.* Retrieved 7.7.2011 http://en.wikiversity.org/wiki/Wikiversity:Main_Page.
Wikimedia (2011o). *Wikiversity: Policies.* Retrieved 30.5.2011 http://en.wikiversity.org/w/index.php?title=Wikiversity:Policies&oldid=693817.
Wikimedia (2011p). *Wikiversity: Research guidelines/En.* Retrieved 30.5.2011 http://beta.wikiversity.org/wiki/Wikiversity:Research_guidelines/En#1.
Wikimedia (2011q). *Wikiversity: Wikiversity community.* Retrieved 11.6.2011 http://en.wikiversity.org/w/index.php?title=Wikiversity:Wikiversity_community&oldid=459640.
Wilbanks, John (2005). *What is Science Commons?* (Blogpost) 9.11. http://creativecommons.org/weblog/entry/5695.
Wouters, Paul F. (1996). Cyberscience. *Kennis en Methode,* 20, 2, 155–186.
Wu Song, Felicia (2010). Theorizing Web 2.0. *Information, Communication & Society (iCS),* 13, 2, 249–275.
Zhao, Dejin, and Mary Rosson (2009). *How and why people Twitter: the role that microblogging plays in informal communication at work.* Paper presented at the GROUP

'09: Proceedings of the ACM 2009 international conference on Supporting group work, Sanibel Island, Florida.

Zheleva, Elena, and Lise Getoor (2009). To Join or Not to Join: The Illusion of Privacy in Social Networks with Mixed Public and Private User Profiles. In *WWW'09 Proceedings of the 18th international conference on World wide web*. New York: ACM http://citeseerx.ist.psu.edu/viewdoc/download?doi=10.1.1.165. 9107&rep=rep1&type=pdf.

Zittrain, Jonathan L. (2008). *The Future of the Internet—And How to Stop It*. New Haven/London: Yale University Press http://futureoftheinternet.org.

Zuckerman, Harriet, and Robert K. Merton (1971). Patterns of Evaluation in Science: Institutionalisation, Structure and Functions of the Referee System. *Minerva*, 9, 1, 66–100.

Index

Social Science

campus

www.campus.de/wissenschaft

Frankfurt. New York